Edward Young, Thomas Stothard, James Neagle, Joseph Collyer

Night thoughts

Edward Young, Thomas Stothard, James Neagle, Joseph Collyer

Night thoughts

ISBN/EAN: 9783337867232

Printed in Europe, USA, Canada, Australia, Japan

Cover: Foto ©ninafisch / pixelio.de

More available books at **www.hansebooks.com**

E D W A R D Y O U N G D.D.

London. Published Feb? 1? 1798. by T. Heptinstall Holborn

Night Thoughts

by

EDWARD YOUNG, D.D.

With the Life of the Author,

AND NOTES CRITICAL & EXPLANATORY.

LONDON.

Printed by C. Whittingham

for

T. HEPTINSTALL, Nº 304, HOLBORN.

1798.

AUTHOR's PREFACE.

As the occasion of this Poem *was real, not ficti-tious; so the method pursued in it was rather im-posed, by what spontaneously arose in the Author's mind, on that occasion, than meditated, or designed. Which will appear very probable from the nature of it. For it differs from the common mode of poetry, which is, from long narration to draw short morals. Here, on the contrary, the narrative is short, and the morality arising from it, makes the bulk of the Poem. The reason of it is, that the facts men-tioned, did naturally pour these moral reflections on the thought of the writer.*

LIFE OF DR. YOUNG.

THE pen of biography cannot be better employed, than in the service of an author, who displayed eminent genius and abilities in the cause of virtue and , religion. Such was Dr. YOUNG, the subject of these Memoirs.

His father, whose name was also EDWARD YOUNG, was Fellow of WINCHESTER COLLEGE, Rector of UPHAM in HAMPSHIRE, and, in the latter part of his life, Dean of SARUM; chaplain to WILLIAM and MARY, and afterward to Queen ANN. JACOB tells us that the latter, when Princess Royal, did him the honour to stand godmother to our poet; and that, upon her ascension to the throne, he was appointed Clerk of the Closet to her Majesty.

It does not appear that this gentleman distinguished himself in the Republic of Letters, otherwise than by a Latin Visitation Sermon, preached in 1686, and by two volumes of Sermons, printed in 1702, and which he dedicated to Lord BRADFORD, through whose interest he probably received some of his promotions. The Dean died at SARUM in 1705, aged 63; after a very short illness, as appears by the exordium of Bishop

Burnet's sermon at the Cathedral on the following
Sunday. "Death (said he) has been of late walking
" round us, and making breach upon breach upon us,
" and has now carried away the head of this body with
" a stroke; so that he, whom you saw *a week ago* dis-
" tributing the holy mysteries, is now laid in the dust.
" But he still lives in the many excellent directions
" he has left us, both how to live and how to die."

Our author, who was an only son, was born at his
father's rectory, in 1681, and received the first part of
his education (as his father had formerly done) at
Winchester College; from whence, in his 19th
year, he was placed on the foundation of New Col-
lege, Oxford; whence again, on the death of the
Warden in the same year, he was removed to Corpus
Christi. In 1708, Archbiſhop Tennison nomi-
nated him to a law fellowship at All Souls, where,
in 1714, he took the degree of Bachelor of Civil Law,
and five years afterward that of Doctor.

Between the acquisition of these academic honours,
Young was appointed to speak the Latin *Oration*
on the foundation of the Codrington Library;
which he afterwards printed, with a dedication to the
Ladies of that family in English.

In this part of his life, our author is said not to
have been that ornament to virtue and religion which
he afterwards became. This is easy to be accounted
for. He had been released from parental authority
by his father's death; and his genius and conversation
had introduced him to the notice of the witty and
profligate Duke of Wharton*, and his gay compa-

* At the instigation of this peer, he was once candidate for a seat
in parliament, but without success, and the expences were paid by
Wharton.

nions, by whom his finances might be improved, but not his morals. This is the period at which POPE is said to have told WARBURTON our young author had " much genius without common-sense:" and it should seem likewise, that he possessed a zeal for religion with little of its practical influence; for, with all his gaiety and ambition, he was an advocate for Revelation and Christianity. Thus when TINDAL, the atheistical philosopher, used to spend much of his time at ALL SOULS, he complained: " The other boys I can always " answer, because I know whence they have their " arguments, which I have read an hundred times; " but that fellow YOUNG, is continually pestering me " with something of his own."

This apparent inconsistency is rendered the more probable from the different kinds of composition in which, at this period, he was engaged: *viz.* a political Panegyric on the new Lord LANSDOWNE, and a sacred Poem on THE LAST DAY, which was written in 1710, but not published till 1713. It was dedicated to the Queen, and acknowledges an obligation, which has been differently understood, either as referring to her having been his godmother, or his patron; for it is inferred from a couplet of SWIFT's, that YOUNG was a pensioned advocate of government:

" Whence GAY was banish'd in disgrace,
" Where POPE will never shew his face,
" Where Y—— must torture his invention,
" To flatter knaves, or lose his pension."

This, however, might be mere report, at this period, since SWIFT was not over nice in his authorities, and nothing is more common than to suppose the advocate, and the flatterer of the great, an hireling. Flattery seems indeed to have been our poet's besetting sin through life; but if interest was his object, he must have been frequently disappointed: and to those disappointments we probably owe some of his best reflections upon human life.

Of his Last Day, (his first considerable performance) Dr. Johnson observes, that it " has an equa- " bility and propriety which he afterwards either " never endeavoured for, or never attained. Many " paragraphs are noble, and few are mean; yet the " whole is languid: the plan is too much extended, " and a succession of images divides and weakens the " general conception: But the great reason why the " reader is disappointed is, that the thought of The " Last Day makes every man more than poetical, " by spreading over his mind a general obscurity of " sacred horror, that oppresses distinction and dis- " dains expression." The subject is indeed truly awful, and was peculiarly affecting to this celebrated critic, who never could, without trembling, meditate upon death or the eternal world. The poet's theological system, moreover, was not, at least when he wrote this, the most consistent and evangelical: I mean he had not those views of the Christian Atonement, and of pardoning grace, which give such a glory to his Night Thoughts, and would much more have illumined this composition. All the preparation he seems to have there in view, is

" By tears and groans, and never-ceasing care,
" And all the pious violence of prayer,"

to fit himself for the Tribunal. Moreover, the project of future misery is too awful for poetic enlarge-

ment, and makes the piece too terrible to be read
with pleasure; while the attempt to *particularize* the
solemnities of judgment, lowers their sublimity, and
makes some parts of the description, as Dr. JOHNSON
has observed, appear mean, and even bordering on
burlesque.—This poem, however, was well received
upon the whole, and the better for being written by a
layman; and it was commended by the ministry and
their party, because the dedication flattered their
mistress and her government—far too much indeed
for the nature of the subject.

Dr. YOUNG's next poem was entitled, THE FORCE
OF RELIGION, and founded on the deaths of Lady
JANE GREY and her husband. " It is written with
" elegance enough," according to Dr. JOHNSON; but
was " never popular:" for " JANE is too heroic to
" be pitied." The dedication of this piece to the
Countess of SALISBURY, was also *inexcuseably* fulsome,
and, I think, profane. Indeed the author himself
seems afterwards to have thought so; for when he
collected his smaller pieces into volumes, he very judi-
ciously suppressed this and most of his other dedica-
tions.

In some part of his life YOUNG certainly went to
IRELAND*, and was there acquainted with the eccen-
trical Dean SWIFT; and his biographers seem agreed,
that this was, most probably, during his connection
with the Duke of WHARTON, who went thither in
1717. But he cannot have long remained there, as in

* From his seventh satire it appears also that he was once abroad,
probably about this time, and saw a field of battle covered with the
slain; and it is affirmed that once, with a classic in his hand, he wan-
dered into the enemy's encampment, and had some difficulty to con-
vince them, that he was only an *absent poet* and not a *spy*.

1719, he brought out his first tragedy of Busiris, at DRURY LANE, and dedicated it to the Duke of NEWCASTLE. This tragedy had been written some years, though now first performed; for it is to our author's credit, that many of his works were laid by him a considerable time before they were obtruded on the public. Our great dramatic critic pronounces this piece " too far removed from known life" to affect the passions.

His next performance was THE REVENGE, the dramatic character of which is sufficiently ascertained by its still keeping possession of the stage. The hint of this is supposed to have been taken from OTHELLO; "⌐but the reflections, the incidents, and the diction, are " original."—The success of this induced him to attempt another tragedy, which was written in 1721, but not brought upon the stage for thirty years afterwards; and then without success, as we shall have farther occasion to observe. It has been remarked, that all his plays conclude with suicide*, and I much fear the frequent introduction of this unnatural crime upon the stage, has contributed greatly to its commission.

We have passed over our Author's PARAPHRASE ON PART OF THE BOOK OF JOB, in order to bring his dramatic performances together. This Paraphrase has been well received, and has often been printed with his NIGHT THOUGHTS. This I could admire, perhaps as much as any of his works, could I forget the original: but there is such a dignified simplicity

---

* Our author seems early to have been enamoured with the Tragic Muse, and with the charms of melancholy. Dr. RIDLEY relates, that, when at OXFORD, he would sometimes shut up his room, and study by a lamp, at mid-day.

even in our prose translation of the poetic parts of scripture, that I can never bear to see them reduced to rhyme, or modern measures.

His next, and one of his best performances, is entitled, THE LOVE OF FAME THE UNIVERSAL PASSION, in Seven characteristic Satires, originally published separately, between the years 1725 and 1728. This, according to Dr. JOHNSON, is a "*very great* per- " formance. It is said to be a series of epigrams, " and if it be, it is what the author intended: His " endeavour was at the production of striking distichs " and pointed sentences; and his distichs have the " weight of solid sentiment, and his points the sharp- " ness of resistless truths. His characters are often " selected with discernment, and drawn with nicety; " his illustrations are often happy, and his reflections " often just. His species of satire is between those " of HORACE and JUVENAL; and he has the gaiety " of HORACE without his laxity of numbers; and the " morality of JUVENAL, with greater variety of " images."—SWIFT indeed has pronounced of these Satires, that they should have been either " more " merry, or more severe:" in that case, they might probably have caught the popular taste more; but this does not prove that they would have been better. The opinion of the Duke of GRAFTON, however, was of more worth than all the opinions of the wits, if it be true as related by Mr. SPENCE, that his grace presented the author with two thousand pounds. " Two thousand pounds for a poem!" said one of the Duke's friends: to whom his grace replied, that he had made an excellent bargain, for he thought them worth four.

b

On the accession of GEORGE I. YOUNG flattered him with an Ode, called OCEAN, to which was prefixed an introductory ODE TO THE KING, and AN ESSAY ON LYRIC POETRY: of these the most observable thing is, that the poet and the critic could not agree: for the Rules of the Essay condemned the Poetry, and the Poetry set at defiance the maxims of the Essay.   The biographer of British poets has truly said, " he had least success in his lyric attempts, in " which he seems to have been under some malig- " nant influence: he is always labouring to be great, " and at last is only turgid."

We now leave a while the works of our author, to contemplate the conduct of the man.   About this time his studies took a more serious turn; and, forsaking the law, which he had never practised, when he was almost fifty he entered into orders, and was in 1728, appointed Chaplain to the King.   One of POPE's biographers relates, that, on this occasion YOUNG applied to his brother poet for direction in his studies, who jocosely recommended THOMAS AQUINAS, which the former taking seriously, he retired to the suburbs with the angelical doctor, till his friend discovered him, and brought him back.

His VINDICATION OF PROVIDENCE, and ESTIMATE OF HUMAN LIFE, were published in this year; they have gone through several editions, and are generally regarded as the best of his prose compositions: But the plan of the latter never was completed.   The following year he printed a very loyal sermon on King CHARLES's Martyrdom, intitled, AN APOLOGY FOR PRINCES.   In 1730, he was presented by his college to the rectory of WELWYN in

HERTFORDSHIRE, worth about £.300 a year, besides the lordship of the manor annexed to it.   This year he relapsed again to poetry, and published a loyal NAVAL ODE, and TWO EPISTLES TO POPE, of which nothing particular need be said.

He was married, in 1731, to Lady ELIZABETH LEE, widow of Colonel LEE, and daughter to the Earl of LITCHFIELD; and it was not long before she brought him a son and heir.

Sometime before his marriage, the Doctor walking in his garden at WELWYN, with this lady and another, a servant came to tell him a gentleman wished to speak to him.   " Tell him," says the Doctor, " I am " too happily engaged to change my situation."   The ladies insisted that he should go, as his visitor was a man of rank, his patron, and his friend; and as persuasion had no effect on him, they took him, one by the right hand, and the other by the left, and led him to the garden-gate.   He laid his hand upon his heart, and in that expressive manner, for which he was so remarkable, spoke the following lines:

> " Thus ADAM look'd when from the garden driv'n,
> " And thus disputed orders sent from Heav'n:
> " Like him I go, but yet to go am loth:
> " Like him I go, for angels drove us both.
> " Hard was his fate, but mine still more unkind;
> " His EVE went with him, but mine stays behind."

Another striking instance of his wit is related in reference to VOLTAIRE: who, while in ENGLAND, (probably at Mr. DODDINGTON's seat in DORSET-SHIRE) ridiculed, with some severity, MILTON's allegorical personages, *Sin* and *Death*; on which YOUNG, who was one of the company, immediately addressed him in the following extemporaneous distich:

" Thou art so witty, profligate, and thin,
" Thou seem'st a MILTON with his *Death* and *Sin*."

Soon after his marriage, our author again indulged
his poetical vein in two odes, called THE SEA PIECE,
with a Poetical Dedication to VOLTAIRE, in which
the above incident seems alluded to in these lines,

" On DORSET downs, when MILTON's page
" With *Sin* and *Death* provok'd thy rage."

In 1734 he printed an ARGUMENT FOR PEACE,
which afterward, with several of his smaller pieces,
and most of his dedications, was consigned by his own
hand to merited oblivion: in which circumstance he
deserves both the thanks and imitation of posterity.

About the year 1741 he had the unhappiness to
lose his wife; her daughter by Colonel LEE, and this
daughter's husband, Mr. TEMPLE. What affliction
he felt for their loss, may be seen in his NIGHT
THOUGHTS, written on this occasion. They are ad-
dressed to LORENZO, a man of pleasure, and the
world; and who, it is generally supposed, was his own
son, then labouring under his father's displeasure. His
son-in-law is said to be characterized by PHILANDER,
and his Lady's daughter was certainly the person he
speaks of under the appellation of NARCISSA.—(See
Night III. line 62.) In her last illness, which was a
consumption, he accompanied her to MONTPELLIER;
or, as Mr. CROFT says, to LYONS, in the South of
FRANCE, at which place she died soon after her ar-
rival.

Being regarded as a heretic, she was denied chris-
tian burial, and her afflicted father was obliged to
steal a grave, and inter her privately with his own
hands. (See Night III. line 162, &c.) In this cele-
brated poem he thus addresses Death:

" Insatiate archer! could not one suffice?
" Thy shaft flew thrice, and thrice my peace was slain;
" And thrice, ere thrice yon moon had fill'd her horn."

These lines have been universally understood of the above deaths; but this supposition can no way be reconciled with Mr. CROFT's dates, who says, Mrs. TEMPLE died in 1736, Mr. TEMPLE in 1740, and Lady YOUNG in 1741. Which quite inverts the order of the poet, who makes NARCISSA's death follow PHILANDER's:

" NARCISSA follows e'er his tomb is clos'd."
                                    Night III. line 62.

There is no possible way to reconcile these contra-dictions: either we must reject Mr. CROFT's dates, for which he gives us no authority, or we must sup-pose the characters and incidents, if not entirely fic-titious, as the author assures us that they were not, were accommodated by poetic licence to his purpose. As to the character of LORENZO, whether taken from real life, or moulded purely in the author's imagina-tion, Mr. CROFT has sufficiently proved that it could not intend his Son, who was but eight years old when most part of the NIGHT THOUGHTS were written, for Night the Seventh is dated, in the original edition, July 1744.

For the literary merits of this work we shall again refer to the criticism of Dr. JOHNSON, which is sel-dom exceptionable when he is not warped by politi-cal prejudices. " In his NIGHT THOUGHTS," says the Doctor, speaking of our author, " he has exhi-" bited a very wide display of original poetry, varie-" gated with deep reflections and striking allusions; " a wilderness of thought, in which the fertility of " fancy scatters flowers of every hue, and of every

" odour. This is one of the few poems in which
" blank verse could not be changed for rhyme, but
" with disadvantage. The wild diffusion of the sen-
" timents, and the digressive sallies of imagination,
" would have been compressed and restrained by
" confinement to rhyme. The excellence of this
" work is not exactness, but copiousness: particular
" lines are not to be regarded; the power is in the
" whole; and in the whole there is a magnificence
" like that ascribed to Chinese plantation, the mag-
" nificence of vast extent and endless diversity."

So far Dr. JOHNSON.—Mr. CROFT says, " Of these
" poems the two or three first have been perused more
" eagerly and more frequently than the rest. When
" he got as far as the fourth or fifth, his original
" motive for taking up the pen was answered; his
" grief was naturally either diminished or exhausted.
" We still find the same pious poet; but we hear less
" of PHILANDER and NARCISSA, and less of the
" mourner whom he loved to pity."

Notwithstanding one might be tempted, from some
passages in the NIGHT THOUGHTS, to suppose he
had taken his leave of terrestrial things, in the alarm-
ing year 1745, he could not refrain from returning
again to politics; but wrote POETICAL REFLECTIONS
on the State of the Kingdom, originally appended to
the NIGHT THOUGHTS, but never re-printed with
them.

In 1753, his tragedy of THE BROTHERS, written
thirty years before, now first appeared upon the
stage. It had been in rehearsal when YOUNG took
orders, and was withdrawn on that occasion. The
Rector of WELWYN devoted £.1000 to " The Society
" for the Propagation of the Gospel," and estimating

the probable produce of this play at such a sum, he perhaps thought the occasion might sanctify the means; and not thinking so unfavourably of the stage as other good men have done, he committed the monstrous absurdity of giving a play for the propagation of the gospel! The author was (as is often the case with authors) deceived in his calculation. THE BROTHERS was never a favourite with the public: but that the society might not suffer, the doctor made up the deficiency from his own pocket.

His next was a prose performance, entitled, " THE " CENTAUR NOT FABULOUS; in Six Letters to a " Friend on the Life in Vogue." The third of these letters describes the death-bed of " the gay, young, " noble, ingenious, accomplished, and most wretched " ALTAMONT," whom report supposed to be Lord EUSTON. But whether ALTAMONT or LORENZO were real or fictitious characters, it is certain the author could be at no loss for models for them among the gay nobility with whom he was acquainted.

In 1759 appeared his lively " CONJECTURES ON " ORIGINAL COMPOSITION;" which, according to Mr. CROFT, appear " more like the production of " untamed, unbridled youth, than of jaded fourscore." This letter contains the pleasing account of the death of ADDISON, and his dying address to Lord WAR- WICK,—" See how a christian can die !"

In 1762, but little before his death, YOUNG published his last, and one of his least esteemed poems— " RESIGNATION," which was written on the following occasion. Observing that Mrs. BOSCAWEN, in the midst of her grief for the loss of the Admiral, derived consolation from a perusal of the NIGHT THOUGHTS, her friend, Mrs. MONTAGUE, proposed a

visit to the author, by whom they were favourably received; and were pleased to confess that his " un-
" bounded genius appeared to greater advantage in
" the companion than even in the author; that the
" Christian was in him a character still more inspired,
" more enraptured, more sublime than the poet, and
" that, in his ordinary conversation,

> ————" Letting down the golden chain from high,
> " He drew his audience upward to the sky."

On this occasion, and at the request of these ladies, the author produced his RESIGNATION, above men-tioned, and which has been so unmercifully treated by the critics; but it has, in some measure, been rescued from their hands by Dr. JOHNSON, who says, " It
" was falsely represented as a proof of decaying facul-
" ties. There is YOUNG in every stanza, such as he
" often was in his highest vigour."

We now approach the closing scene of our author's life, of which, unhappily, we have few particulars. For three or four years before his death, he appears to have been incapacitated, by the infirmities of age, for public duty; yet he perfectly enjoyed his intel-lects to the last, and even his vivacity: for in his last illness, a friend mentioning the recent decease of a person who had long been in a decline, and observ-ing, that he was quite worn to a *shell* before he died; " Very likely," replied the doctor; " but what is be-
" come of the *kernel?*"—He is said to have regretted to another friend, that his NIGHT THOUGHTS, of all his works most calculated to do good, were written so much above the understanding of common readers, as to contract their sphere of usefulness: This, how-ever, ought not perhaps to be regretted, since there

is a great sufficiency of good books for common rea-
ders, and the style of that work will always introduce
it where plainer compositions would not be read.

He died at his Parsonage House at WELWYN,
April 12, 1765, and was buried, according to his
desire, by the side of his lady, under the altar-piece
of that church: Which is said to be ornamented in a
singular manner with an elegant piece of needle-
work by Lady YOUNG, and some appropriate inscrip-
tions, painted by the direction of the doctor.

His best monument is to be found in his works;
but a less durable one, in marble, was erected by his
only son and heir, with a very modest and sensible in-
scription.   This son, Mr. FREDERICK YOUNG, had
the first part of his education at WINCHESTER school,
and, becoming a scholar upon the foundation, was
sent, in consequence thereof, to NEW COLLEGE, in
OXFORD; but there being no vacancy (though the
society waited for one no less than two years,) he
was admitted in the meantime in BALIOL, where he
behaved so imprudently as to be forbidden the col-
lege *.   This misconduct disobliged his father so
much, that it is said he never would see him after-
wards: However, by his will he bequeathed to him
the bulk of his fortune, which was considerable, re-
serving only a legacy to his friend STEVENS, the
hatter at TEMPLE-GATE; and 1000l. to his house-
keeper, with his dying charge to see all his manu-

---

* Mr. CROFT denies this circumstance, and calls the poet's son his
friend. He does not however pretend to vindicate the conduct of the
youth; but he relates his repentance and regret, which is far better.
Perhaps it is not possible wholly to vindicate the father. Great genius,
even accompanied with piety, is not always most ornamental to do-
mestic life: and " the prose of ordinary occurrences," says CROFT,
" is beneath the dignity of poets."

C

scripts destroyed; which may have been some loss
to posterity, though none perhaps to his own fame.

Dr. YOUNG, as a christian and divine, has been
reckoned an example of primeval piety.—He was
an able orator, but it is not known whether he com-
posed many sermons: and it is certain that he pub-
lished very few. The following incident does honour
to his feelings: when preaching in his turn one Sunday
at St. JAMES's, finding he could not gain the attention
of his audience, his pity for their folly got the better
of all decorum; he sat back in the pulpit, and burst
into a flood of tears.

His turn of mind was naturally solemn; and he
usually, when at home in the country, spent many
hours walking among the tombs in his own church-
yard. His conversation, as well as writings, had all
a reference to a future life; and this turn of mind
mixed itself even with his improvements in garden-
ing: He had, for instance, an alcove, with a bench so
well painted in it, that at a distance it seemed to be
real, but upon a nearer approach the deception was
perceived, and this motto appeared:

INVISIBILIA NON DECIPIUNT.
The things unseen do not deceive us.

In another part of his garden was also this inscrip-
tion:

AMBULANTES IN HORTO AUDIERUNT VOCEM DEI.
They heard the voice of GOD walking in the garden.

This seriousness occasioned him to be charged with
gloominess of temper, yet was he fond of rural sports
and innocent amusements. He would sometimes
frequent the assembly and the bowling-green; and we
see in his satires that he knew how to laugh at folly.

His wit was poignant, and always levelled at those who shewed any contempt for decency or religion; an instance of which we have remarked in his extemporary epigram on Voltaire.

Dr. YOUNG rose betimes, and engaged with his domestics in the duties of Morning Prayer. He is said to have read but little; but he noted what he read, and many of his books were so swelled with folding down his favourite passages, that they would hardly shut. He was moderate in his meals, and rarely drank wine, except when he was ill; being (as he used to say) unwilling to waste the succours of sickness on the stability of health. After a slight refreshment, he retired to rest early in the evening, even though he might have company who wished to prolong his stay.

He lived at a moderate expence, rather inclined to parsimony than profusion; and seems to have possessed just conceptions of the vanity of the world: yet, (such is the inconsistency of man!) he courted honours and preferments at the borders of the grave, even so late as 1758; but none were then conferred. It has however been asserted that he had a pension of 200l. a year from government, conferred under the auspices of WALPOLE.

At last, when he was full fourscore, the author of the NIGHT THOUGHTS,

" Who thought e'en gold itself might come a day too late,"

Was made Clerk of the Closet to the Princess Dowager of WALES. What retarded his promotion so long it is not easy to determine. Some attribute it to his attachment to the Prince of WALES and his friends: and others assert, that the king thought him sufficiently provided for. Certain it is, that he knew no straits in pecuniary matters; and that, in the method he has recommended of estimating human life, honours are of little value.

His merits as an Author have already been considered in a review of his works: and nothing seems necessary to be added, but the following general characters of his composition, from BLAIR and JOHNSON.

Dr. BLAIR says (in his celebrated lectures): " Among moral and didactic poets, Dr. YOUNG is " of too great eminence to be passed over without " notice. In all his works, the marks of strong ge- " nius appear. His UNIVERSAL PASSION, pos- " sesses the full merit of that animated conciseness " of style, and lively description of characters, which " I mention as requisite in satirical and didactic " compositions. Though his wit may often be " thought too sparkling, and his sentences too point- " ed, yet the vivacity of his fancy is so great, as to " entertain every reader. In his NIGHT THOUGHTS, " there is much energy of expression; in the three " first, there are several pathetic passages; and scat- " tered through them all, happy images and allusions, " as well as pious reflections occur. But the senti- " ments are frequently over-strained, and turgid; and " the style is too harsh and obscure to be pleasing."

The same critic has said of our author in another place, that his " merit in figurative language is great " and deserves to be remarked. No writer, ancient " or modern, had a stronger imagination than Dr. " YOUNG, or one more fertile in figures of every

" kind, his metaphors are often new, and often natu-
" ral and beautiful. But his imagination was strong
" and rich, rather than delicate and correct."

These strictures may be thought severe; but it
should be remembered, that an author derives far
more honour from such a discriminate character, from
a judicious critic, than from the indiscriminate com-
mendation of an admirer. The following is the con-
clusion of Dr. JOHNSON's critique, and shall conclude
these memoirs.

" It must be allowed of YOUNG's poetry that it
" abounds in thought, but without much accuracy
" or selection. When he lays hold of a thought,
" he pursues it beyond expectation, [and] sometimes
" happily, as in his parallel of *quicksilver* with *pleasure*
" . . . . which is very ingenious, very subtle, and
" almost exact . . . . . .

" His versification is his own; neither his blank
" nor his rhyming lines have any resemblance to
" those of former writers; he picks up no hemi-
" sticks, he copies no favourite expressions; he
" seems to have laid up no stores of thought or
" diction, but to owe all to the fortuitous sugges-
" tions of the present moment. Yet I have reason
" to believe that, when once he had formed a new
" design, he then laboured it with very patient in-
" dustry, and that he composed with great labour
" and frequent revisions.

" His verses are formed by no certain model; he
" is no more like himself in his different produc-
" tions, than he is like others. He seems never
" to have studied prosody, nor to have any direc-
" tion, but from his own ear. But with all his
" defects he was a man of genius, and a poet."

P. S. The materials of the above Life are taken from the ARTICLE referring to our author in JOHNSON's Lives of the Poets, written by Mr. HERBERT CROFT, with the Critique of Dr. JOHNSON, and compared with the BIOGRAPHIA BRITANNICA, and other respectable authorities.

CONTENTS.

THE

COMPLAINT.

NIGHT I.

ON

LIFE, DEATH, AND IMMORTALITY.

TIR'D Nature's sweet restorer, balmy Sleep!
He—like the world, his ready visit pays
Where Fortune smiles; the wretched he forsakes:
Swift on his downy pinions flies from woe,
And lights on lids unsully'd with a tear.   5
    From short (as usual) and disturb'd repose
I wake—How happy they, who wake no more!
Yet that were vain, if dreams infest the grave.
I wake, emerging from a sea of dreams
Tumultuous; where my wreck'd desponding thought,
From wave to wave of fancy'd misery,   11
At random drove, her helm of reason lost:
Though now restor'd, 'tis only change of pain;
(A bitter change!) severer for severe.

B

The day too short for my distress; and Night,   15
Ev'n in the zenith of her dark domain,
Is sunshine to the colour of my fate.
    Night, sable goddess! from her ebon throne,
In rayless majesty, now stretches forth
Her leaden sceptre o'er a slumb'ring world.   20
Silence, how dread! and darkness, how profound!
Nor eye, nor list'ning ear, an object finds;
Creation sleeps.   'Tis as the gen'ral pulse
Of life stood still, and Nature made a pause;
An awful pause! prophetic of her end.   25
And let her prophecy be soon fulfill'd:
Fate! drop the curtain; I can lose no more.
    Silence and Darkness! solemn sisters! twins
From ancient Night, who nurse the tender thought
To Reason, and on Reason build Resolve,   30
(That column of true majesty in Man,)
Assist me: I will thank you in the grave;
The grave, your kingdom: There this frame shall fall
A victim sacred to your dreary shrine.
But what are ye!—   35
    THOU, who didst put to flight
Primæval Silence, when the morning stars,
Exulting, shouted o'er the rising ball;
O THOU! whose word from solid darkness struck
That spark, the sun, strike wisdom from my soul; 40
My soul, which flies to THEE, her trust, her treasure,
As misers to their gold, while others rest.
    Through this opaque of Nature and of Soul,
This double night, transmit one pitying ray,
To lighten, and to cheer.   O lead my mind,   45
(A mind that fain would wander from its woe,)

Lead it through various scenes of life and death;
And from each scene, the noblest truths inspire.
Nor less inspire my conduct than my song;
Teach my best reason, reason; my best will   50
Teach rectitude; and fix my firm resolve
Wisdom to wed, and pay her long arrear:
Nor let the phial of thy vengeance pour'd
On this devoted head, be pour'd in vain.
    The bell strikes one—We take no note of time, 55
But from its loss—To give it then a tongue,
Is wise in man—As if an angel spoke,
I feel the solemn sound.   If heard aright,
It is the knell of my departed hours:
Where are they? With the years beyond the flood. 60
It is the signal that demands dispatch:
How much is to be done! My hopes and fears
Start up alarm'd, and o'er life's narrow verge
Look down—On what? A fathomless abyss;
A dread eternity! how surely mine!   65
And can eternity belong to me,
Poor pensioner on the bounties of an hour?
    How poor, how rich, how abject, how august,
How complicate, how wonderful, is Man!
How passing wonder HE, who made him such!   70
Who center'd in our make such strange extremes!
From diff'rent natures marvellously mix'd,
Connection exquisite of distant worlds!
Distinguish'd link in being's endless chain!
Midway from Nothing to the Deity!   75
A beam ethereal, sully'd and absorpt!
Though sully'd and dishonour'd still divine!
Dim miniature of greatness absolute!

An heir of glory! a frail child of dust!
Helpless immortal! insect infinite!   80
A worm! a god!—I tremble at myself,
And in myself am lost! At home, a stranger,
Thought wanders up and down, surpris'd, aghast,
And wond'ring at her own: How reason reels!
O what a miracle to Man is Man,   85
Triumphantly distress'd! what joy, what dread!
Alternately transported, and alarm'd!
What can preserve my life? or what destroy?
An angel's arm can't snatch me from the grave,
Legions of angels can't confine me there.   90
'Tis past conjecture; all things rise in proof:
While o'er my limbs Sleep's soft dominion spreads,
What though my soul fantastic measures trod
O'er fairy fields; or mourn'd along the gloom
Of pathless woods; or down the craggy steep   95
Hurl'd headlong, swam with pain the mantled pool;
Or scal'd the cliff; or danc'd on hollow winds,
With antic shapes—wild natives of the brain!
Her ceaseless flight, though devious, speaks her nature
Of subtler essence than the trodden clod;   100
Active, aërial, tow'ring, unconfin'd,
Unfetter'd with her gross companion's fall.
Ev'n silent Night proclaims my soul immortal:
Ev'n silent Night proclaims eternal day.
For human weal, Heav'n husbands all events: 105
Dull Sleep instructs, nor sport vain dreams in vain.
    Why then their loss deplore that are not lost?
Why wanders wretched thought their tombs around,
In infidel distress? Are angels there?
Slumber's rak'd up in dust, ethereal fire?   110

Yet. Man. fool. Man, here buries all his thoughts;

Page 5.

London Published Oct.ʳ 25ᵗʰ 1797 by T. Heptinstall Nᵒ 30ⁱ Holborn.

They live! they greatly live! a life on earth
Unkindled, unconceiv'd! and from an eye
Of tenderness, let heav'nly pity fall
On me, more justly number'd with the dead.
This is the desert, this the solitude: 115
How populous, how vital, is the grave!
This is creation's melancholy vault,
The vale funereal, the sad cypress gloom;
The land of apparitions, empty shades!
All, all on earth is shadow, all beyond   120
Is substance: The reverse is Folly's creed:
How solid all, where change shall be no more!
   This is the bud of being, the dim dawn,
The twilight of our day, the vestibule;
Life's theatre as yet is shut, and Death,   125
Strong Death alone can heave the massy bar,
This gross impediment of clay remove,
And make us, embryos of existence, free.
From real life, but little more remote
Is he, not yet a candidate for light,   130
The future embryo, slumb'ring in his sire.
Embryos we must be, till we burst the shell,
Yon ambient azure shell, and spring to life,
The life of gods, (O transport!) and of man.
   Yet Man, fool Man! here buries all his thoughts;
Inters celestial hopes without one sigh.   136
Pris'ner of earth, and pent beneath the moon,
Here pinions all his wishes: Wing'd by Heav'n
To fly at infinite; and reach it there,
Where seraphs gather immortality.   140
On Life's fair tree, fast by the throne of God,
What golden joys ambrosial clust'ring glow

In His full beam, and ripen for the just!
Where momentary ages are no more!
Where Time, and Pain, and Chance, and Death expire!
And is it in the flight of threescore years,   146
To push eternity from human thought,
And smother souls immortal in the dust?
A soul immortal, spending all her fires,
Wasting her strength in strenuous idleness,   150
Thrown into tumult, raptur'd, or alarm'd
At aught this scene can threaten, or indulge,
Resembles ocean into tempest wrought,
To waft a feather, or to drown a fly.

    Where falls this censure? it o'erwhelms myself; 155
How was my heart incrusted by the world!
O how self-fetter'd was my grov'ling soul!
How, like a worm, was I wrapt round and round
In silken thought, which reptile Fancy spun!
Till darken'd Reason lay quite clouded o'er   160
With soft conceit of endless comfort here,
Nor yet put forth her wings to reach the skies!

    Night-visions may befriend (as sung above:)
Our waking dreams are fatal.   How I dreamt
Of things impossible! (could Sleep do more?)   165
Of joys perpetual in perpetual change!
Of stable pleasures on the tossing wave!
Eternal sunshine in the storms of Life!
How richly were my noontide trances hung
With gorgeous tapestries of pictur'd joys,   170
Joy behind joy, in endless perspective!
Till at Death's toll, whose restless iron tongue
Calls daily for his millions at a meal,
Starting I woke, and found myself undone.

Where's now my frenzy's pompous furniture? 175
The cobwebb'd cottage, with its ragged wall
Of mould'ring mud, is royalty to me.
The spider's most attenuated thread,
Is cord, is cable, to man's tender tie
On earthly bliss; it breaks at every breeze. 180
    O ye blest scenes of permanent delight!
Full, above measure! lasting, beyond bound!
A perpetuity of bliss, is bliss.
Could you, so rich in rapture, fear an end,
That ghastly thought would drink up all your joy, 185
And quite unparadise the realms of light.
Safe are you lodg'd above these rolling spheres;
The baleful influence of whose giddy dance
Sheds sad vicissitude on all beneath.
Here teems with revolutions ev'ry hour; 190
And rarely for the better; or the best,
More mortal than the common births of Fate.
Each moment has its sickle, emulous
Of Time's enormous scythe, whose ample sweep
Strikes empires from the root; each moment plays 195
His little weapon in the narrower sphere
Of sweet domestic comfort, and cuts down
The fairest bloom of sublunary bliss.
    Bliss! sublunary bliss!—proud words, and vain!
Implicit treason to divine decrees! 200
A bold invasion of the rights of heav'n!
I clasp'd the phantoms, and I found them air;
O had I weigh'd it ere my fond embrace!
What darts of agony had miss'd my heart!
Death! great proprietor of all! 'tis thine 205
To tread out empire, and to quench the stars.

The sun himself by thy permission shines;
And, one day, thou shalt pluck him from his sphere.
Amidst such mighty plunder, why exhaust
Thy partial quiver on a mark so mean?   210
Why thy peculiar rancour wreak'd on me?
Insatiate archer! could not one suffice?
Thy shaft flew thrice; and thrice my peace was slain;
And thrice, e'er thrice yon moon had fill'd her horn.
O Cynthia! why so pale? Dost thou lament   215
Thy wretched neighbour? grieve to see thy wheel
Of ceaseless change outwhirl'd in human life?
How wanes my borrow'd bliss! from Fortune's smile,
Precarious courtesy! not Virtue's sure,
Self-given, solar, ray of sound delight.   220

In ev'ry vary'd posture, place, and hour,
How widow'd ev'ry thought of ev'ry joy!
Thought, busy thought! too busy for my peace;
Through the dark postern of time long elaps'd,
Led softly by the stillness of the night,   225
Led, like a murderer, (and such it proves!)
Strays (wretched rover!) o'er the pleasing past;
In quest of wretchedness perversely strays;
And finds all desert now; and meets the ghosts
Of my departed joys, a numerous train!   230
I rue the riches of my former fate;
Sweet comfort's blasted clusters I lament;
I tremble at the blessings once so dear;
And ev'ry pleasure pains me to the heart.

Yet why complain? or why complain for one? 235
Hangs out the sun his lustre but for me,
The single man? Are angels all beside?
I mourn for millions: 'Tis the common lot;

In this shape, or in that, has Fate entail'd
The mother's throes on all of woman born,　　240
Not more the children, than sure heirs of pain.
　War, Famine, Pest, Volcano, Storm, and Fire,
Intestine Broils, Oppression, with her heart
Wrapt up in triple brass, besiege mankind.
GOD's image, disinherited of day,　　245
Here, plung'd in mines, forgets a sun was made;
There, beings, deathless as their haughty lord,
Are hammer'd to the galling oar for life;
And plough the winter's wave, and reap despair.
Some for hard masters, broken under arms,　　250
In battle lopp'd away, with half their limbs,
Beg bitter bread through realms their valour sav'd,
If so the tyrant, or his minions, doom.
Want, and incurable Disease, (fell pair!)
On hopeless multitudes remorseless seize　　255
At once; and make a refuge of the grave.
How groaning hospitals eject their dead!
What numbers groan for sad admission there!
What numbers, once in Fortune's lap high-fed,
Solicit the cold hand of Charity!　　260
To shock us more, solicit it in vain!
Ye silken sons of pleasure, since in pains
You rue more modish visits, visit here,
And breathe from your debauch: Give, and reduce
Surfeit's dominion o'er you: But so great　　265
Your impudence, you blush at what is right.
　Happy! did sorrow seize on such alone.
Not prudence can defend, or virtue save;
Disease invades the chastest temperance;
And punishment the guiltless; and alarm,　　270

C

Through thickest shades, pursues the fond of peace.
Man's caution often into danger turns,
And, his guard falling, crushes him to death.
Not Happiness itself makes good her name;
Our very wishes give us not our wish.   275
How distant oft the thing we doat on most,
From that for which we doat, felicity!
The smoothest course of Nature has its pains;
And truest friends, through error, wound our rest.
Without misfortune, what calamities!   280
And what hostilities, without a foe!
Nor are foes wanting to the best on earth.
But endless is the list of human ills,
And sighs might sooner fail than cause to sigh.
    A part how small of the terraqueous globe   285
Is tenanted by Man! the rest a waste;
Rocks, deserts, frozen seas, and burning sands!
Wild haunts of monsters, poisons, stings, and death.
Such is Earth's melancholy map! But, far
More sad! this earth is a true map of Man: 290
So bounded are his haughty lord's delights
To Woe's wide empire; where deep troubles toss,
Loud sorrows howl, invenom'd passions bite,
Rav'nous calamities our vitals seize,
And threat'ning Fate wide opens to devour.   295
    What then am I, who sorrow for myself?
In age, in infancy, from others aid
Is all our hope; to teach us to be kind.
That, Nature's first, last lesson to mankind;
The selfish heart deserves the pain it feels.   300
More gen'rous sorrow, while it sinks, exalts;
And conscious virtue mitigates the pang.

Nor Virtue, more than Prudence, bids me give
Swoln thought a second channel; who divide,
They weaken too, the torrent of their grief.　　305
Take then, O world! thy much indebted tear:
How sad a sight is human happiness,
To those whose thought can pierce beyond an hour!
O thou, whate'er thou art, whose heart exults!
Wouldst thou I should congratulate thy fate?　310
I know thou wouldst; thy pride demands it from me.
Let thy pride pardon, what thy nature needs,
The salutary censure of a friend.
Thou happy wretch! by blindness thou art blest;
By dotage dandled to perpetual smiles.　　315
Know, smiler! at thy peril art thou pleas'd;
Thy pleasure is the promise of thy pain.
Misfortune, like a creditor severe,
But rises in demand for her delay;
She makes a scourge of past prosperity,　　320
To sting thee more, and double thy distress.
　　Lorenzo, fortune makes her court to thee.
Thy fond heart dances while the syren sings.
Dear is thy welfare; think me not unkind;
I would not damp, but to secure thy joys.　325
Think not that Fear is sacred to the storm.
Stand on thy guard against the smiles of Fate.
Is Heav'n tremendous in its frowns? most sure;
And in its favours formidable too:
Its favours here are trials, not rewards;　　330
A call to duty, not discharge from care;
And should alarm us full as much as woes;
Awake us to their cause and consequence;
And make us tremble, weigh'd with our desert;

Awe Nature's tumults, and chastise her joys,   335
Lest, while we clasp, we kill them; nay, invert
To worse than simple misery, their charms.
Revolted joys, like foes in civil war,
Like bosom friendships to resentment sour'd,
With rage invenom'd rise against our peace.   340
Beware what earth calls happiness; beware
All joys, but joys that never can expire.
Who builds on less than an immortal base,
Fond as he seems, condemns his joys to death.

    Mine dy'd with thee, PHILANDER! thy last sigh
Dissolv'd the charm; the disenchanted earth   346
Lost all her lustre.   Where, her glittering tow'rs?
Her golden mountains, where? All darken'd down
To naked waste; a dreary vale of tears:
The great magician's dead! Thou poor pale piece 350
Of out-cast earth, in darkness! what a change
From yesterday! thy darling hope so near,
(Long-labour'd prize!) O how ambition flush'd
Thy glowing cheek! ambition, truly great,
Of virtuous praise.   Death's subtle seed within,   355
(Sly, treach'rous miner!) working in the dark,
Smil'd at thy well-concerted scheme, and beckon'd
The worm to riot on that rose so red,
Unfaded ere it fell; one moment's prey!

    Man's foresight is conditionally wise;   360
LORENZO! wisdom into folly turns
Oft, the first instant; its idea fair
To lab'ring thought is born.   How dim our eye!
The present moment terminates our sight;
Clouds, thick as those on doomsday, drown the next;
We penetrate, we prophesy in vain.   366

Time is dealt out by particles; and each,
Ere mingled with the streaming sands of life,
By Fate's inviolable oath is sworn
Deep silence, " Where eternity begins."   370
　　By Nature's law, what may be, may be now;
There's no prerogative in human hours.
In human hearts what bolder thought can rise,
Than Man's presumption on to-morrow's dawn?
Where is to-morrow? In another world.   375
For numbers this is certain; the reverse
Is sure to none; and yet on this perhaps,
This peradventure, infamous for lies,
As on a rock of adamant we build
Our mountain hopes; spin our eternal schemes, 380
As we the fatal sisters would out-spin,
And, big with life's futurities, expire.
　　Not ev'n PHILANDER had bespoke his shroud,
Nor had he cause; a warning was deny'd:
How many fall as sudden, not as safe!   385
As sudden, though for years admonish'd home.
Of human ills the last extreme beware,
Beware, LORENZO! a slow sudden death.
How dreadful that delib'rate surprise!
Be wise to-day; 'tis madness to defer;   390
Next day the fatal precedent will plead;
Thus on, till wisdom is push'd out of life.
Procrastination is the thief of time;
Year after year it steals, till all are fled,
And to the mercies of a moment leaves   395
The vast concerns of an eternal scene.
If not so frequent, would not this be strange?
That 'tis so frequent, this is stranger still.

Of Man's miraculous mistakes, this bears
The palm, " That all men are about to live,"   400
For ever on the brink of being born.
All pay themselves the compliment to think
They one day shall not drivel; and their pride
On this reversion takes up ready praise;
At least their own; their future selves applauds;   405
How excellent that life they ne'er will lead!
Time lodg'd in their own hands is Folly's vails;
That lodg'd in Fate's, to Wisdom they consign;
The thing they can't but purpose, they postpone:
'Tis not in folly, not to scorn a fool;   410
And scarce in human wisdom to do more.
All promise is poor dilatory Man,
And that through ev'ry stage: When young, indeed,
In full content, we sometimes, nobly rest,
Unanxious for ourselves; and only wish,   415
As duteous sons, our fathers were more wise.
At thirty, Man suspects himself a fool;
Knows it at forty, and reforms his plan;
At fifty chides his infamous delay,
Pushes his prudent purpose to resolve;   420
In all the magnanimity of thought
Resolves; and re-resolves; then dies the same.
    And why? Because he thinks himself immortal.
All men think all men mortal, but themselves;
Themselves, when some alarming shock of fate   425
Strikes thro' their wounded hearts the sudden dread;
But their hearts wounded, like the wounded air,
Soon close; where past the shaft, no trace is found.
As from the wing no scar the sky retains;
The parted wave no furrow from the keel;   430

So dies in human hearts the thought of death.
Ev'n with the tender tear, which Nature sheds
O'er those we love, we drop it in their grave.
Can I forget PHILANDER? That were strange:
O my full heart! But should I give it vent,   435
The longest night, though longer far, would fail,
And the Lark listen to my midnight song.

   The sprightly Lark's shrill matin wakes the morn;
Grief's sharpest thorn hard pressing on my breast,
I strive, with wakeful melody, to cheer   440
The sullen gloom, sweet Philomel! like thee,
And call the stars to listen: Ev'ry star
Is deaf to mine, enamour'd of thy lay.
Yet be not vain; there are, who thine excel,
And charm thro' distant ages: Wrapt in shade,   445
Pris'ner of darkness! to the silent hours,
How often I repeat their rage divine,
To lull my griefs, and steal my heart from woe!
I roll their raptures, but not catch their fire.
Dark, though not blind, like thee, Mæonides!   450
Or, Milton! thee; ah! could I reach your strain!
Or his, who made Mæonides our own.
Man too he sung: Immortal Man I sing.
Oft bursts my song beyond the bounds of life;
What now, but immortality can please!   455
O had he press'd his theme, pursu'd the track
Which opens out of darkness into day!
O had he mounted on his wing of fire,
Soar'd, where I sink, and sung immortal Man!
How had it blest mankind, and rescu'd me!   460

COMPLAINT.

NIGHT II.

ON

TIME, DEATH, AND FRIENDSHIP.

" WHEN the cock crew, he wept"—Smote by
     that eye
Which looks on me, on all: That Pow'r who bids
This midnight centinel, with clarion shrill
(Emblem of that which shall awake the dead),
Rouse souls from slumber into thoughts of Heav'n. 5
Shall I too weep? Where then is fortitude?
And, fortitude abandon'd, what is Man!
I know the terms on which he sees the light;
He that is born, is listed; life is war;
Eternal war with woe. Who bears it best,   10
Deserves it least.—On other themes I'll dwell.
LORENZO! let me turn my thoughts on thee,
And thine, on themes may profit; profit there,

D

Where most thy need. Themes, too, the genuine growth
Of dear PHILANDER's dust. He, thus, though dead, 15
May still befriend.—What themes? Time's wondrous
     price,
Death, Friendship, and PHILANDER's final scene.
    So could I touch these themes, as might obtain
Thine ear, nor leave thy heart quite disengag'd,
The good deed would delight me; half-impress 20
On my dark cloud an Iris; and from grief
Call glory—Dost thou mourn PHILANDER's fate?
I know thou say'st it: Says thy life the same?
He mourns the dead who lives as they desire.
Where is that thrift, that Avarice of Time 25
(O glorious avarice!) thought of death inspires,
As rumour'd robberies endear our gold?
O Time! than gold more sacred; more a load
Than lead, to fools; and fools reputed wise.
What moment granted Man without account? 30
What years are squander'd, Wisdom's debt unpaid!
Our wealth in days all due to that discharge.
Haste, haste, he lies in wait, he's at the door,
Insidious Death! should his strong hand arrest,
No composition sets the pris'ner free. 35
Eternity's inexorable chain
Fast binds; and Vengeance claims the full arrear.
    How late I shudder'd on the brink! how late
Life call'd for her last refuge in despair.
That time is mine, O MEAD! to thee I owe; 40
Fain would I pay thee with Eternity.
But ill my genius answers my desire;
My sickly song is mortal, past thy cure.
Accept the will;—that dies not with my strain.

For what calls thy disease, LORENZO? Not   45
For Esculapian, but for moral aid.
Thou think'st it folly to be wise too soon.
Youth is not rich in time; it may be, poor;
Part with it as with money, sparing; pay
No moment but in purchase of its worth;   50
And what its worth, ask death-beds; they can tell.
Part with it as with life: Reluctant; big
With holy hope of nobler time to come;
Time higher aim'd, still nearer the great mark
Of Men and Angels; virtue more divine.

   Is this our duty, wisdom, glory, gain?   55
(These Heav'n benign in vital union binds,)
And sport we like the natives of the bough,
When vernal suns inspire? Amusement reigns
Man's great demand; to trifle is to live: 60
And is it then a trifle, too, to die?

   Thou say'st I preach, LORENZO! 'Tis confest.
What if, for once, I preach thee quite awake?
Who wants amusement in the flame of battle?
Is it not treason to the soul immortal,   65
Her foes in arms, eternity the prize?
Will toys amuse, when med'cines cannot cure?
When spirits ebb, when life's enchanting scenes
Their lustre lose, and lessen in our sight,
As lands and cities with their glitt'ring spires   70
To the poor shatter'd bark, by sudden storm
Thrown off to sea, and soon to perish there;
Will toys amuse? No: Thrones will then be toys,
And earth and skies seem dust upon the scale.

   Redeem we time?—Its loss we dearly buy.   75
What pleads LORENZO for his high-priz'd sports?

He pleads Time's num'rous blanks; he loudly pleads
The straw-like trifles on life's commonstream.
From whom those blanks and trifles, but from thee?
No blank, no trifle, Nature made or meant.   80
Virtue, or purpos'd virtue, still be thine;
This cancels thy complaint at once; this leaves
In act no trifle, and no blank in time.
This greatens, fills, immortalizes all;
·This, the blest art of turning all to gold: 85
This, the good heart's prerogative to raise
A royal tribute from the poorest hours;
Immense revenue! every moment pays.
If nothing more than purpose in thy pow'r;
Thy purpose firm, is equal to the deed: 90
Who does the best his circumstance allows,
Does well, acts nobly; angels could no more.
Our outward act, indeed, admits restraint:
'Tis not in things o'er thought to dominecr;
Guard well thy thought; our thoughts are heard in
        Heav'n.   95
    On all-important Time, through ev'ry age,
Though much, and warm, the wise have urg'd; the man
Is yet unborn, who duly weighs an hour.
" I've lost a day"—the Prince who nobly cry'd,
Had been an emperor without his crown;   100
Of Rome? Say, rather, lord of human race:
He spoke, as if deputed by Mankind.
So should all speak: So Reason speaks in all;
From the soft whispers of that God in Man,
Why fly to folly, why to frenzy fly,   105
For rescue from the blessings we possess?
Time, the supreme!—Time is eternity;

Pregnant with all eternity can give;
Pregnant with all that makes archangels smile.
Who murders Time, he crushes in the birth   110
A pow'r ethereal, only not ador'd.
    Ah, how unjust to Nature, and himself,
Is thoughtless, thankless, inconsistent Man!
Like children babbling nonsense in their sports,
We censure Nature for a span too short;   115
That span too short, we tax as tedious too;
Torture invention, all expedients tire,
To lash the ling'ring moments into speed,
And whirl us (happy riddance!) from ourselves.
Art, brainless Art! our furious charioteer   120
(For Nature's voice unstifled would recal),
Drives headlong tow'rds the precipice of Death;
Death most our dread; Death thus more dreadful made;
O what a riddle of absurdity!
Leisure is pain; takes off our chariot-wheels;   125
How heavily we drag the load of life!
Blest leisure is our curse; like that of CAIN,
It makes us wander; wander earth around
To fly that tyrant, Thought. As Atlas groan'd
The world beneath, we groan beneath an hour. 130
We cry for mercy to the next amusement;
The next amusement mortgages our fields!
Slight inconvenience! Prisons hardly frown,
From hateful Time if prisons set us free.
Yet when Death kindly tenders us relief,   135
We call him cruel; years to moments shrink,
Ages to years. The telescope is turn'd,
To Man's false optics (from his folly false)
Time, in advance, behind him hides his wings,

And seems to creep decrepit with his age: 140
Behold him, when past by; what then is seen,
But his broad pinions swifter than the winds?
And all Mankind, in contradiction strong,
Rueful, aghast! cry out on his career.

  Leave to thy foes these errors, and these ills;   145
To Nature just, their cause and cure explore.
Not short Heav'n's bounty, boundless our expence;
No niggard, Nature; Men are prodigals.
We waste (not use) our time; we breathe, not live.
Time wasted is existence, us'd is life.   150
And bare existence, Man, to live ordain'd,
Wrings and oppresses with enormous weight.
And why; since time was giv'n for use, not waste.
Injoin'd to fly; with tempest, tide, and stars,
To keep his speed, nor ever wait for Man;   155
Time's use was doom'd a pleasure; waste, a pain;
That Man might feel his error, if unseen:
And, feeling, fly to labour for his cure;
Not, blund'ring, split on idleness for ease.
Life's cares are comforts, such by Heav'n design'd; 160
He that has none, must make them, or be wretched.
Cares are employments; and without employ
The soul is on the rack; the rack of rest,
To souls most adverse; action all their joy.

  Here, then, the riddle, mark'd above, unfolds; 165
Then Time turns torment, when Man turns a fool.
We rave, we wrestle with great Nature's plan;
We thwart the Deity; and 'tis decreed,
Who thwart His will shall contradict their own.
Hence our unnat'ral quarrel with ourselves;   170
Our thoughts at enmity; our bosom-broil;

We push Time from us, and we wish him back;
Lavish of lustrums, and yet fond of life;
Life we think long and short—Death seek—and shun;
Body, and soul, like peevish man and wife,   175
United jar, and yet are loth to part.
    O the dark days of vanity! while here,
How tasteless! and how terrible when gone!
Gone! they ne'er go; when past, they haunt us still;
The spirit walks of ev'ry day deceas'd;   180
And smiles an angel, or a fury frowns.
Nor death, nor life, delight us. If time past,
And time possest, both pain us, what can please!
That which the Deity to please ordain'd,
Time us'd. The Man who consecrates his hours 185
By vig'rous effort, and an honest aim,
At once he draws the sting of life and death;
He walks with Nature; and her paths are peace.
    Our error's cause and cure are seen. See next
Time's nature, origin, importance, speed;   190
And thy great gain from urging his career.
All-sensual Man, because untouch'd, unseen;
He looks on Time as nothing.   Nothing else
Is truly Man's; 'tis Fortune's—Time's a god.
Hast thou ne'er heard of Time's omnipotence?   195
For, or against, what wonders can he do!
And will: To stand blank neuter he disdains.
Not on those terms was Time (Heav'n's stranger!) sent
On his important embassy to Man.
LORENZO! no: On the long-destin'd hour,   200
From everlasting ages growing ripe,
That memorable hour of wondrous birth,
When the dread SIRE, on emanation bent,

And big with Nature, rising in his might,
Call'd forth creation (for then Time was born),   205
By Godhead streaming through a thousand worlds;
Not on those terms, from the great days of Heav'n,
From old Eternity's mysterious orb,
Was Time cut off, and cast beneath the skies;
The skies, which watch him in his new abode,   210
Measuring his motions by revolving spheres;
That horologe machinery divine.
Hours, days, and months, and years, his children play,
Like num'rous wings, around him, as he flies:
Or, rather, as unequal plumes they shape   215
His ample pinions, swift as darted flame,
To gain his goal, to reach his ancient rest,
And join anew Eternity his sire;
In his immutability to nest,
When worlds, that count his circles now, unhing'd 220
(Fate the loud signal sounding) headlong rush
To timeless night and chaos, whence they rose.

　　Why spur the speedy? Why with levities
New-wing thy short, short day's too rapid flight?
Know'st thou, or what thou dost, or what is done? 225
Man flies from Time, and Time from Man; too soon
In sad divorce this double flight must end;
And then, where are we? where, LORENZO! then
Thy sports, thy pomps?—I grant thee, in a state
Not unambitious; in the ruffled shroud,   230
Thy Parian tomb's triumphant arch beneath.
Has Death his fopperies? Then well may Life
Put on her plume, and in her rainbow shine.

　　Ye well-array'd! Ye lilies of our land!
Ye lilies male! who neither toil nor spin,   235

(As sister lilies might,) if not so wise
As Solomon, more sumptuous to the sight!
Ye delicate! who nothing can support,
Yourselves most insupportable! for whom
The winter rose must blow, the Sun put on   240
A brighter beam in Leo, silky soft
Favonius breathe still softer, or be chid,
And other worlds send odours, sauce and song,
And robes, and notions, fram'd in foreign looms!
O ye LORENZO's of our age! who deem   245
One moment unamus'd, a misery
Not made for feeble Man! who call aloud
For ev'ry bauble, drivell'd o'er by sense,
For rattles, and conceits of ev'ry cast,
For change of follies, and relays of joy,   250
To drag your patient through the tedious length
Of a short winter's day—say, sages say!
Wit's oracles; say, dreamers of gay dreams;
How will you weather an eternal night,
Where such expedients fail?   255
    O treach'rous Conscience! while she seems to sleep
On rose and myrtle, lull'd with syren song;
While she seems, nodding o'er her charge to drop
On headlong Appetite the slacken'd rein,
And give us up to License, unrecall'd,   260
Unmark'd;—see, from behind her secret stand,
The sly informer minutes ev'ry fault,
And her dread diary with horror fills.
Not the gross act alone employs her pen;
She reconnoitres Fancy's airy band,   265
A watchful foe! The formidable spy,
List'ning, o'erhears the whispers of our camp:

E

Our dawning purposes of heart explores,
And steals our embryos of iniquity.
As all-rapacious usurers conceal   270
Their doomsday-book from all-consuming heirs;
Thus, with indulgence most severe, she treats
Us spendthrifts of inestimable Time;
Unnoted, notes each moment misapply'd;
In leaves more durable than leaves of brass,   275
Writes our whole history; which Death shall read
In ev'ry pale delinquent's private ear,
And judgment publish; publish to more worlds
Than this; and endless age in groans resound.
LORENZO, such that sleeper in thy breast!   280
Such is her slumber; and her vengeance such
For slighted counsel; such thy future peace!
And think'st thou still thou canst be wise too soon?
    But why on Time so lavish is my song?
On this great theme kind Nature keeps a school, 285
To teach her sons herself. Each night we die,
Each morn are born anew: Each day, a life!
And shall we kill each day? If trifling kills,
Sure vice must butcher. O what heaps of slain
Cry out for vengeance on us! Time destroy'd   290
Is suicide, where more than blood is spilt.
Time flies, Death urges, knells call, Heav'n invites,
Hell threatens: All exerts; in effort, all;
More than creation labours!—labours more?
And is there in creation, what, amidst   295
This tumult universal, wing'd dispatch,
And ardent energy, supinely yawns?—
Man sleeps; and Man alone; and Man, whose fate,
Fate irreversible, intire, extreme,

Endless—hair-hung—breeze-shaken—o'er the gulph
A moment trembles—drops——and Man—for whom
All else is in alarm—Man—the sole cause 302
Of this surrounding storm—And yet he sleeps,
As the storm rock'd to rest!—Throw Years away?
Throw Empires, and be blameless. Moments seize; 305
Heav'n's on their wing: A moment we may wish,
When worlds want wealth to buy. Bid Day stand still,
Bid him drive back his car, and reimport
The period past, regive the given hour.
LORENZO, more than miracles we want; 310
LORENZO—O for yesterdays to come!
　　Such is the language of the Man awake;
His ardour such for what oppresses thee.
And is his ardour vain? LORENZO! No;
That more than miracle the Gods indulge; 315
To-day is yesterday return'd; return'd
Full power'd to cancel, expiate, raise, adorn,
And reinstate us on the rock of peace.
Let it not share its predecessor's fate;
Nor, like its eldest sisters, die a fool. 320
Shall it evaporate in fume? fly off
Fuliginous, and stain us deeper still?
Shall we be poorer for the plenty pour'd?
More wretched for the clemencies of Heav'n?
　　Where shall I find him? Angels! tell me where. 325
You know him—He is near you—Point him out—
Shall I see glories beaming from his brow?
Or trace his footsteps by the rising flow'rs?
Your golden wings, now hov'ring o'er him, shed
Protection; now, are waving in applause 330
To that blest son of foresight! lord of Fate!

That awful independent on to-morrow!
Whose work is done; who triumphs in the past;
Whose yesterdays look backward with a smile;
Nor, like the Parthian, wound him as they fly;   335
That common, but opprobrious lot! Past hours,
If not by guilt, yet wound us by their flight.
If Folly bounds our prospect by the grave,
All feeling of futurity benumb'd;
All god-like passion for eternals quench'd;   340
All relish of realities expir'd;
Renounc'd all correspondence with the skies;
Our freedom chain'd; quite wingless our desire;
In sense dark-prison'd all that ought to soar;
Prone to the centre; crawling in the dust;   345
Dismounted ev'ry great and glorious aim;
Embruted ev'ry faculty divine;
Heart-bury'd in the rubbish of the world—
The world, that gulp of souls, immortal souls,
Souls elevate, angelic, wing'd with fire   350
To reach the distant skies, and triumph there
On thrones, which shall not mourn their masters chang'd;
Though we from earth; ethereal, they that fell.
Such veneration due, O Man! to Man.

Who venerate themselves the world despise.   355
For what, gay friend! is this escutcheon'd world,
Which hangs out Death in one eternal night?
A night, that glooms us in the noon-tide ray,
And wraps our thought, at banquets, in the shroud.
Life's little stage is a small eminence,   360
Inch-high the grave above; that home of Man,
Where dwells the multitude: We gaze around;
We read their monuments; we sigh; and while

'Whose yesterdays look backward with a Smile
Nor, like the Parthian, wound him as they fly;

Page. 23

London, Published. Aug.st 30.th 1797. by T. Heptinstall, N.o 304. High Holborn.

We sigh, we sink; and are what we deplor'd;
Lamenting, or lamented, all our lot!   365
  Is Death at distance? No: He has been on thee;
And giv'n sure earnest of his final blow.
Those hours, which lately smil'd, where are they now?
Palid to thought, and ghastly! drown'd, all drown'd
In that great deep, which nothing disembogues! 370
And, dying, they bequeath'd thee small renown.
The rest are on the wing: How fleet their flight!
Already has the fatal train took fire;
A moment—and the world's blown up to thee—
The sun is darkness—and the stars are dust.   375
  'Tis greatly wise to talk with our past hours;
And ask them, what report they bore to Heav'n;
And how they might have borne more welcome news.
Their answers form what Men experience call;
If Wisdom's friend, her best; if not, worst foe.   380
O reconcile them! kind Experience cries,
" There's nothing here, but what as nothing weighs;
" The more our joy, the more we know it vain;
" And by success are tutor'd to despair."
Nor is it only thus, but must be so.   385
Who knows not this, though grey, is still a child.
Loose then from earth the grasp of fond desire,
Weigh anchor, and some happier clime explore.
  Art thou so moor'd thou canst not disengage,
Nor give thy thoughts a ply to future scenes!   390
Since, by life's passing breath, blown up from earth,
Light, as the summer's dust, we take in air
A moment's giddy flight, and fall again;
Join the dull mass, increase the trodden soil,
And sleep till Earth herself shall be no more.   395

Since then (as emmets, their small world o'erthrown)
We, sore-amaz'd, from out Earth's ruins crawl,
And rise to fate extreme of foul or fair,
As Man's own choice, (controller of the skies!)
As Man's despotic will, perhaps one hour,   400
(O how omnipotent is Time!) decrees;
Should not each warning give a strong alarm?
Warning, far less than that of bosom torn
From bosom, bleeding o'er the sacred dead!
Should not each dial strike us as we pass,   405
Portentous as the written wall, which struck,
O'er midnight bowls, the proud Assyrian pale,
Erewhile high-flush'd with insolence and wine?
Like that, the dial speaks; and points to thee,
LORENZO! loth to break thy banquet up: 410
" O Man, thy kingdom is departing from thee;
" And, while it lasts, is emptier than my shade."
Its silent language such: Nor need'st thou call
Thy Magi, to decypher what it means.
Know, like the Medean, Fate is in thy walls: 415
Dost ask, How? whence? Belshazzar-like, amaz'd!
Man's make incloses the sure seeds of Death;
Life feeds the murderer: Ingrate! he thrives
On her own meal, and then his nurse devours.

     But here, LORENZO, the delusion lies;   420
That solar shadow, as it measures life,
It life resembles too: Life speeds away
From point to point, though seeming to stand still.
The cunning fugitive is swift by stealth:
Too subtle is the movement to be seen;   425
Yet soon Man's hour is up, and we are gone.
Warnings point out our danger; gnomons, time:

As these are useless when the sun is set;
So those, but when more glorious Reason shines.
Reason should judge in all; in Reason's eye   430
That sedentary shadow travels hard.
But such our gravitation to the wrong,
So prone our hearts to whisper what we wish,
'Tis later with the wise, than he's aware;
A WILMINGTON goes slower than the sun: 435
And all mankind mistake their time of day;
Ev'n age itself.   Fresh hopes are hourly sown
In furrow'd brows.   So gentle life's descent,
We shut our eyes, and think it is a plain.
We take fair days in winter, for the spring;   440
And turn our blessings into bane.   Since oft
Man must compute that age he cannot feel,
He scarce believes he's older for his years.
Thus, at life's latest eve, we keep in store
One disappointment sure, to crown the rest;   445
The disappointment of a promis'd hour.
On this, or similar, PHILANDER! thou,
Whose mind was moral, as the preacher's tongue;
And strong, to wield all science, worth the name;
How often we talk'd down the summer's sun,   450
And cool'd our passions by the breezy stream!
How often thaw'd and shorten'd winter's eve,
By conflict kind, that struck out latent truth,
Best found, so sought; to the recluse more coy!
Thoughts disentangle, passing o'er the lip;   455
Clean runs the thread; if not, 'tis thrown away,
Or kept to tie up nonsense for a song;
Song, fashionably fruitless; such as stains

The fancy, and unhallow'd passion fires;
Chiming her saints to Cytherea's fane.   460
    Know'st thou, LORENZO! what a friend contains?
As bees mix'd nectar draw from fragrant flow'rs,
So men from Friendship, Wisdom and Delight;
Twins ty'd by Nature; if they part, they die.
Hast thou no friend to set thy mind abroach?   465
Good sense will stagnate. Thoughts shut up, want air,
And spoil, like bales unopen'd to the sun.
Had thought been all, sweet speech had been deny'd;
Speech, thought's canal! Speech, thought's criterion too!
Thought in the mine, may come forth gold or dross;
When coin'd in words, we know its real worth.   471
If sterling, store it for thy future use;
'Twill buy thee benefit; perhaps renown.
Thought too, deliver'd, is the more possest;
Teaching, we learn; and, giving, we retain   475
The births of intellect; when dumb, forgot.
Speech ventilates our intellectual fire;
Speech burnishes our mental magazine;
Brightens, for ornament, and whets, for use.
What numbers, sheath'd in erudition, lie   480
Plung'd to the hilts in venerable tomes,
And rusted; who might have borne an edge,
And play'd a sprightly beam, if born to speech!
If born blest heirs to half their mother's tongue!
'Tis thought's exchange, which, like th' alternate push
Of waves conflicting, breaks the learned scum,   486
And defecates the student's standing pool.
    In Contemplation is his proud resource?
'Tis poor, as proud, by converse unsustain'd.

Rude thought runs wild in Contemplation's field; 490
Converse, the menage, breaks it to the bit
Of due restraint; and Emulation's spur
Give's graceful energy, by rivals aw'd.
'Tis converse qualifies for solitude;
As exercise for salutary rest. 495
By that untutor'd, Contemplation raves;
And Nature's fool, by Wisdom's is outdone.
    Wisdom, though richer than Peruvian mines,
And sweeter than the sweet ambrosial hive,
What is she, but the means of happiness? 500
That unobtain'd, than folly more a fool;
A melancholy fool, without her bells.
Friendship, the means of wisdom, richly gives
The precious end, which makes our wisdom wise.
Nature, in zeal for human amity, 505
Denies, or damps, an undivided joy.
Joy is an import; joy is an exchange;
Joy flies monopolists: It calls for two;
Rich fruit! Heav'n planted! never pluck'd by one.
Needful auxiliars are our friends, to give 510
To social Man true relish of himself.
Full on ourselves descending in a line,
Pleasure's bright beam is feeble in delight:
Delight intense, is taken by rebound;
Reverberated pleasures fire the breast. 515
    Celestial Happiness, whene'er she stoops
To visit earth, one shrine the goddess finds,
And one alone, to make her sweet amends
For absent Heav'n—the bosom of a friend;
Where heart meets heart, reciprocally soft, 520
Each other's pillow to repose divine.

F

Beware the counterfeit: In Passion's flame
Hearts melt; but melt like ice, soon harder froze.
True love strikes root in Reason; Passion's foe:
Virtue alone entenders us for life: 525
I wrong her much—entenders us for ever:
Of Friendship's fairest fruits, the fruit most fair
Is Virtue kindling at a rival fire,
And emulously rapid in her race.
O the soft enmity! endearing strife!   530
This carries Friendship to her noon-tide point,
And gives the rivet of eternity.

    From Friendship, which outlives my former themes,
Glorious survivor of old Time, and Death!
From Friendship, thus, that flow'r of heav'nly seed, 535
The wise extract Earth's most Hyblean bliss,
Superior wisdom, crown'd with smiling joy.

    But for whom blossoms this Elysian flow'r?
Abroad they find, who cherish it at home.
LORENZO! pardon what my love extorts,   540
An honest love, and not afraid to frown.
Though choice of follies fasten on the great,
None clings more obstinate, than fancy fond,
That sacred friendship is their easy prey;
Caught by the wafture of a golden lure,   545
Or fascination of a high-born smile.
Their smiles, the great, and the coquet, throw out
For other hearts, tenacious of their own;
And we no less of ours, when such the bait.
Ye Fortune's cofferers! Ye pow'rs of wealth!   550
You do your rent-rolls most felonious wrong,
By taking our attachment to yourselves.
Can gold gain friendship? Impudence of hope!

As well mere Man an angel might beget.
Love, and love only, is the loan for love.   555
LORENZO! pride repress; nor hope to find
A friend, but what has found a friend in thee.
All like the purchase; few the price will pay;
And this makes friends such miracles below.

 What if (since daring on so nice a theme)   560
I shew thee friendship delicate, as dear,
Of tender violations apt to die?
Reserve will wound it; and Distrust, destroy.
Deliberate on all things with thy friend.
But since friends grow not thick on ev'ry bough,   565
Nor ev'ry friend unrotten at the core;
First, on thy friend, delib'rate with thyself;
Pause, ponder, sift; not eager in the choice,
Nor jealous of the chosen; fixing, fix;
Judge before friendship, then confide till death.   570
Well, for thy friend; but nobler far, for thee;
How gallant danger for Earth's highest prize!
A friend is worth all hazard we can run.
" Poor is the friendless master of a world:
" A world in purchase for a friend is gain."   575
 So sung he (angels hear that angel sing!
Angels from friendship gather half their joy,)
So sung PHILANDER, as his friend went round
In the rich ichor, in the gen'rous blood
Of BACCHUS, purple god of joyous wit,   580
A brow solute, and ever-laughing eye.
He drank long health, and virtue to his friend;
His friend, who warm'd him more, who more inspir'd.
Friendship's the wine of life; but friendship new
(Not such was his) is neither strong, nor pure.   585

O! for the bright complexion, cordial warmth,
And elevating spirit, of a friend,
For twenty summers rip'ning by my side;
All feculence of falsehood long thrown down;
All social virtues rising in his soul;   590
As crystal clear; and smiling, as they rise!
Here nectar flows; it sparkles in our sight;
Rich to the taste, and genuine from the heart.
High-flavour'd bliss for gods! on earth how rare!
On earth how lost!—PHILANDER is no more.   595
    Think'st thou the theme intoxicates my song?
And I too warm?—Too warm I cannot be.
I lov'd him much; but now I love him more.
Like birds, whose beauties languish, half conceal'd,
Till, mounted on the wing, their glossy plumes   600
Expanded shine with azure, green, and gold;
How blessings brighten as they take their flight!
His flight PHILANDER took; his upward flight,
If ever soul ascended.   Had he dropt,
(That eagle genius!) O had he let fall   605
One feather as he flew! I, then, had wrote,
What friends might flatter; prudent foes forbear;
Rivals scarce damn; and Zoilus reprieve.
Yet what I can, I must: It were profane
To quench a glory lighted at the skies,   610
And cast in shadows his illustrious close.
Strange! the theme most affecting, most sublime,
Momentous most to man, should sleep unsung!
And yet it sleeps, by genius unawak'd,
Painim or Christian; to the blush of wit.   615
Man's highest triumph! Man's profoundest fall!
The death-bed of the just! is yet undrawn

By mortal hand: It merits a divine:
Angels should paint it, angels ever there;
There, on a post of honour, and of joy.   620
   Dare I presume, then? But PHILANDER bids;
And glory tempts, and inclination calls—
Yet am I struck; as struck the soul, beneath
Aërial groves' impenetrable gloom;
Or, in some mighty ruin's solemn shade;   625
Or, gazing by pale lamps on high-born dust,
In vaults; thin courts of poor unflatter'd kings!
Or, at the midnight altar's hallow'd flame.
It is religion to proceed: I pause—
And enter, aw'd, the temple of my theme.   630
Is it his death-bed? No: It is his shrine:
Behold him, there, just rising to a god.
   The chamber where the good man meets his fate,
Is privileg'd beyond the common walk
Of virtuous life, quite in the verge of Heav'n.   635
Fly, ye profane! If not, draw near with awe.
Receive the blessing, and adore the chance,
That threw in this Bethesda your disease;
If unrestor'd by this, despair your cure.
For, here, resistless demonstration dwells;   640
A death-bed's a detector of the heart.
   Here tir'd Dissimulation drops her mask,
Through life's grimace, that mistress of the scene!
Here real, and apparent, are the same.
You see the Man; you see his hold on Heav'n;   645
If sound his virtue; as PHILANDER's, sound.
Heav'n waits not the last moment; owns her friends
On this side death; and points them out to men;

A lecture silent, but of sov'reign pow'r!
To vice, confusion; and to virtue, peace.   650
    Whatever farce the boastful hero plays,
Virtue alone has majesty in death;
And greater still, the more the tyrant frowns.
PHILANDER! he severely frown'd on thee.
" No warning giv'n! Unceremonious fate!   655
" A sudden rush from life's meridian joys!
" A wrench from all we love! from all we are!
" A restless bed of pain! A plunge opaque
" Beyond conjecture! Feeble Nature's dread!
" Strong Reason's shudder at the dark unknown! 660
" A sun extinguish'd! a just op'ning grave!
" And oh! the last, last; what? (can words express?
" Thought reach?) the last, last—silence of a friend!"
Where are those horrors,that amazement where,
This hideous group of ills (which singly shock)   665
Demands from Man?—I thought him Man till now.
    Through Nature's wreck, thro' vanquish'd agonies
(Like the stars struggling thro' this midnight gloom),
What gleams of joy! what more than human peace!
Where, the frail mortal? the poor abject worm?   670
No, not in death, the mortal to be found.
His conduct is a legacy for all,
Richer than Mammon's for his single heir.
His comforters he comforts; great in ruin,
With unreluctant grandeur, gives, not yields   675
His soul sublime; and closes with his fate.
    How our hearts burnt within us at the scene!
Whence, this brave bound o'er limits fix'd to Man?
His God sustains him in his final hour!

His final hour brings glory to his God!   680
Man's glory Heav'n vouchsafes to call her own.
We gaze; we weep; mixt tears of grief and joy!
Amazement strikes! Devotion bursts to flame!
Christians adore, and infidels believe.

   As some tall tow'r, or lofty mountain's brow,   685
Detains the sun, illustrious from its height;
While rising vapours and descending shades,
With damps, and darkness, drown the spacious vale;
Undamp'd by doubt, undarken'd by despair,
PHILANDER thus, augustly rears his head,   690
At that black hour, which gen'ral horror sheds
On the low level of th' inglorious throng:
Sweet Peace, and heav'nly Hope, and humble Joy,
Divinely beam on his exalted soul;
Destruction gild, and crown him for the skies,   695
With incommunicable lustre bright.

COMPLAINT.

NIGHT III.

NARCISSA.

Ignoscenda quidem, scirent si ignoscere manes!
VIRGIL.

FROM dreams, where thought in Fancy's maze runs
    mad,
To Reason, that heav'n-lighted lamp in Man,
Once more I wake; and at the destin'd hour,
Punctual as lovers to the moment sworn,
I keep my assignation with my woe.   5
   O! lost to virtue, lost to manly thought,
Lost to the noble sallies of the soul!
Who think it solitude, to be alone.
Communion sweet! communion large, and high!
Our reason, guardian angel, and our god!   10
Then, nearest these, when others most remote;
And all, ere long, shall be remote, but these.

G

How dreadful, then, to meet them all alone,
A stranger! unacknowledg'd, unapprov'd!
Now woo them; wed them; bind them to thy breast;
To win thy wish, creation has no more.   16
Or, if we wish a fourth, it is a friend—
But friends, how mortal! dang'rous the desire.

    Take Phœbus to yourselves, ye basking bards!
Inebriate at fair Fortune's fountain-head,   20
And reeling through the wilderness of joy
Where Sense runs savage, broke from Reason's chain,
And sings false peace, till smother'd by the pall.—
My fortune is unlike—unlike my song—
Unlike the deity my song invokes.   25
I, to Day's soft-ey'd sister pay my court,
(Endymion's rival!) and her aid implore;
Now first implor'd in succour to the Muse.

    Thou, who didst lately borrow Cynthia's form,
And modestly forego thine own! O thou   30
Who didst thyself, at midnight hours, inspire!
Say, why not Cynthia, patroness of song?
As thou her crescent, she thy character
Assumes; still more a goddess by the change.

    Are there demurring wits, who dare dispute   35
This revolution in the world inspir'd?
Ye train Pierian! to the lunar sphere,
In silent hour, address your ardent call
For aid immortal; less her brother's right.
She, with the spheres harmonious, nightly leads   40
The mazy dance, and hears their matchless strain;
A strain for gods, deny'd to mortal ear.
Transmit it heard, thou silver queen of heav'n!
What title, or what name, endears thee most?

Cynthia! Cyllene! Phœbe!—or dost hear   45
With higher gust, fair P———D of the skies?
Is that the soft enchantment calls thee down,
More pow'rful than of old Circean charm?
Come; but from heav'nly banquets with thee bring
The soul of song, and whisper in mine ear   50
The theft divine; or in propitious dreams
(For dreams are thine) transfuse it through the breast
Of thy first votary—but not thy last;
If, like thy namesake, thou art ever kind.
    And kind thou wilt be—kind on such a theme— 55
A theme so like thee, a quite lunar theme,
Soft, modest, melancholy, female, fair!
A theme that rose all pale, and told my soul
'Twas night; on her fond hopes perpetual night;
A night which struck a damp, a deadlier damp   60
Than that which smote me from PHILANDER's tomb.
NARCISSA follows, ere his tomb is clos'd.
Woes cluster; rare are solitary woes;
They love a train, they tread each other's heel;
Her death invades his mournful right, and claims 65
The grief that started from my lids for him:
Seizes the faithless, alienated tear,
Or shares it, ere it falls.   So frequent death,
Sorrow he more than causes, he confounds;
For human sighs his rival strokes contend,   70
And make distress, distraction.   Oh PHILANDER!
What was thy fate? A double fate to me;
Portent, and pain! a menace, and a blow!
Like the black raven hov'ring o'er my peace,
Not less a bird of omen, than of prey.   75
It call'd NARCISSA long before her hour;

It call'd her tender soul, by break of bliss,
From the first blossom, from the buds of joy;
Those few our noxious fate unblasted leaves
In this inclement clime of human life.   80

　　Sweet harmonist! and beautiful as sweet!
And young as beautiful! and soft as young!
And gay as soft! and innocent as gay!
And happy (if aught happy here) as good!
For fortune fond had built her nest on high,   85
Like birds quite exquisite of note and plume;
Transfix'd by Fate (who loves a lofty mark),
How from the summit of the grove she fell,
And left it unharmonious! all its charm
Extinguish'd in the wonders of her song!   90
Her song still vibrates in my ravish'd ear,
Still melting there, and with voluptuous pain
(O to forget her!) thrilling through my heart!

　　Song, beauty, youth, love, virtue, joy! this group
Of bright ideas, flow'rs of Paradise,   95
As yet unforfeit, in one blaze we bind,
Kneel, and present it to the skies; as all
We guess of Heav'n: And these were all her own.
And she was mine; and I was—was most blest—
Gay title of the deepest misery!   100
As bodies grow more pond'rous robb'd of life;
Good lost weighs more in grief, than gain'd in joy.
Like blossom'd trees o'erturn'd by vernal storm,
Lovely in death the beauteous ruin lay;
And if in death still lovely, lovelier there;   105
Far lovelier! Pity swells the tide of love.
And will not the severe excuse a sigh?
Scorn the proud man that is asham'd to weep:

Our tears indulg'd indeed deserve our shame.
Ye that e'er lost an angel! pity me.   110
　　Soon as the lustre languish'd in her eye,
Dawning a dimmer day on human sight;
And on her cheek, the residence of spring,
Pale Omen sat, and scatter'd fears around
On all that saw; (and who would cease to gaze, 115
That once had seen!) with haste, parental haste,
I flew, I snatch'd her from the rigid north,
Her native bed, on which bleak Boreas blew,
And bore her nearer to the sun; the sun
(As if the sun could envy) check'd his beam,   120
Deny'd his wonted succour, or with more
Regret beheld her drooping, than the bells
Of lilies, fairest lilies not so fair.
　　Queen lilies! and ye painted populace!
Who dwell in fields, and lead ambrosial lives;   125
In morn and ev'ning dew, your beauties bathe,
And drink the sun; which gives your cheeks to glow,
And out-blush (mine excepted) ev'ry fair;
You gladlier grew, ambitious of her hand,
Which often crop'd your odours, incense meet   130
To thought so pure.　Ye lovely fugitives!
Coëval race with Man! for Man you smile;
Why not smile at him too? You share indeed
His sudden pass; but not his constant pain.
　　So Man is made, nought ministers delight   135
But what his glowing passions can engage;
And glowing passions, bent on aught below,
Must, soon or late, with anguish turn the scale;
And anguish, after rapture, how severe!
Rapture—Bold Man! who tempts the wrath divine,

By plucking fruit deny'd to mortal taste,   141
Whilst here, presuming on the rights of Heav'n!
For transport dost thou call on ev'ry hour,
LORENZO? At thy friend's expence be wise;
Lean not on earth; 'twill pierce thee to the heart; 145
A broken reed at best; but oft a spear;
On its sharp point peace bleeds, and hope expires.
    Turn, hopeless thought! turn from her: Thought
          repell'd,
Resenting rallies, and wakes ev'ry woe.
Snatch'd ere thy prime! and in thy bridal hour! 150
And when kind fortune, with thy lover, smil'd!
And when high-flavour'd thy fresh op'ning joys!
And when blind Man pronounc'd thy bliss complete!
And on a foreign shore; where strangers wept!
Strangers to thee; and, more surprising still,   155
Strangers to kindness, wept: Their eyes let fall
Inhuman tears; strange tears; that trickled down
From marble hearts! obdurate tenderness!
A tenderness that call'd them more severe;
In spite of Nature's soft persuasion, steel'd;   160
While Nature melted, Superstition rav'd;
That mourn'd the dead; and this deny'd a grave!
    Their sighs incens'd; sighs foreign to the will!
Their will the tyger suck'd, outrag'd the storm.
For oh! the curst ungodliness of zeal!   165
While sinful flesh relented, spirit nurs'd
In blind Infallibility's embrace,
The sainted spirit petrify'd the breast;
Deny'd the charity of dust, to spread
O'er dust! a charity their dogs enjoy.   170
What could I do? what succour? what resource?

While Nature melted Superstition rave.
That mournd the dead, and this denyd a grave.

Page 83

London Published Feb'ry 1 1798 by T. Heptinstall, no 3 Holborn

With pious sacrilege a grave I stole;
With impious piety that grave I wrong'd;
Short in my duty, coward in my grief!
More like her murderer than friend, I crept   175
With soft suspended step, and, muffl'd deep
In midnight darkness, whisper'd my last sigh.
I whisper'd what should echo thro' their realms:
Nor writ her name, whose tomb should pierce the skies.
Presumptuous fear! how durst I dread her foes,   180
While Nature's loudest dictates I obey'd?
Pardon necessity, blest shade! of grief
And indignation rival bursts I pour'd;
Half-execration mingl'd with my pray'r;
Kindl'd at man, while I his God ador'd: 185
Sore grudg'd the savage land her sacred dust;
Stamp'd the curs'd soil; and with humanity
(Deny'd Narcissa) wish'd them all a grave.
    Glows my resentment into guilt? what guilt
Can equal violations of the dead!   190
The dead how sacred! sacred is the dust
Of this heav'n-labour'd form, erect, divine!
This heav'n-assum'd, majestic robe of earth,
HE deign'd to wear, who hung the vast expanse
With azure bright, and cloth'd the sun in gold.   195
When ev'ry passion sleeps that can offend;
When strikes us ev'ry motive that can melt;
When man can wreak his rancour uncontroul'd,
That strongest curb on insult and ill-will;   200
Then, spleen to dust—the dust of innocence—
An angel's dust!—This Lucifer transcends;
When he contended for the Patriarch's bones,

'Twas not the strife of malice, but of pride;
The strife of pontiff pride, not pontiff gall.   205
　　Far less than this, is shocking in a race
Most wretched, but from streams of mutual love,
And uncreated, but for love divine;
And, but for love divine, this moment lost,
By Fate resorb'd, and sunk in endless night.   210
Man, hard of heart to man! of horrid things
Most horrid! 'mid stupendous, highly strange!
Yet oft his courtesies are smoother wrongs;
Pride brandishes the favours he confers,
And contumelious his humanity: 215
What then his vengeance? Hear it not, ye stars,
And thou, pale Moon! turn paler at the sound.
Man is to man, the sorest surest ill.
A previous blast foretels the rising storm:
O'erwhelming turrets threaten ere they fall;   220
Volcanos bellow ere they disembogue;
Earth trembles ere her yawning jaws devour;
And smoke betrays the wide-consuming fire:
Ruin from man is most conceal'd when near,
And sends the dreadful tidings in the blow.   225
Is this the flight of fancy? Would it were!
Heav'n's sov'reign saves all beings, but himself,
That hideous sight, a naked human heart.

　　Fir'd is the Muse? And let the Muse be fir'd:
Who, not inflam'd when what he speaks he feels, 230
And in the nerve most tender, in his friends?
Shame to mankind! PHILANDER had his foes;
He felt the truths I sing, and I in him:
But he nor I feel more. Past ills, NARCISSA!

Are sunk in thee, thou recent wound of heart!
Which bleeds with other cares, with other pangs; 235
Pangs num'rous, as the num'rous ills that swarm'd
O'er thy distinguish'd fate, and, clust'ring there
Thick as the locust on the land of Nile,
Make death more deadly, and more dark the grave.
Reflect (if not forgot my touching tale) 240
How was each circumstance with aspics arm'd!
An aspic—each and all—an Hydra woe.
What strong Herculean virtue could suffice?
Or is it virtue to be conquer'd here?
This hoary cheek a train of tears bedews; 245
And each tear mourns its own distinct distress;
And each distress, distinctly mourn'd, demands
Of grief still more, as heighten'd by the whole.
A grief like this proprietors excludes:
Not friends alone such obsequies deplore; 250
They make mankind the mourner; carry sighs
Far as the fatal Fame can wing her way;
And turn the gayest thought of gayest age,
Down the right channel, through the vale of death.

The vale of Death! that hush'd cimmerian vale, 255
Where Darkness, brooding o'er unfinish'd fates,
With raven wing incumbent, waits the day
(Dread day!) that interdicts all future change!
That subterranean world, that land of ruin!
Fit walk, LORENZO, for proud human thought! 260
There let my thought expatiate; and explore
Balsamic truths, and healing sentiments,
Of all most wanted, and most welcome, here.
For gay LORENZO's sake, and for thy own,
My soul! " The fruits of dying friends survey; 265

" Expose the vain of life; weigh life and death:
" Give Death his eulogy; thy fear subdue;
" And labour that first palm of noble minds,
" A manly scorn of terror from the tomb."
This harvest reap from thy NARCISSA's grave. 270
As poets feign'd, from Ajax' streaming blood
Arose, with grief inscrib'd, a mournful flow'r;
Let wisdom blossom from my mortal wound.
And first, of dying friends; what fruit from these?
It brings us more than triple aid; an aid   275
To chase our thoughtlessness, fear, pride, and guilt.
    Our dying friends come o'er us like a cloud,
To damp our brainless ardours; and abate
That glare of life, which often blinds the wise.
Our dying friends are pioneers to smooth   280
Our rugged pass to death; to break those bars
Of terror, and abhorrence, Nature throws
Cross our obstructed way; and thus to make
Welcome, as safe, our port from ev'ry storm.
Each friend by fate snatch'd from us, is a plume 285
Pluck'd from the wing of human vanity,
Which makes us stoop from our aërial heights,
And, damp'd with omen of our own decease,
On drooping pinions of ambition lower'd,
Just skim earth's surface, ere we break it up,   290
O'er putrid earth to scratch a little dust,
And save the world a nuisance.   Smitten friends
Are angels sent on errands full of love:
For us they languish, and for us they die:
And shall they languish, shall they die, in vain? 295
Ungrateful, shall we grieve their hov'ring shades,
Which wait the revolution in our hearts?

Shall we disdain their silent soft address;
Their posthumous advice, and pious pray'r?
Senseless, as herds that graze their hallow'd graves, 300
Tread under-foot their agonies and groans;
Frustrate their anguish, and destroy their deaths?
   LORENZO! no; the thought of death indulge;
Give it its wholesome empire! let it reign,
That kind chastiser of thy soul in joy!   305
Its reign will spread thy glorious conquests far,
And still the tumults of thy ruffled breast;
Auspicious æra! golden days, begin!
The thought of death shall, like a god, inspire.
And why not think on death? Is life the theme 310
Of ev'ry thought? and wish of ev'ry hour?
And song of ev'ry joy? Surprising truth!
The beaten spaniel's fondness not so strange.
To wave the num'rous ills that seize on life
As their own property, their lawful prey;   315
Ere Man has measur'd half his weary stage,
His luxuries have left him no reserve,
No maiden relishes, unbroach'd delights;
On cold-serv'd repetitions he subsists,
And in the tasteless present, chews the past;   320
Disgusted chews, and scarce can swallow down.
Like lavish ancestors, his earlier years
Have disinherited his future hours,
Which starve on orts, and glean their former field.
   Live ever here, LORENZO!—Shocking thought!
So shocking, they who wish, disown it too;   326
Disown from shame, what they from folly crave.
Live ever in the womb, nor see the light!

For what live ever here?—With lab'ring step
To tread our former footsteps? Pace the round   330
Eternal? To climb life's worn, heavy wheel,
Which draws up nothing new? To beat, and beat,
The beaten track? To bid each wretched day
The former mock? To surfeit on the same,
And yawn our joys; or thank a misery   335
For change, though sad? To see what we have seen?
Hear, till unheard, the same old slabber'd tale?
To taste the tasted, and at each return
Less tasteful? O'er our palates to decant
Another vintage? Strain a flatter year,   340
Through loaded vessels, and a laxer tone?
Crazy machines to grind earth's wasted fruits!
Ill-ground, and worse concocted! load, not life!
The rational foul kennels of excess!
Still-streaming thoroughfares of dull debauch!   345
Trembling each gulp, lest Death should snatch the bowl.
     Such of our fine ones is the wish refin'd!
So would they have it: Elegant desire!
Why not invite the bellowing stalls, and wilds?
But such examples might their riot awe.   350
Through want of virtue, that is, want of thought
(Though on bright thought they father all their flights,)
To what are they reduc'd? To love, and hate,
The same vain world; to censure, and espouse,
This painted shrew of life, who calls them fool   355
Each moment of each day; to flatter bad
Through dread of worse? To cling to this rude rock,
Barren, to them, of good, and sharp with ills,
And hourly blacken'd with impending storms,

And infamous for wrecks of human hope—   · 360
Scar'd at the gloomy gulph, that yawns beneath.
Such are their triumphs! such their pangs of joy!
    'Tis time, high time, to shift this dismal scene.
This hugg'd, this hideous state, what art can cure?
One only; but that one, what all may reach;   365
Virtue—she, wonder-working goddess! charms
That rock to bloom; and tames the painted shrew;
And what will more surprise, LORENZO! gives
To life's sick, nauseous iteration, change;
And straitens Nature's circle to a line.   370
Believ'st thou this, LORENZO? Lend an ear,
A patient ear, thou'lt blush to disbelieve.
    A languid, leaden iteration reigns,
And ever must, o'er those whose joys are joys
Of sight, smell, taste: The cuckow-seasons sing   375
The same dull note to such as nothing prize,
But what those seasons from the teeming earth,
To doating sense indulge.   But nobler minds,
Which relish fruits unripen'd by the sun,
Make their days various; various as the dyes   380
On the dove's neck, which wanton in his rays.
On minds of dove-like innocence possest,
On lighten'd minds, that bask in Virtue's beams,
Nothing hangs tedious, nothing old revolves
In that, for which they long; for which they live. 385
Their glorious efforts, wing'd with heav'nly hope,
Each rising morning sees still higher rise;
Each bounteous dawn its novelty presents
To worth maturing, new strength, lustre, fame;
While Nature's circle, like a chariot-wheel   390
Rolling beneath their elevated aims,

Makes their fair prospect fairer ev'ry hour;
Advancing virtue, in a line to bliss;
Virtue, which Christian motives best inspire!
And bliss, which Christian schemes alone ensure! 395
    And shall we then, for Virtue's sake, commence
Apostates? and turn infidels for joy?
A truth it is, few doubt, but fewer trust;
" He sins against this life, who slights the next."
What is this life? How few their fav'rite know! 400
Fond in the dark, and blind in our embrace,
By passionately loving life, we make
Lov'd life unlovely; hugging her to death.
We give to time eternity's regard;
And, dreaming, take our passage for our port. 405
Life has no value, as an end, but means;
An end deplorable! a means divine!
When 'tis our all, 'tis nothing: Worse than nought;
A nest of pains: When held as nothing, much:
Like some fair hum'rists, life is most enjoy'd 410
When courted least: most worth, when disesteem'd;
Then 'tis the seat of comfort, rich in peace;
In prospect richer far; important! awful!
Not to be mention'd, but with shouts of praise!
Not to be thought on, but with tides of joy! 415
The mighty basis of eternal bliss!
    Where now the barren rock? the painted shrew?
Where now, LORENZO! life's eternal round?
Have I not made my triple promise good?
Vain is the world; but only to the vain. 420
To what compare we then this varying scene,
Whose worth ambiguous rises, and declines?
Waxes, and wanes? (In all propitious, Night

Assists me here:) Compare it to the moon;
Dark in herself, and indigent; but rich   425
In borrow'd lustre from a higher sphere.
When gross guilt interposes, lab'ring earth,
O'ershadow'd, mourns a deep eclipse of joy;
Her joys, at brightest, pallid, to that font
Of full effulgent glory, whence they flow.   430
   Nor is that glory distant: Oh LORENZO!
A good man, and an angel!—these between
How thin the barrier!—What divides their fate?
Perhaps a moment, or perhaps a year;
Or, if an age, it is a moment still;   435
A moment, or eternity's forgot.
Then be, what once *they* were, who now are gods;
Be what PHILANDER was, and claim the skies.
Starts timid Nature at the gloomy pass?
The soft transition call it, and be cheer'd: 440
Such it is often, and why not to thee?
To hope the best is pious, brave, and wise;
And may itself procure what it presumes.
Life is much flatter'd, Death is much traduc'd:
Compare the rivals, and the kinder crown.   445
" Strange competition!"—True, LORENZO! Strange!
So little life can cast into the scale.
   Life makes the soul dependent on the dust;
Death gives her wings to mount above the spheres.
Through chinks, styl'd organs, dim Life peeps at light;
Death bursts th' involving cloud, and all is day; 451
All eye, all ear, the disembody'd pow'r.
Death has feign'd evils, Nature shall not feel;
Life, ills substantial, Wisdom cannot shun.
Is not the mighty Mind, that son of heav'n,   455

By tyrant Life dethron'd, imprison'd, pain'd?
By Death enlarg'd, ennobled, deify'd?
Death but intombs the body; life, the soul.
    " Is Death then guiltless? How he marks his way
" With dreadful waste of what deserves to shine! 460
" Art, genius, fortune, elevated pow'r!
" With various lustres these light up the world,
" Which Death puts out, and darkens human race."
I grant, LORENZO! this indictment just:
The sage, peer, potentate, king, conqueror,   465
Death humbles these; more barb'rous Life, the Man.
Life is the triumph of our mould'ring clay;
Death, of the spirit infinite, divine!
Death has no dread, but what frail Life imparts;
Nor Life true joy, but what kind Death improves. 470
No bliss has Life to boast, till Death can give
Far greater; Life's a debtor to the grave,
Dark lattice! letting in eternal day.
    LORENZO! blush at fondness for a life,
Which sends celestial souls on errands vile,   475
To cater for the sense; and serve at boards,
Where ev'ry ranger of the wilds, perhaps
Each reptile, justly claims our upper hand.
Luxurious feast! a soul, a soul immortal,
In all the dainties of a brute bemir'd!   480
LORENZO! blush at terror for a death,
Which gives thee to repose in festive bow'rs,
Where nectars sparkle, angels minister,
And more than angels share, and raise, and crown,
And eternize, the birth, bloom, bursts of bliss. 485
What need I more? O Death, the palm is thine!
    Then welcome, Death! thy dreaded harbingers,

Age, and Disease; Disease, though long my guest;
That plucks my nerves, those tender strings of life;
Which, pluck'd a little more, will toll the bell,   490
That calls my few friends to my funeral;
Where feeble Nature drops, perhaps, a tear,
While Reason and Religion, better taught,
Congratulate the dead, and crown his tomb
With wreath triumphant.   Death is victory;   495
It binds in chains the raging ills of life:
Lust and Ambition, Wrath and Avarice,
Dragg'd at his chariot-wheel, applaud his pow'r.
That ills corrosive, cares importunate,
Are not immortal too, O Death! is thine.   500
Our day of dissolution!—Name it right;
'Tis our great pay-day; 'tis our harvest, rich
And ripe: What though the sickle, sometimes keen,
Just scars us as we reap the golden grain;
More than thy balm, O Gilead! heals the wound. 505
Birth's feeble cry, and Death's deep dismal groan,
Are slender tributes low-taxt Nature pays
For mighty gain: The gain of each, a life!
But O! the last, the former so transcends,
Life dies, compar'd! Life lives beyond the grave. 510
    And feel I, Death! no joy from thought of thee?
Death, the great counsellor, who Man inspires
With nobler thought, and fairer deed!
Death, the deliverer, who rescues Man!
Death, the rewarder, who the rescu'd crowns!   515
Death, that absolves my birth; a curse without it!
Rich Death, that realizes all my cares,
Toils, virtues, hopes; without it a chimera!
Death, of all pain the period, not of joy;

I

Joy's source, and subject, still subsist unhurt;   520
One, in my soul; and one, in her great Sire;
Though the four winds were warring for my dust.
Yes, and from winds, and waves, and central night,
Though prison'd there, my dust too I reclaim
(To dust when drop proud Nature's proudest spheres,)
And live entire.   Death is the crown of life: 526
Were Death deny'd, poor Man would live in vain;
Were Death deny'd, to live would not be life;
Were Death deny'd, ev'n fools would wish to die.
Death wounds to cure: We fall; we rise; we reign!
Spring from our fetters; fasten in the skies;   531
Where blooming Eden withers in our sight.
Death gives us more than was in Eden lost;
This king of terrors is the prince of peace.
When shall I die to vanity, pain, death?   535
When shall I die?—When shall I live for ever?

THE

COMPLAINT.

NIGHT IV.

THE CHRISTIAN TRIUMPH.

CONTAINING

OUR ONLY CURE FOR THE FEAR OF DEATH;

AND

PROPER SENTIMENTS OF HEART ON THAT INESTI-
MABLE BLESSING.

A Much-indebted Muse, O YORKE! intrudes.
Amid the smiles of Fortune, and of Youth,
Thine ear is patient of a serious song.
How deep implanted in the breast of Man
The dread of Death! I sing its sov'reign cure.   5
    Why start at Death? Where is he? Death arriv'd, ‑
Is past; not come, or gone, he's never here.
Ere hope, sensation fails; black-boding Man
Receives, not suffers, Death's tremendous blow.

The knell, the shroud, the mattock, and the grave,   10
The deep damp vault, the darkness, and the worm—
These are the bugbears of a winter's eve,
The terrors of the living, not the dead.
Imagination's fool, and Error's wretch,
Man makes a death, which Nature never made;   15
Then on the point of his own fancy falls;
And feels a thousand deaths, in fearing one.
    But were Death frightful, what has Age to fear?
If prudent, Age should meet the friendly foe,
And shelter in his hospitable gloom.   20
I scarce can meet a monument, but holds
My younger; ev'ry date cries—" Come away."
And what recals me? Look the world around,
And tell me what: The wisest cannot tell.
Should any born of woman give his thought   25
Full range, on just dislike's unbounded field;
Of things, the vanity; of men, the flaws;
Flaws in the best; the many, flaw all o'er;
As leopards, spotted, or as Æthiops, dark;
Vivacious, ill; good dying immature   30
(How immature, NARCISSA's marble tells);
And at its death bequeathing endless pain;
His heart, though bold, would sicken at the sight,
And spend itself in sighs for future scenes.
    But grant to life (and just it is to grant   35
To lucky life) some perquisites of joy;
A time there is, when, like a thrice-told tale,
Long-rifled life of sweet can yield no more,
But from our comment on the comedy,
Pleasing reflections on parts well-sustain'd,   40
Or purpos'd emendations where we fail'd,

Or hopes of plaudits from our candid Judge,
When, on their exit, souls are bid unrobe,
Toss fortune back her tinsel, and her plume,
And drop this mask of flesh behind the scene.   45
With me, that time is come; my world is dead;
A new world rises, and new manners reign:
Foreign comedians (a spruce band) arrive,
To push me from the scene, or hiss me there.
What a pert race starts up! The strangers gaze,   50
And I at them; my neighbour is unknown;
Nor that the worst: Ah me! the dire effect
Of loit'ring here, of Death defrauded long;
Of old so gracious, (and let that suffice)
My very master knows me not.——   55
    Shall I dare say, peculiar is the fate?
I've been so long remember'd, I'm forgot.
An object ever pressing dims the sight,
And hides behind its ardour to be seen.
When in his courtiers' ears I pour my plaint,   60
They drink it as the nectar of the great;
And squeeze my hand, and beg me come to-morrow:
Refusal! canst thou wear a smoother form?
    Indulge me, nor conceive I drop my theme:
Who cheapens life, abates the fear of death: 65
Twice-told the period spent on stubborn Troy,
Court-favour, yet untaken, I besiege;
Ambition's ill-judg'd effort to be rich.
Alas! ambition makes my little, less; ˬ
Embitt'ring the possess'd: Why wish for more?   70
Wishing, of all employments, is the worst;
Philosophy's reverse; and health's decay!
Were I as plump as stall'd Theology,

Wishing would waste me to this shade again.
Were I as wealthy as a South Sea dream,   75
Wishing is an expedient to be poor.
Wishing, that constant hectic of a fool;
Caught at a court; purg'd off by purer air,
And simpler diet; gifts of rural life!
  Blest be that hand divine, which gently laid   80
My heart at rest, beneath this humble shed.
The world's a stately bark, on dang'rous seas,
With pleasure seen, but boarded at our peril:
— Here, on a single plank, thrown safe ashore,
I hear the tumult of the distant throng,   85
As that of seas remote, or dying storms;
And meditate on scenes, more silent still;
Pursue my theme, and fight the Fear of Death.
Here, like a shepherd gazing from his hut,
Touching his reed, or leaning on his staff,   90
Eager Ambition's fiery chase I see;
I see the circling hunt of noisy men,
Burst law's inclosure, leap the mounds of right,
Pursuing, and pursu'd, each other's prey;
As wolves, for rapine; as the fox, for wiles;   95
— Till Death, that mighty hunter, earths them all.
  Why all this toil for triumphs of an hour?
What, though we wade in wealth, or soar in fame,
Earth's highest station ends in, " Here he lies:"
And " Dust to dust" concludes her noblest song. 100
If this song lives, posterity shall know
One (though in Britain born, with courtiers bred)
Who thought e'en gold might come a day too late;
Nor on his subtle death-bed plann'd his scheme
For future vacancies in church or state;   105

Some avocation deeming it—to die;
Unbit by rage canine of dying rich;
Guilt's blunder! and the loudest laugh of Hell.
   O my coëvals! remnants of yourselves!
Poor human ruins, tott'ring o'er the grave!   110
Shall we, shall aged men, like aged trees,
Strike deeper their vile root, and closer cling,
Still more enamour'd of this wretched soil?
Shall our pale wither'd hands be still stretch'd out
Trembling, at once, with eagerness and age?   115
With av'rice, and convulsions, grasping hard?
Grasping at air! for what has earth beside?
Man wants but little; nor that little, long;
How soon must he resign his very dust,
Which frugal Nature lent him for an hour!   120
Years unexperienc'd rush on num'rous ills;
And soon as Man, expert from Time, has found
The key of Life, it opes the gates of Death.
   When in this vale of years I backward look,
And miss such numbers, numbers too of such,   125
Firmer in health, and greener in their age,
And stricter on their guard, and fitter far
To play Life's subtle game, I scarce believe
I still survive: And am I fond of Life,
Who scarce can think it possible I live?   130
Alive by miracle! or what is next,
Alive by MEAD! If I am still alive,
Who long have bury'd what gives Life to live,
Firmness of nerve, and energy of thought.
Life's lee is not more shallow than impure,   135
And vapid; Sense and Reason shew the door, —
Call for my bier, and point me to the dust.

O Thou great Arbiter of Life and Death!
Nature's immortal, immaterial Sun!
Whose all prolific beam late call'd me forth   140
From darkness, teeming darkness, where I lay
The worm's inferior, and, in rank, beneath
The dust I tread on, high to bear my brow,
To drink the spirit of the golden day,
And triumph in existence; and couldst know   145
No motive but my bliss; and hast ordain'd
A rise in blessing! with the patriarch's joy,
Thy call I follow to the land unknown;
I trust in Thee, and know in whom I trust;
Or Life, or Death, is equal; neither weighs;   150
All weight in this—O let me live to Thee!

    Though Nature's terrors, thus, may be represt;
Still frowns grim Death; guilt points the tyrant's spear.
And whence all human guilt? From Death forgot.
—Ah me! too long I set at nought the swarm   155
Of friendly warnings, which around me flew;
And smil'd unsmitten: Small my cause to smile!
Death's admonitions, like shafts upwards shot,
More dreadful by delay, the longer ere
They strike our hearts, the deeper is their wound; 160
O think how deep, Lorenzo! here it stings:
Who can appease its anguish? How it burns!
What hand the barb'd, invenom'd, thought can draw?
What healing hand can pour the balm of peace;
And turn my sight undaunted on the tomb?   165

    With joy—with grief, that healing hand I see;
Ah! too conspicuous! It is fix'd on high.
On high?—What means my phrenzy? I blaspheme;
Alas! how low! how far beneath the skies!

The skies it form'd; and now it bleeds for me— 170
But bleeds the balm I want—yet still it bleeds.
Draw the dire steel—Ah no!—the dreadful blessing
What heart or can sustain, or dares forego?
There hangs all human hope; that nail supports
The falling universe: That gone, we drop! 175
Horror receives us, and the dismal wish
Creation had been smother'd in her birth—
Darkness his curtain, and his bed the dust;
When stars and sun are dust beneath his throne!
In Heav'n itself can such indulgence dwell? 180
O what a groan was there! A groan not his.
He seiz'd our dreadful right; the load sustain'd;
And heav'd the mountain from a guilty world.
A thousand worlds, so bought, were bought too dear.
Sensations new in angels bosoms rise; 185
Suspend their song, and make a pause in bliss.
    O for their song to reach my lofty theme!
Inspire me, Night! with all thy tuneful spheres inspire;
Whilst I with seraphs share seraphic themes,
And shew to men the dignity of Man; 190
Lest I blaspheme my subject with my song.
Shall Pagan pages glow celestial flame,
And Christian languish? On our hearts, not heads,
Falls the foul infamy: My heart! awake.
What can awake thee, unawak'd by this, 195
" Expended Deity on human weal?"
Feel the great truths, which burst the tenfold night
Of Heathen error, with a golden flood
Of endless day; To feel, is to be fir'd;
And to believe, LORENZO! is to feel. 200

K

Thou most indulgent, most tremendous Pow'r!
Still more tremendous, for thy wondrous love!
That arms, with awe more awful, thy commands;
And foul transgression dips in sev'nfold night;
How our hearts tremble at thy love immense!   205
In love immense, inviolably just,   .
Thou, rather than thy justice should be stain'd,
Didst stain the cross; and, work of wonders far
The greatest! that thy dearest far might bleed.

Bold thought! Shall I dare speak it, or repress? 210
Should Man more execrate, or boast, the guilt
Which rous'd such vengeance? which such love in-
      flam'd?
O'er guilt (how mountainous!) with out-stretcht arms,
Stern Justice, and soft-smiling Love, embrace,
Supporting, in full majesty, thy throne,   215
When seem'd its majesty to need support,
Or that, or Man, inevitably lost.
What, but the fathomless of thought divine,
Could labour such expedient from despair,
And rescue both! both rescue! both exalt!   220
O how are both exalted by the deed!
The wondrous deed! or shall I call it more?
A wonder in Omnipotence itself!
A mystery, no less to gods than men!

Not, thus, our infidels th' Eternal draw,   225
A God all o'er, consummate, absolute,
Full-orb'd, in his whole round of rays complete:
They set at odds Heav'n's jarring attributes;
And, with one excellence, another wound;
Maim Heav'n's perfection, break its equal beams, 230

Bid Mercy triumph—over God himself,
Undeify'd by their opprobrious praise:
A God all mercy, is a God unjust.
    Ye brainless wits! ye baptiz'd infidels!   —
Ye worse for mending! wash'd to fouler stains!   235
The ransom was paid down; the fund of Heav'n,
Heav'n's inexhaustible exhausted fund,
Amazing, and amaz'd, pour'd forth the price,
All price beyond: Though curious to compute,
Archangels fail'd to cast the mighty sum: 240
Its value vast ungraspt by minds create,
For ever hides, and glows, in the Supreme.
    And was the ransom paid? It was: And paid
(What can exalt the bounty more?) for you.
The sun beheld it—No—the shocking scene   — 245
Drove back his chariot: Midnight veil'd his face;
Not such as this; not such as Nature makes;
A midnight, Nature shudder'd to behold;
A midnight new! a dread eclipse (without
Opposing spheres) from her Creator's frown!   250
Sun! didst thou fly thy Maker's pain? or start
At that enormous load of human guilt,
Which bow'd his blessed head; o'erwhelm'd his cross;
Made groan the centre; burst earth's marble womb,
With pangs, strange pangs! deliver'd of her dead? 255
Hell howl'd; and Heav'n that hour let fall a tear;
Heav'n wept, that Men might smile! Heav'n bled, that Man
      Might never die!—
    And is devotion virtue? 'Tis compell'd;   259
What heart of stone, but glows at thoughts like these!
Such contemplations mount us; and should mount

The mind still higher; nor ever glance on Man,
Unraptur'd, uninflam'd.—Where roll my thoughts
To rest from wonders? Other wonders rise;
And strike where'er they roll: My soul is caught: 265
Heav'n's sov'reign blessings, clust'ring from the cross,
Rush on her, in a throng, and close her round,
The pris'ner of amaze!—In his blest life,
I see the path, and, in his death, the price,
And in his great ascent, the proof supreme   270
Of immortality.—And did he rise?
Hear, O ye nations! hear it, O ye dead!
He rose! He rose! He burst the bars of Death.
Lift up your heads, ye everlasting gates!
And give the King of Glory to come in—   275
Who is the King of Glory?—He who left
His throne of glory, for the pang of death.
Lift up your heads, ye everlasting gates!
And give the King of Glory to come in—
Who is the King of Glory?—He who slew   280
The rav'nous foe, that gorg'd all human race!
The King of Glory, HE, whose glory fill'd
Heav'n with amazement at his love to Man;
And with divine complacency beheld
Powers most illumin'd, wilder'd in the theme.   285
    The theme, the joy, how then shall Man sustain?
Oh the burst gates, crush'd sting, demolish'd throne,
Last gasp of vanquish'd Death! Shout, Earth and Heav'n!
This sum of good to Man: Whose nature, then,
Took wing, and mounted with him from the tomb! 290
Then, then I rose; then first Humanity
Triumphant past the crystal ports of light,
(Stupendous guest!) and seiz'd eternal youth, .

C.Stothard R.A.del.   J.N.

He rose, He rose, He burst the bars of Death.
Lift up your heads, ye everlasting gates,
And give the King of Glory to come in.
Page 65

London.Published Nov.2.6.1797.by T.Heptinstall N.o.304.Holborn.

Seiz'd in our name. E'er since, 'tis blasphemous
To call Man mortal. Man's mortality,   295
Was then transferr'd to Death; and Heav'n's duration
Unalienably seal'd to this frail frame,
This child of dust.—Man, all-immortal! hail;
Hail, Heav'n! all-lavish of strange gifts to Man!
Thine all the glory; Man's the boundless bliss.   300
    Where am I rapt by this triumphant theme,   —
On Christian joy's exulting wing? Above
Th' Aonian mount!—Alas, small cause for joy!
What if to pain immortal? if extent
Of being, to preclude a close of woe?   305
Where, then, my boast of immortality?
I boast it still, though cover'd o'er with guilt;
For guilt, not innocence, his life he pour'd!
'Tis guilt alone can justify his death;
Nor that, unless his death can justify   310
Relenting guilt in Heav'n's indulgent sight.
If, sick of folly, I relent; he writes
My name in Heav'n, with that inverted spear
(A spear deep-dipt in blood!) which pierc'd his side,
And open'd there a font for all mankind,   315
Who strive, who combat crimes, to drink, and live:
This, only this, subdues the Fear of Death.
    And what is this?—Survey the wondrous cure;
And at each step, let higher wonder rise!
" Pardon for infinite offence! and pardon   320
" Through means, that speak its value infinite!
" A pardon bought with blood! with blood divine!
" With blood divine of Him I made my foe!
" Persisted to provoke! though woo'd, and aw'd,
" Blest, and chastis'd, a flagrant rebel still!   325

" A rebel, 'midst the thunders of his throne!
" Nor I alone! a rebel universe!
" My species up in arms! not one exempt!
" Yet, for the foulest of the foul, he dies;
" Most joy'd, for the redeem'd from deepest guilt! 330
" As if our race were held of highest rank;
" And Godhead dearer, as more kind to Man!"
　　Bound, ev'ry heart! and, ev'ry bosom, burn!
Oh what a scale of miracles is here!
Its lowest round, high planted on the skies;   335
Its tow'ring summit lost beyond the thought
Of Man or Angel! Oh that I could climb
The wonderful ascent with equal praise!
Praise! flow for ever (if astonishment
Will give thee leave,) my praise! for ever flow; 340
Praise ardent, cordial, constant, to high Heav'n
More fragrant than Arabia sacrific'd;
And all her spicy mountains in a flame.
　　So dear, so due to Heav'n, shall praise descend,
With her soft plume (from plausive angels' wing 345
First pluck'd by Man) to tickle mortal ears,
Thus diving in the pockets of the great?
Is praise the perquisite of ev'ry paw,
Though black as hell, that grapples well for gold?
Oh love of gold! thou meanest of amours!   350
Shall praise her odours waste on virtues dead?
Embalm the base, perfume the stench of guilt,
Earn dirty bread by washing Æthiops fair,
Removing filth, or sinking it from sight,
A scavenger in scenes where vacant posts,   355
Like gibbets yet untenanted, expect
Their future ornaments? From courts and thrones,

Return, apostate praise! thou vagabond!
Thou prostitute! to thy first love return,
Thy first, thy greatest, once unrival'd theme.   360
    There flow redundant; like Meander flow,
Back to thy fountain; to that parent Pow'r,
Who gives the tongue to sound, the thought to soar,
The soul to be.   Men homage pay to men,
Thoughtless beneath whose dreadful eye they bow 365
In mutual awe profound, of clay to clay,
Of guilt to guilt; and turn their backs on Thee,
Great SIRE! whom thrones celestial ceaseless sing;
To prostrate angels, an amazing scene!
O the presumption of Man's awe for Man!   370
Man's Author, End, Restorer, Law, and Judge!
Thine, all; day thine, and thine this gloom of night,
With all her wealth, with all her radiant worlds;
What, night eternal, but a frown from THEE!
What, Heav'n's meridian glory, but thy smile!   375
And shall not praise be thine? not human praise?
While Heav'n's high host on hallelujahs live?
    O may I breathe no longer, than I breathe
My soul in praise to HIM, who gave my soul,
And all her infinite of prospect fair,   380
Cut through the shades of hell, great love! by THEE,
Oh most adorable! most unador'd!
Where shall that praise begin, which ne'er should end?
Where'er I turn, what claim on all applause!
How is Night's sable mantle labour'd o'er,   385
How richly wrought with attributes divine!
What wisdom shines! what love! This midnight pomp,
This gorgeous arch, with golden worlds inlay'd!
Built with divine ambition! nought to THEE;

For others this profusion: Thou, apart,   390
Above, beyond! Oh tell me, mighty Mind!
What art thou? Shall I dive into the deep?
Call to the sun, or ask the roaring winds,
For their Creator? Shall I question loud
The thunder, if in that th' Almighty dwells?   395
Or holds he furious storms in streighten'd reins,
And bids fierce whirlwinds wheel his rapid car?
    What mean these questions?—Trembling I retract;
My prostrate soul adores the present God:
Praise I a distant Deity? He tunes   400
My voice (if tun'd); the nerve that writes, sustains:
Wrapp'd in his being, I resound his praise:
But though past all diffus'd, without a shore,
His essence; local is his throne (as meet,)
To gather the disperst (as standards call   405
The listed from afar;) to fix a point,
A central point, collective of his sons,
Since finite ev'ry nature, but his own.
The nameless He, whose nod is Nature's birth;
And Nature's shield, the shadow of his hand;   410
Her dissolution, his suspended smile!
The great First-Last! pavilion'd high he sits
In darkness, from excessive splendour, borne,
By gods unseen, unlessthrough lustre lost.
His glory, to created glory, bright,   415
As that to central horrors; He looks down
On all that soars; and spans immensity.
    Though Night unnumber'd worlds unfolds to view,
Boundless creation! what art thou? A beam,
A mere effluvium of his majesty: 420
And shall an atom of this atom-world

Mutter, in dust and sin, the theme of Heav'n?
Down to the centre should I send my thought,
Through beds of glitt'ring ore, and glowing gems—
Their beggar'd blaze wants lustre for my lay— 425
Goes out in darkness: If, on tow'ring wing,
I send it through the boundless vault of stars—
The stars, though rich what dross their gold to THEE!
Great, good, wise, wonderful, eternal King.
If to those conscious stars thy throne around 430
Praise ever-pouring, and imbibing bliss;
And ask their strain—they want it, more they want,
Poor their abundance, humble their sublime,
Languid their energy, their ardour cold,
Indebted still, their highest rapture burns; 435
Short of its mark, defective, though divine.
    Still more—this theme is Man's, and Man's alone;
Their vast appointments reach it not: They see
On earth a bounty not indulg'd on high;
And downward look for Heav'n's superior praise! 440
First-born of ether! high in fields of light!
View Man, to see the glory of your God!
Could angels envy, they had envy'd here;
And some did envy; and the rest, though gods,
Yet still gods unredeem'd (there triumphs Man, 445
Tempted to weigh the dust against the skies,)
They less would feel, though more adorn my theme.
They sung Creation (for in that they shar'd;)
How rose in melody the child of love,
Creation's great superior, Man! is thine; 450
Thine is Redemption; they just gave the key;
'Tis thine to raise, and eternize, the song;
Though human, yet divine; for should not this

Raise Man o'er Man, and kindle seraphs here?
Redemption! 'twas creation more sublime;   455
Redemption! 'twas the labour of the skies;
Far more than labour—It was death in Heav'n.
A truth so strange! 'twere bold to think it true;
If not far bolder still to disbelieve.   459

　　Here pause, and ponder: Was there death in Heav'n?
What then on earth? On earth, which struck the blow?
Who struck it? Who?—O how is Man enlarg'd,
Seen through this medium! how the pigmy tow'rs!
How counterpois'd his origin from dust!
How counterpois'd to dust his sad return!   465
How voided his vast distance from the skies!
How near he presses on the seraph's wing!
Which is the seraph? which the born of clay?
How this demonstrates, through the thickest cloud
Of guilt, and clay condens'd, the son of Heav'n! 470
The double son; the made, and the re-made!
And shall Heav'n's double property be lost?
Man's double madness only can destroy.
To Man the bleeding cross has promis'd all;
The bleeding cross has sworn eternal grace;   475
Who gave his life, what grace shall he deny?
O ye! who, from this Rock of ages leap,
Disdainful, plunging headlong in the deep!
What cordial joy, what consolation strong,
Whatever winds arise, or billows roll,   480
Our int'rest in the master of the storm!
Cling there, and in wreck'd Nature's ruins smile;
While vile apostates tremble in a calm.

　　Man! Know thyself. All wisdom centres there;
To none Man seems ignoble, but to Man;   485

Angels, that grandeur, men o'erlook, admire:
How long shall human nature be their book,
Degen'rate mortal! and unread by thee?
The beam dim Reason sheds shews wonders there.
What high contents! illustrious faculties!   490
But the grand comment, which displays at full
Our human height, scarce sever'd from divine,
By Heav'n compos'd, was publish'd on the cross.
    Who looks on that, and sees not in himself
An awful stranger, a terrestrial god?   495
A glorious partner with the Deity
In that high attribute, immortal life?
If a God bleeds, he bleeds not for a worm:
I gaze, and, as I gaze, my mounting soul
Catches strange fire, Eternity! at thee;   500
And drops the world—or rather more enjoys:
How chang'd the face of Nature! how improv'd!
What seem'd a chaos, shines a glorious world,
Or what a world, an Eden; heighten'd all!
It is another scene! another self!   505
And still another, as time rolls along;
And that a self far more illustrious still.
Beyond long ages, yet roll'd up in shades
Unpierc'd by bold Conjecture's keenest ray,
What evolutions of surprising fate!   510
How Nature opens, and receives my soul
In boundless walks of raptur'd thought! where gods
Encounter, and embrace me! What new births
Of strange adventure, foreign to the sun,
Where what now charms, perhaps whate'er exists, 515
Old Time, and fair Creation, are forgot!

Is this extravagant? Of Man we form
Extravagant conception, to be just:
Conception unconfin'd wants wings to reach him:
Beyond its reach, the Godhead only, more.   520
He, the great Father! kindled at one flame
The world of rationals; one spirit pour'd
From spirit's awful Fountain; pour'd himself
Through all their souls; but not in equal stream,
Profuse, or frugal, of th' inspiring God,   525
As his wise plan demanded; and when past
Their various trials in their various spheres,
If they continue rational, as made,
Resorbs them all into himself again;
His throne their centre, and his smile their crown. 530
    Why doubt we, then, the glorious truth to sing,
Though yet unsung, as deem'd, perhaps, too bold?
Angels are men of a superior kind:
Angels are men in lighter habit clad,
High o'er celestial mountains wing'd in flight;   535
And men are angels, loaded for an hour,
Who wade this miry vale, and climb with pain,
And slipp'ry step, the bottom of the steep.
Angels their failings, mortals have their praise;
While here, of corps ethereal, such inroll'd,   540
And summon'd to the glorious standard soon,
Which flames eternal crimson through the skies.
Nor are our brothers thoughtless of their kin,
Yet absent; but not absent from their love.
MICHAEL has fought our battles; RAPHAEL sung 545
Our triumphs; GABRIEL on our errands flown,
Sent by the SOV'REIGN: And are these, O Man!

Thy friends, thy warm allies? and thou (shame burn
The cheek to cinder!) rival to the brute!
Religion's all.   Descending from the skies   550
To wretched Man, the goddess in her left
Holds out this world, and in her right, the next;
Religion! the sole voucher Man is Man;
Supporter sole of Man above himself;
Ev'n in this night of frailty, change, and death,   555
She gives the soul, a soul that acts a god.
Religion—Providence—an after-state—
Here is firm footing; here is solid rock;
This can support us; all is sea besides;
Sinks under us; bestorms, and then devours.   560
His hand the good Man fastens on the skies,
And bids Earth roll, nor feels her idle whirl.

As when a wretch, from thick, polluted air,
Darkness, and stench, and suffocating damps,
And dungeon-horrors, by kind Fate discharg'd,   565
Climbs some fair eminence, where ether pure
Surrounds him, and Elysian prospects rise,
His heart exults, his spirits cast their load;
As if new-born, he triumphs in the change;
So joys the soul, when from inglorious aims,   570
And sordid sweets, from feculence and froth
Of ties terrestrial, set at large, she mounts
To Reason's region, her own element,
Breathes hopes immortal, and affects the skies.

Religion! thou the soul of happiness;   575
And, groaning Calvary, of thee! There shine
The noblest truths; there strongest motives sting;
There sacred violence assaults the soul;
There, nothing but compulsion is forborn.

Can love allure us? Or can terror awe?   580
He weeps!—the falling drop puts out the sun;
He sighs!—the sigh earth's deep foundation shakes.
If in his love so terrible, what then
His wrath inflam'd! his tenderness on fire;
Like soft, smooth oil, outblazing other fires?   585
Can pray'r, can praise avert it?—Thou, my all!
My theme! my inspiration! and my crown!
My strength in age! my rise in low estate!
My soul's ambition, pleasure, wealth!—my world!
My light in darkness! and my life in death!   590
My boast through time! bliss through eternity!
Eternity, too short to speak thy praise!
Or fathom thy profound of love to Man;
To man of men the meanest, ev'n to me!
My sacrifice! my God! what things are these!   595
    What then art Thou? by what name shall I call thee?
Knew I the name devout archangels use,
Devout archangels should the name enjoy,
By me unrivall'd: Thousands more sublime,
None half so dear, as that, which, though unspoke, 600
Still glows at heart: O how Omnipotence
Is lost in love! Thou great PHILANTHROPIST!
Father of Angels! but the friend of Man!
Like JACOB, fondest of the younger born!
—Thou, who didst save him, snatch the smoking brand
From out the flames, and quench it in thy blood! 606
How art thou pleas'd, by bounty to distress!
To make us groan beneath our gratitude,
Too big for birth! to favour, and confound;
To challenge, and to distance, all return!   610
Of lavish love stupendous heights to soar,

And leave praise panting in the distant vale!
Thy right too great defrauds thee of thy due;
And sacrilegious our sublimest song.
But since the naked will obtains thy smile,　　　615
Beneath this monument of praise unpaid,
And future life symphonious to my strain,
(That noblest hymn to Heav'n!) for ever lie
Intomb'd, my fear of death! and ev'ry fear,
The dread of ev'ry evil, but thy frown.　　　620
　　Whom see I yonder, so demurely smile?
Laughter a labour, and might break their rest.
Ye quietists, in homage to the skies!
Serene! of soft address! who mildly make
An unobtrusive tender of your hearts,　　　625
Abhorring violence! who halt indeed;
But, for the blessing, wrestle not with Heav'n!
Think you my song too turbulent? too warm?
Are passions, then, the pagans of the soul?
Reason alone baptiz'd? alone ordain'd　　　630
To touch things sacred? Oh for warmer still!
Guilt chills my zeal, and age benumbs my pow'rs;
Oh for an humbler heart, and prouder song!
THOU, my much-injur'd theme! with that soft eye,
Which melted o'er doom'd Salem, deign to look 635
Compassion to the coldness of my breast;
And pardon to the winter in my strain!
Oh ye cold-hearted, frozen, formalists!
On such a theme, 'tis impious to be calm;
— Passion, is reason, transport, temper, here.　　　640
Shall Heav'n, which gave us ardour, and has shewn
Her own for Man so strongly, not disdain
What smooth emollients in theology,

Recumbent Virtue's downy doctors preach,
That prose of piety, a lukewarm praise?   645
Rise odours sweet from incense uninflam'd?
Devotion, when lukewarm, is undevout;
But when it glows, its heat is struck to Heav'n;
To human hearts her golden harps are strung;
High Heav'n's orchestra chants Amen to Man.   650
   Hear I, or dream I hear, their distant strain,
Sweet to the soul, and tasting strong of Heav'n,
Soft-wafted on celestial Pity's plume,
Through the vast spaces of the universe,
To cheer me in this melancholy gloom?   655
Oh when will Death (now stingless,) like a friend,
Admit me of their choir? Oh when will Death
— This mould'ring, old partition-wall throw down!
Give beings, one in nature, one abode?
Oh Death divine! that giv'st us to the skies!   660
Great Future! glorious Patron of the past,
And present! when shall I thy shrine adore?
From Nature's continent, immensely wide,
Immensely blest, this little isle of life,
This dark, incarcerating colony,   665
Divides us.   Happy day! that breaks our chain;
That manumits; that calls from exile home;
That leads to Nature's great metropolis,
— And re-admits us, through the guardian hand
Of elder brothers, to our Father's throne;   670
Who hears our Advocate, and, through his wounds
Beholding Man, allows that tender name.
'Tis this makes Christian Triumph a command:
'Tis this makes joys a duty to the wise;
'Tis impious, in a good man, to be sad.   675

Seest thou, LORENZO! where hangs all our hope?
Touch'd by the cross, we live, or more than die;
That touch which touch'd not angels; more divine
Than that, which touch'd confusion into form,
And darkness into glory; partial touch!   680
Ineffably pre-eminent regard!
Sacred to Man, and sov'reign through the whole
Long golden chain of miracles, which hangs
From Heav'n through all duration, and supports,
In one illustrious and amazing plan,   685
Thy welfare, Nature! and thy God's renown;
That touch, with charm celestial, heals the soul ••
Diseas'd, drives pain from guilt, lights life in death,
Turns earth to Heav'n, to heav'nly thrones transforms
The ghastly ruins of the mould'ring tomb!   690
    Dost ask me when? When HE who dy'd returns;
Returns, how chang'd! Where then the man of woe?
In glory's terrors all the Godhead burns;
And all his courts, exhausted by the tide
Of deities triumphant in his train,   695
Leave a stupendous solitude in Heav'n;
Replenish'd soon, replenish'd with increase
Of pomp, and multitude; a radiant band
Of angels new; of angels from the tomb.
    Is this by fancy thrown remote? and rise   700
Dark doubts between the promise and event?
I send thee not to volumes for thy cure;
Read Nature! Nature is a friend to truth;
Nature is Christian; preaches to mankind;
And bids dead matter aid us in our creed.   705
Hast thou ne'er seen the comet's flaming flight? —
Th' illustrious stranger passing, terror sheds

M

On gazing nations, from his fiery train
Of length enormous, takes his ample round
Through depths of ether; coasts unnumber'd worlds,
Of more than solar glory; doubles wide   711
Heav'n's mighty cape, and then revisits earth,
From the long travel of a thousand years.
Thus, at the destin'd period, shall return
HE, once on earth, who bids the comet blaze: 715
And, with him, all our triumph o'er the tomb.
     Nature is dumb on this important point;
Or hope precarious in low whisper breathes;
Faith, speaks aloud, distinct; ev'n adders hear,
But turn, and dart into the dark again.   720
Faith builds a bridge across the gulph of Death,
To break the shock blind Nature cannot shun,
And lands thought smoothly on the farther shore.
Death's terror is the mountain Faith removes;
That mountain-barrier between Man and Peace. 725
'Tis Faith disarms destruction; and absolves,
From ev'ry clam'rous charge, the guiltless tomb.
     Why disbelieve? LORENZO!—" Reason bids,
" All-sacred Reason."—Hold her sacred still;
Nor shalt thou want a rival in thy flame: 730
All-sacred Reason; source, and soul, of all
Demanding praise, on earth, or earth above!
My heart is thine: Deep in its inmost folds,
Live thou with life; live dearer of the two.
Wear I the blessed cross, by fortune stampt   735
On passive Nature, before thought was born?
My birth's blind bigot! fir'd with local zeal!
No; Reason rebaptiz'd me when adult;
Weigh'd true, and false, in her impartial scale;

My heart became the convert of my head; 740
And made that choice, which once was but my fate.
" On argument alone my faith is built:"
Reason pursu'd is Faith; and unpursu'd,
Where proof invites, 'tis Reason, then, no more:
And such our proof, that, or our faith is right, 745
Or Reason lies, and Heav'n design'd it wrong:
Absolve we this? What, then, is blasphemy!
    Fond as we are, and justly fond of Faith,
Reason, we grant, demands our first regard;
The mother honour'd, as the daughter dear. 750
Reason the root; fair Faith is but the flow'r:
The fading flow'r shall die; but Reason lives
Immortal as her Father in the skies.
When Faith is virtue, Reason makes it so. —
Wrong not the Christian; think not Reason yours; 755
'Tis Reason our great Master holds so dear;
'Tis Reason's injur'd rights his wrath resents;
'Tis Reason's voice obey'd, his glories crown;
To give lost Reason life, he pour'd his own;
Believe, and shew the reason of a man; 760
Believe, and taste the pleasure of a god;
Believe, and look with triumph on the tomb.
Through Reason's wounds alone thy Faith can die;
Which dying, tenfold terror gives to Death,
And dips in venom his twice-mortal sting. 765
    Learn hence what honours, what loud pæans, due
To those who push our antidote aside;
Those boasted friends to Reason, and to Man,
Whose fatal love stabs ev'ry joy, and leaves
Death's terror heighten'd gnawing on his heart. 770

These pompous sons of Reason idoliz'd
And vilify'd at once; of Reason dead
Then deify'd, as monarchs were of old;
What conduct plants proud laurels on their brow?
While love of truth thro' all their camp resounds, 775
They draw Pride's curtain o'er the noon-tide ray,
Spike up their inch of reason, on the point
Of philosophic wit call'd argument;
And then, exulting in their taper, cry,
" Behold the sun!" and, Indian-like, adore.   780
    Talk they of morals? O thou bleeding Love!
Thou maker of new morals to mankind!
The grand morality is love of THEE.
As wise as SOCRATES, if such they were
(Nor will they 'bate of that sublime renown;)   785
As wise as SOCRATES, might justly stand
The definition of a modern fool.
    A Christian is the highest style of Man.
And is there, who the blessed cross wipes off,
As a foul blot, from his dishonour'd brow?   790
If angels tremble, 'tis at such a sight:
The wretch they quit, desponding of their charge,
More struck with grief or wonder, who can tell?
    Ye sold to sense! ye citizens of earth!
(For such alone the Christian banner fly;)   795
Know ye how wise your choice, how great your gain?
Behold the picture of earth's happiest man:
    " He calls his wish, it comes; he sends it back,
    " And says he call'd another; that arrives,
    " Meets the same welcome; yet he still calls on; 800
    " Till one calls him, who varies not his call,

" But holds him fast, in chains of darkness bound,
" Till Nature dies, and Judgment sets him free;
" A freedom far less welcome than his chain."
But grant Man happy; grant him happy long; 805
Add to life's highest prize her latest hour;
That hour, so late, is nimble in approach,
That, like a post, comes on in full career:
How swift the shuttle flies that weaves thy shroud!
Where is the fable of thy former years? 810
Thrown down the gulph of time; as far from thee
As they had ne'er been thine; the day in hand,
Like a bird struggling to get loose, is going;
Scarce now possess'd, so suddenly 'tis gone;
And each swift moment fled, is death advanc'd 815
By strides as swift: Eternity is all;
And whose eternity? Who triumphs there?
Bathing for ever in the font of bliss!
For ever basking in the Deity!
LORENZO! who?—Thy conscience shall reply. 820
O give it leave to speak; 'twill speak ere long,
Thy leave unask'd: LORENZO! hear it now,
While useful its advice, its accent mild.
By the great edict, the divine decree,
Truth is deposited with Man's last hour; 825
An honest hour, and faithful to her trust;
Truth, eldest daughter of the Deity;
Truth of his council, when he made the worlds;
Nor less when he shall judge the worlds he made;
Though silent long, and sleeping ne'er so sound, 830
Smother'd with errors, and oppress'd with toys,
That heav'n-commission'd hour no sooner calls,
But from her cavern in the soul's abyss,

Like him they fable under Ætna whelm'd,
—The goddess bursts in thunder, and in flame;   835
Loudly convinces, and severely pains.
Dark Dæmons I discharge, and Hydra-stings;
The keen vibration of bright truth—is hell:
Just definition! though by schools untaught.
Ye deaf to truth! peruse this parson'd page,   840
And trust, for once, a prophet, and a priest;
" Men may live fools, but fools they cannot die."

COMPLAINT.

NIGHT V.

THE RELAPSE.

LORENZO! to recriminate is just.
Fondness of fame is avarice of air.
I grant the man is vain who writes for praise.
Praise no man e'er deserv'd, who sought no more.
   As just thy second charge.   I grant the Muse   5
Has often blush'd at her degen'rate sons,
Retain'd by Sense to plead her filthy cause;
To raise the low, to magnify the mean,
And subtilize the gross into refin'd:
As if to magic numbers' pow'rful charm   10
'Twas giv'n, to make a civet of their song
Obscene, and sweeten ordure to perfume.
Wit, a true pagan, deifies the brute,
And lifts our swine-enjoyments from the mire.

The fact notorious, nor obscure the cause.   15
We wear the chains of Pleasure, and of Pride:
These share the man; and these distract him too;
Draw diff'rent ways, and clash in their commands.
Pride, like an eagle, builds among the stars;
But Pleasure, lark-like, nests upon the ground.   20
Joys shar'd by brute-creation, Pride resents;
Pleasure embraces: Man would both enjoy,
And both at once: A point how hard to gain!
But what can't wit, when stung by strong desire?
Wit dares attempt this arduous enterprise.   25
Since joys of Sense can't rise to Reason's taste;
In subtle Sophistry's laborious forge,
Wit hammers out a reason new, that stoops
To sordid scenes, and meets them with applause.
Wit calls the Graces the chaste zone to loose;   30
Nor less than a plump god to fill the bowl:
A thousand phantoms, and a thousand spells,
A thousand opiates scatters to delude,
To fascinate, inebriate, lay asleep,
And the fool'd mind of Man delightfully confound.   35
Thus that which shock'd the judgment, shocks no more;
That which gave Pride offence, no more offends.
Pleasure and Pride, by nature mortal foes,
At war eternal, which in Man shall reign,
By Wit's address, patch up a fatal peace,   40
And hand in hand lead on the rank debauch,
From rank, refin'd to delicate and gay.
Art, cursed Art! wipes off th' indebted blush
From Nature's cheek, and bronzes ev'ry shame.
Man smiles in ruin, glories in his guilt,   45
And Infamy stands candidate for praise.

All writ by Man in favour of the soul,
These sensual ethics far, in bulk, transcend.
The flow'rs of eloquence, profusely pour'd
O'er spotted vice, fill half the letter'd world.   50
Can pow'rs of genius exorcise their page,
And consecrate enormities with song?

    But let not these inexpiable strains
Condemn the muse that knows her dignity;
Nor meanly stops at Time, but holds the world   55
As 'tis, in Nature's ample field—a point—
A point in her esteem; from whence to start,
And run the round of universal space,
To visit Being universal there,
And Being's Source, that utmost flight of mind!   60
Yet, spite of this so vast circumference,
Well knows, but what is moral, nought is great.
Sing syrens only? Do not angels sing?
There is in Poesy a decent pride,
Which well becomes her when she speaks to Prose, 65
Her younger sister; haply not more wise.

    Think'st thou, LORENZO! to find pastimes here?
No guilty passion blown into a flame,
No foible flatter'd, dignity disgrac'd,
No fairy field of fiction, all on flow'r,   70
No rainbow colours, here, or silken tale;
But solemn counsels, images of awe,
Truths, which eternity lets fall on Man
With double weight, through these revolving spheres,
This death-deep silence, and incumbent shade;   75
Thoughts, such as shall revisit your last hour;
Visit uncall'd, and live when life expires;

And thy dark pencil, Midnight! darker still
In melancholy dipt, embrowns the whole.

    Yet this, ev'n this, my laughter-loving friends! 80
LORENZO! and thy brothers of the smile!
If what imports you most can most engage,
Shall steal your ear, and chain you to my song.
Or, if you fail me, know, the wise shall taste
The truths I sing; the truths I sing shall feel;   85
And, feeling, give assent; and their assent
Is ample recompence; is more than praise.
But chiefly thine, O LITCHFIELD! nor mistake;
Think not unintroduc'd I force my way;
NARCISSA, not unknown, not unally'd,   90
By virtue, or by blood, illustrious youth!
To thee, from blooming amaranthine bow'rs,
Where all the language Harmony, descends
Uncall'd, and asks admittance for the muse:
A muse that will not pain thee with thy praise; 95
Thy praise she drops, by nobler still inspir'd.

    O THOU! blest Spirit! whether the Supreme,
Great antemundane FATHER! in whose breast
Embryo creation, unborn being, dwelt,
And all its various revolutions roll'd   100
Present, though future; prior to themselves;
Whose breath can blow it into nought again;
Or, from his throne, some delegated pow'r,
Who, studious of our peace, dost turn the thought
From vain and vile, to solid and sublime!   105
Unseen THOU lead'st me to delicious draughts
Of inspiration, from a purer stream,
And fuller of the god, than that which burst

From fam'd Castalia: nor is yet allay'd
My sacred thirst; though long my soul has rang'd 110
Through pleasing paths of moral and divine,
By THEE sustain'd, and lighted by the stars.
   By them best lighted are the paths of thought;
Nights are their days, their most illumin'd hours.
By day, the soul, o'erborne by life's career, 115
Stunn'd by the din, and giddy with the glare,
Reels far from reason, jostled by the throng.
By day the soul is passive, all her thoughts
Impos'd, precarious, broken, ere mature.
By night from objects free, from passion cool, 120
Thoughts uncontroll'd, and unimpress'd, the births
Of pure election, arbitrary range,
Not to the limits of one world confin'd;
But from ethereal travels, light on earth,
As voyagers drop anchor for repose. 125
   Let Indians, and the gay, like Indians, fond
Of feather'd fopperies, the sun adore:
Darkness has more divinity for me;
It strikes thought inward; it drives back the soul
To settle on herself, our point supreme! 130
There lies our theatre, there sits our Judge.
Darkness the curtain drops o'er life's dull scene;
'Tis the kind hand of Providence stretch'd out
'Twixt Man and vanity; 'tis Reason's reign,
And Virtue's too; these tutelary shades 135
Are Man's asylum from the tainted throng.
Night is the good man's friend, and guardian too;
It no less rescues virtue, than inspires.
   Virtue, for ever frail, as fair below,
Her tender nature suffers in the crowd, 140

Nor touches on the world, without a stain:
The world's infectious; few bring back at eve,
Immaculate, the manners of the morn.
Something we thought, is blotted; we resolv'd,
Is shaken; we renounc'd, returns again.   145
Each salutation may slide in a sin
Unthought before, or fix a former flaw.
Nor is it strange: Light, motion, concourse, noise,
All scatter us abroad; thought outward-bound,
Neglectful of our home-affairs, flies off   150
In fume and dissipation, quits her charge,
And leaves the breast unguarded to the foe.

   Present example gets within our guard,
And acts with double force, by few repell'd.
Ambition fires ambition; love of gain   155
Strikes, like a pestilence, from breast to breast;
Riot, Pride, Perfidy, blue vapours breathe;
And Inhumanity is caught from Man,
From smiling Man. A slight, a single glance,
And shot at random, often has brought home   160
A sudden fever to the throbbing heart,
Of envy, rancour, or impure desire.
We see, we hear, with peril; safety dwells
Remote from multitude; the world's a school
Of wrong, and what proficients swarm around!   165
We must or imitate, or disapprove;
Must list as their accomplices, or foes;
That stains our innocence; this wounds our peace.
From Nature's birth, hence, Wisdom has been smit
With sweet recess, and languish'd for the shade.   170
   This sacred shade, and solitude, what is it?
'Tis the felt presence of the Deity.

Few are the faults we flatter when alone.
Vice sinks in her allurements, is ungilt,
And looks, like other objects, black by night.   175
By night, an atheist half-believes a God.
   Night is fair Virtue's immemorial friend;
The conscious moon, through ev'ry distant age,
Has held a lamp to Wisdom, and let fall,
On Contemplation's eye, her purging ray.   180
The fam'd Athenian, he who woo'd from Heav'n
Philosophy the fair, to dwell with Men,
And form their manners, not inflame their pride,
While o'er his head, as fearful to molest
His lab'ring mind, the stars in silence slide,   185
And seem all gazing on their future guest,
See him soliciting his ardent suit
In private audience: all the live-long night,
Rigid in thought, and motionless, he stands;
Nor quits his theme, or posture, till the sun   190
(Rude drunkard! rising rosy from the main!)
Disturbs his nobler intellectual beam,
And gives him to the tumult of the world.
Hail, precious moments stol'n from the black waste
Of murder'd Time! auspicious Midnight, hail!   195
The world excluded—ev'ry passion hush'd—
And open'd a calm intercourse with Heav'n—
Here—the soul sits in council; ponders past,
Predestines future action; sees, not feels,
Tumultuous life, and reasons with the storm;   200
All her lies answers, and thinks down her charms.
   What awful joy! what mental liberty!
I am not pent in darkness; rather say
(If not too bold) in darkness I'm embower'd.

Delightful gloom! the clust'ring thoughts around   205
Spontaneous rise, and blossom in the shade;
But droop by day, and sicken in the sun.
Thought borrows light elsewhere; from that First Fire,
Fountain of animation! whence descends
URANIA, my celestial guest! who deigns   210
Nightly to visit me, so mean; and now
Conscious how needful discipline to Man,
From pleasing dalliance with the charms of Night
My wand'ring thought recalls, to what excites
Far other beat of heart; NARCISSA's tomb!   215
   Or is it feeble Nature calls me back,
And breaks my spirit into grief again?
Is it a Stygian vapour in my blood?
A cold, slow puddle, creeping through my veins!
Or is it thus with all Men?—Thus with all.   220
What are we? How unequal! Now we soar,
And now we sink; to be the same, transcends
Our present prowess.   Dearly pays the soul
For lodging ill; too dearly rents her clay.
Reason, a baffled counsellor! but adds   225
The blush of weakness to the bane of woe.
The noblest spirit fighting her hard fate,
In this damp, dusky region, charg'd with storms,
But feebly flutters, yet untaught to fly;
Or, flying, short her flight, and sure her fall.   230
Our utmost strength, when down, to rise again;
And not to yield, though beaten, all our praise.
   'Tis vain to seek in Men for more than Man.
Though proud in promise, big in previous thought,
Experience damps our triumph. I, who late,   235
Emerging from the shadows of the grave,

Where Grief detain'd me pris'ner, mounting high,
Threw wide the gates of everlasting day,
And call'd mankind to glory, shook off Pain,
Mortality shook off, in æther pure,   240
And struck the stars; now feel my spirits fail;
They drop me from the zenith; down, I rush,
Like him whom fable fledg'd with waxen wings,
In sorrow drown'd—but not, in sorrow, lost.
How wretched is the Man, who never mourn'd! 245
I dive for precious pearl, in Sorrow's stream:
Not so the thoughtless Man that only grieves;
Takes all the torment, and rejects the gain
(Inestimable gain!) and gives Heav'n leave
To make him but more wretched, not more wise.

　　If wisdom is our lesson (and what else   251
Ennobles Man? What else have angels learnt?)
Grief! more proficients in thy school are made,
Than Genius, or proud Learning, e'er could boast.
Voracious Learning, often over-fed,   255
Digests not into sense her motley meal.
This Book-case, with dark booty almost burst,
This Forager on others wisdom, leaves
Her native farm, her Reason, quite untill'd.
With mix'd manure she surfeits the rank soil,   260
Dung'd, but not drest; and rich to beggary.
A pomp untameable of weeds prevails.
Her Servant's wealth, incumber'd Wisdom mourns.

　　And what says Genius? " Let the dull be wise."
Genius, too hard for Right, can prove it wrong; 265
And loves to boast, where blush men less inspir'd.
It pleads exemption from the laws of Sense;
Considers Reason as a leveller;

And scorns to share a blessing with the crowd.
That wise it could be, thinks an ample claim   270
To Glory, and to Pleasure gives the rest.
CRASSUS but sleeps, ARDELIO is undone.
Wisdom less shudders at a fool, than wit.

But Wisdom smiles, when humbled mortals weep;
When Sorrow wounds the breast, as ploughs the glebe,
And hearts obdurate feel her soft'ning shower;   276
Her seed celestial, then, glad Wisdom sows;
Her golden harvest triumphs in the soil.
If so, NARCISSA! welcome my Relapse;
I'll raise a tax on my calamity,   280
And reap rich compensation from my pain.
I'll range the plenteous intellectual field,
And gather ev'ry thought of sov'reign power
To chase the moral maladies of man;
Thoughts, which may bear transplanting to the skies,
Tho' natives of this coarse penurious soil: 286
Nor wholly wither there, where seraphs sing,
Refin'd, exalted, not annull'd, in Heav'n.
Reason, the sun that gives them birth, the same
In either clime, though more illustrious there.   290
These choicely cull'd, and elegantly rang'd,
Shall form a garland for NARCISSA's tomb;
And, peradventure, of no fading flow'rs.

Say, on what themes shall puzzled choice descend?
" Th' importance of contemplating the tomb;   295
" Why men decline it; Suicide's foul birth;
" The various kinds of grief; the faults of age;
" And Death's dread character—invite my song."
And, first, th' importance of our end survey'd.
Friends counsel quick dismission of our grief: 300

Mistaken kindness! our hearts heal too soon.
Are they more kind than he, who struck the blow?
Who bid it do his errand in our hearts,
And banish peace, till nobler guests arrive,
And bring it back, a true, and endless peace?   305
Calamities are friends: as glaring day
Of these unnumber'd lustres robs our sight:
Prosperity puts out unnumber'd thoughts
Of import high, and light divine, to Man.
    The Man how blest, who, sick of gaudy scenes, 310
(Scenes apt to thrust between us and ourselves!)
Is led by choice to take his fav'rite walk,
Beneath Death's gloomy, silent, cypress shades,
Unpierc'd by Vanity's fantastic ray;
To read his monuments, to weigh his dust,   315
Visit his vaults, and dwell among the tombs!
LORENZO! read with me NARCISSA's stone;
(NARCISSA was thy fav'rite) let us read
Her moral stone; few doctors preach so well;
Few orators so tenderly can touch   320
The feeling heart.   What pathos in the date!
Apt words can strike; and yet in them we see
Faint images of what we here enjoy.
What cause have we to build on length of life?
Temptations seize, when Fear is laid asleep;   325
And ill foreboded is our strongest guard.
    See from her tomb, as from an humble shrine,
Truth, radiant goddess! sallies on my soul,
And puts Delusion's dusky train to flight;
Dispels the mist our sultry passions raise,   330
From objects low, terrestrial, and obscene;
And shews the real estimate of things;

o

Which no man, unafflicted ever saw;
Pulls off the veil from Virtue's rising charms;
Detects Temptation in a thousand lyes.   335
Truth bids me look on Men, as autumn leaves,
And all they bleed for, as the summer's dust,
Driv'n by the whirlwind: Lighted by her beams,
I widen my horizon, gain new powers,
See things invisible, feel things remote,   340
Am present with futurities; think nought
To Man so foreign as the joys possest;
Nought so much his as those beyond the grave.
    No folly keeps its colour in her sight;
Pale worldly Wisdom loses all her charms;   345
In pompous promise from her schemes profound,
If future fate she plans, 'tis all in leaves,
Like Sybil, unsubstantial, fleeting bliss!
At the first blast it vanishes in air.
Not so, celestial: Wouldst thou know, LORENZO? 350
How differ worldly Wisdom and divine?
Just as the waning and the waxing moon.
More empty worldly Wisdom ev'ry day;
And ev'ry day more fair her rival shines.
When later, there's less time to play the fool.   355
Soon our whole term for Wisdom is expir'd
(Thou know'st she calls no council in the grave:)
And everlasting fool is writ in fire,
Or real Wisdom wafts us to the skies.
    As worldly schemes resemble Sybil's leaves,   360
The good man's days to Sibyl's books compare
(In ancient story read, thou know'st the tale,)
In price still rising, as in number less,
Inestimable quite his final hour.

For that who thrones can offer, offer thrones;   365
Insolvent worlds the purchase cannot pay.
" Oh let me die his death !" all Nature cries.
" Then live his life"—All Nature faulters there.
Our great Physician daily to consult,
To commune with the grave our only cure.   370
    What grave prescribes the best?—A friend's; and yet,
From a friend's grave how soon we disengage!
Ev'n to the dearest, as his marble, cold.
Why are friends ravish'd from us? 'Tis to bind,
By soft Affection's ties, on human hearts,   375
The thought of death, which Reason, too supine,
Or misemploy'd, so rarely fastens there.
Nor reason, nor affection, no, nor both
Combin'd, can break the witchcrafts of the world.
Behold th' inexorable hour at hand !   380
Behold th' inexorable hour forgot !
And to forget it, the chief aim of life,
Though well to ponder it, is life's chief end.
    Is Death, that ever threat'ning, ne'er remote,
That all-important, and that only sure   385
(Come when he will,) an unexpected guest?
Nay, though invited by the loudest calls
Of blind Imprudence, unexpected still?
Though num'rous messengers are sent before,
To warn his great arrival. What the cause,   390
The wondrous cause, of this mysterious ill?
All Heav'n looks down astonish'd at the sight.
    Is it, that Life has sown her joys so thick,
We can't thrust in a single care between?
Is it, that Life has such a swarm of cares,   395
The thought of Death can't enter for the throng?

Is it, that Time steals on with downy feet,
Nor wakes Indulgence from her golden dream?
To-day is so like yesterday, it cheats;
We take the lying sister for the same.   400
Life glides away, LORENZO! like a brook;
For ever changing, unperceiv'd the change.
In the same brook none ever bath'd him twice:
To the same life none ever twice awoke.
We call the brook the same; the same we think 405
Our life, though still more rapid in its flow;
Nor mark the much irrevocably laps'd,
And mingled with the sea.   Or shall we say
(Retaining still the brook to bear us on)
That Life is like a vessel on the stream?   410
In Life embark'd, we smoothly down the tide
Of Time descend, but not on Time intent;
Amus'd, unconscious of the gliding wave;
Till on a sudden we perceive a shock;
We start, awake, look out; what see we there? 415
Our brittle bark is burst on CHARON's shore.
    Is this the cause Death flies all human thought?
Or is it Judgment by the Will struck blind,
That domineering mistress of the soul,
Like him so strong by DALILAH the fair?   420
Or is it Fear turns startled Reason back,
From looking down a precipice so steep?
'Tis dreadful; and the dread is wisely plac'd,
By Nature, conscious of the make of Man.
A dreadful friend it is, a terror kind,   425
A flaming sword to guard the tree of life.
By that unaw'd, in Life's most smiling hour,
The good man would repine; would suffer joys,

And burn impatient for his promis'd skies.
The bad, on each punctilious pique of pride,   430
Or gloom of humour, would give rage the reign,
Bound o'er the barrier, rush into the dark,
And mar the scenes of Providence below.
  What groan was that, LORENZO!—Furies! rise;
And drown, in your less execrable yell,   435
BRITANNIA's shame.   There took her gloomy flight,
On wing impetuous, a black sullen soul,
Blasted from hell, with horrid lust of death.
Thy friend, the brave, the gallant ALTAMONT,
So call'd, so thought—and then he fled the field, 440
Less base the fear of Death, than fear of Life.
O BRITAIN, infamous for suicide!
An island in thy manners! far disjoin'd
From the whole world of rationals beside!
In ambient waves plunge thy polluted head,   445
Wash the dire stain, nor shock the continent.
  But thou be shock'd, while I detect the cause
Of Self-assault, expose the monster's birth,
And bid Abhorrence hiss it round the world.
Blame not thy clime, nor chide the distant sun; 450
The sun is innocent, thy clime absolv'd :
Immoral climes kind Nature never made.
The cause I sing, in Eden might prevail,
And proves it is thy folly, not thy fate.
  The soul of Man (let Man in homage bow,   455
Who names his soul,) a native of the skies!
High-born, and free, her freedom should maintain,
Unsold, unmortgag'd for Earth's little bribes.
Th' illustrious stranger, in this foreign land,
Like strangers, jealous of her dignity,   460

Studious of home, and ardent to return,
Of Earth suspicious, Earth's enchanted cup
With cool reserve light touching, should indulge,
On Immortality, her godlike taste;
There take large draughts; make her chief banquet there.
   But some reject this sustenance divine;   466
To beggarly vile appetites descend;
Ask alms of Earth, for guests that came from Heav'n;
Sink into slaves; and sell, for present hire,
Their rich reversion, and (what shares its fate)   470
Their native freedom, to the prince who sways
This nether world. And when his payments fail,
When his foul basket gorges them no more,
Or their pall'd palates loath the basket full;
Are instantly, with wild demoniac rage,   475
For breaking all the chains of Providence,
And bursting their confinement; though fast barr'd
By laws divine and human; guarded strong
With horrors doubled to defend the pass,
The blackest, Nature, or dire Guilt, can raise   480
And moated round with fathomless destruction,
Sure to receive, and whelm them in their fall.
   Such, Britons! is the cause, to you unknown,
Or worse, o'erlook'd; o'erlook'd by magistrates,
Thus criminals themselves. I grant the deed   485
Is madness; but the madness of the heart.
And what is that? Our utmost bound of guilt.
A sensual unreflecting life is big
With monstrous births, and Suicide, to crown
The black infernal brood. The bold to break   490
Heav'n's law supreme, and desperately rush
Through sacred Nature's murder, on their own,

Because they never think of Death, they die.
'Tis equally Man's duty, glory, gain,
At once to shun, and meditate, his end.   495
When by the bed of languishment we sit
(The seat of wisdom! if our choice, not fate,)
Or o'er our dying friends in anguish hang,
Wipe the cold dew, or stay the sinking head,
Number their moments, and, in ev'ry clock,   500
Start at the voice of an eternity;
See the dim lamp of life just feebly lift
An agonizing beam, at us to gaze,
Then sink again, and quiver into death,
That most pathetic herald of our own;   505
How read we such sad scenes? As sent to Man
In perfect vengeance? No; in pity sent,
To melt him down like wax, and then impress,
Indelible, Death's image on his heart;
Bleeding for others, trembling for himself.   510
We bleed, we tremble; we forget, we smile.
The mind turns fool, before the cheek is dry.
Our quick-returning folly cancels all;
As the tide rushing razes what is writ
In yielding sands, and smooths the letter'd shore. 515
    LORENZO! hast thou ever weigh'd a sigh?
Or study'd the philosophy of tears?
(A science yet unlectur'd in our schools!)
Hast thou descended deep into the breast,
And seen their source? If not, descend with me, 520
And trace these briny riv'lets to their springs.
    Our fun'ral tears from diff'rent causes rise.
As if from sep'rate cisterns in the soul,
Of various kinds, they flow.   From tender hearts,

By soft contagion call'd, some burst at once,   525
And stream obsequious to the leading eye.
Some ask more time, by curious art distill'd.
Some hearts in secret hard, unapt to melt,
Struck by the magic of the public eye,
Like MOSES' smitten rock, gush out amain.   530
Some weep to share the fame of the deceas'd,
So high in merit, and to them so dear.
They dwell on praises, which they think they share;
And thus, without a blush, commend themselves.
Some mourn in proof that something they could love;
They weep not to relieve their grief, but shew.   536
Some weep in perfect justice to the dead,
As conscious all their love is in arrear.
Some mischievously weep, not unappriz'd,
Tears, sometimes, aid the conquest of an eye.   540
With what address the soft EPHESIANS drew
Their sable net-work o'er entangled hearts!
As seen through chrystal, how their roses glow,
While liquid pearl runs trickling down their cheek!
Of her's not prouder EGYPT's wanton queen,   545
Carousing gems, herself dissolv'd in love.
Some weep at death, abstracted from the dead,
And celebrate, like CHARLES, their own decease.
By kind construction some are deem'd to weep,
Because a decent veil conceals their joy.   550
    Some weep in earnest, and yet weep in vain;
As deep in indiscretion, as in woe.
Passion, blind Passion, impotently pours
Tears, that deserve more tears; while Reason sleeps;
Or gazes, like an ideot, unconcern'd;   555
Nor comprehends the meaning of the storm;

Knows not it speaks to her, and her alone.
Irrationals all sorrow are beneath,
That noble gift! that privilege of Man!
From Sorrow's pang, the birth of endless joy.   560
But these are barren of that birth divine:
They weep impetuous, as the summer storm,
And full as short! The cruel grief soon tam'd,
They make a pastime of the stingless tale;
Far as the deep-resounding knell, they spread   565
The dreadful news, and hardly feel it more:
No grain of wisdom pays them for their woe.
    Half-round the globe, the tears pumpt up by Death
Are spent in wat'ring vanities of life;
In making Folly flourish still more fair.   570
When the sick soul, her wonted stay withdrawn,
Reclines on earth, and sorrows in the dust;
Instead of learning, there, her true support,
Though there thrown down her true support to learn,
Without Heav'n's aid impatient to be blest,   575
She crawls to the next shrub, or bramble vile,
Though from the stately cedar's arms she fell:
With stale, forsworn embraces, clings anew,
The stranger weds, and blossoms, as before,
In all the fruitless fopperies of Life: 580
Presents her weed, well-fancy'd, at the ball,
And raffles for the death's-head on the ring.
    So wept AURELIA, till the destin'd Youth
Stept in, with his receipt for making smiles,
And blanching sables into bridal bloom.   585
So wept LORENZO fair CLARISSA's fate;
Who gave that angel boy on whom he doats;
And dy'd to give him, orphan'd in his birth!

P

Not such, NARCISSA, my distress for thee.
I'll make an altar of thy sacred tomb,   590
To sacrifice to Wisdom,—What wast thou?
" Young, gay, and fortunate!" Each yields a theme.
I'll dwell on each, to shun thought more severe;
(Heav'n knows I labour with severer still!)
I'll dwell on each, and quite exhaust thy death. 595
A soul without reflection, like a pile
Without inhabitant, to ruin runs.

    And first, thy youth.   What says it to grey hairs?
NARCISSA, I'm become thy pupil now—
Early, bright, transient, chaste, as morning dew, 600
She sparkled, was exhal'd, and went to Heav'n.
Time on this head has snow'd; yet still 'tis borne
Aloft; nor thinks but on another's grave.
Cover'd with shame I speak it, Age severe
Old worn-out vice sets down for virtue fair;   605
With graceless gravity chastising youth,
That youth chastis'd surpassing in a fault,
Father of all, forgetfulness of death;
As if, like objects pressing on the sight,
Death had advanc'd too near us to be seen: 610
Or, that life's loan Time ripen'd into right;
And men might plead prescription from the grave;
Deathless, from repetition of reprieve.
Deathless? far from it! such are dead already;
Their hearts are bury'd, and the world's their grave.

    Tell me, some god! my guardian angel! tell, 616
What thus infatuates? What enchantment plants
The phantom of an age 'twixt us and Death
Already at the door? He knocks, we hear him,
And yet we will not hear.   What mail defends 620.

Our untouch'd hearts? What miracle turns off
The pointed thought, which from a thousand quivers
Is daily darted, and is daily shunn'd?
We stand, as in a battle, throngs on throngs
Around us falling; wounded oft ourselves;   625
Though bleeding with our wounds, immortal still!
We see Time's furrows on another's brow,
And Death intrench'd, preparing his assault;
How few themselves in that just mirror see!
Or, seeing, draw their inference as strong!   630
There death is certain; doubtful here: He must,
And soon; we may, within an age, expire.
Tho' grey our heads, our thoughts and aims are green;
Like damag'd clocks, whose hand and bell dissent,
Folly sings six, while Nature points at twelve.   635
     Absurd longevity! More, more, it cries:
More life, more wealth, more trash of ev'ry kind.
And wherefore mad for more, when relish fails?
Object and Appetite must club for joy;
Shall Folly labour hard to mend the bow,   640
Baubles, I mean, that strike us from without,   .
While Nature is relaxing ev'ry string,
Ask Thought for joy; grow rich, and hoard within.
Think you the soul, when this life's rattles cease,
Has nothing of more manly to succeed?   645
Contract the taste immortal; learn ev'n now
To relish what alone subsists hereafter.
Divine, or none, henceforth your joys for ever.
Of age the glory is, to wish to die.
That wish is praise and promise; it applauds   650
Past life, and promises our future bliss.
What weakness see not children in their sires!

Grand-climacterical absurdities!
Grey-hair'd authority, to faults of youth,
How shocking! It makes folly thrice a fool;   655
And our first childhood might our last despise.
Peace and esteem is all that age can hope.
Nothing but Wisdom gives the first; the last,
Nothing, but the repute of being wise.
Folly bars both; our age is quite undone.   660
    What folly can be ranker? Like our shadows,
Our wishes lengthen, as our sun declines.
No wish should loiter, then, this side the grave.
Our hearts should leave the world, before the knell
Calls for our carcases to mend the soil.   665
Enough to live in tempest, die in port;
Age should fly concourse, cover in retreat
Defects of judgment, and the will subdue;
Walk thoughtful on the silent, solemn shore
Of that vast ocean it must sail so soon;   670
And put good works on board; and wait the wind
That shortly blows us into worlds unknown:
If unconsider'd too, a dreadful scene!
    All should be prophets to themselves; foresee
Their future fate; their future fate foretaste;   675
This art would waste the bitterness of death.
The thought of death alone, the fear destroys.
A disaffection to that precious thought
Is more than midnight darkness on the soul,
Which sleeps beneath it, on a precipice,   680
Puff'd off by the first blast, and lost for ever.
    Dost ask, LORENZO, why so warmly prest,
By repetition hammer'd on thine ear,
The thought of Death? That thought is the machine,

The grand machine, that heaves us from the dust, 685
And rears us into men. That thought ply'd home,
Will soon reduce the ghastly precipice
O'crhanging hell; will soften the descent,
And gently slope our passage to the grave:
How warmly to be wish'd! What heart of flesh ·690
Would trifle with tremendous! dare extremes!
Yawn o'er the fate of infinite! What hand,
Beyond the blackest brand of censure bold
(To speak a language too well known to thee,)
Would at a moment give its all to chance,   695
And stamp the die for an eternity!

 Aid me, NARCISSA! aid me to keep pace
With destiny; and ere her scissars cut
My thread of life, to break this tougher thread
Of moral death, that ties me to the world.   700
Sting thou my slumb'ring Reason to send forth
A thought of observation on the foe;
To sally, and survey the rapid march
Of his ten thousand messengers to Man;
Who, JEHU like, behind him turns them all.   705
All accident apart, by Nature sign'd,
My warrant is gone out, though dormant yet;
Perhaps behind one moment lurks my fate.

 Must I then forward only look for Death?
Backward I turn mine eye, and find him there. 710
Man is a self-survivor ev'ry year.
Man, like a stream, is in perpetual flow.
Death's a destroyer of quotidian prey.
My youth, my noon-tide, his; my yesterday;
The bold invader shares the present hour.   715

Each moment on the former shuts the grave.
While Man is growing, life is in decrease;
And cradles rock us nearer to the tomb.
Our birth is nothing but our death begun;
As tapers waste, that instant they take fire.   720
    Shall we then fear, lest that should come to pass,
Which comes to pass each moment of our lives?
If fear we must, let that death turn us pale,
Which murders strength and ardour; what remains
Should rather call on Death, than dread his call. 725
Ye partners of my fault, and my decline!
Thoughtless of death, but when your neighbour's knell
(Rude visitant!) knocks hard at your dull sense,
And with its thunder scarce obtains your ear!
Be Death your theme in ev'ry place and hour;   730
Nor longer want, ye monumental sires!
A brother tomb to tell you, you shall die.
That Death you dread (so great is Nature's skill!)
Know, you shall court, before you shall enjoy.
    But you are learn'd; in volumes deep you sit; 735
In wisdom, shallow: Pompous ignorance!
Would you be still more learned than the learn'd?
Learn well to know how much need not be known,
And what that knowledge which impairs your sense.
Our needful knowledge, like our needful food,   740
Unhedg'd, lies open in life's common field;
And bids all welcome to the vital feast.
You scorn what lies before you in the page
Of Nature and Experience, moral truth!
Of indispensible, eternal fruit!   745
Fruit, on which mortals feeding, turn to gods;

And dive in science for distinguish'd names,
Dishonest fomentation of your pride;
Sinking in virtue, as you rise in fame.
Your learning, like the lunar beam, affords   750
Light, but not heat; it leaves you undevout,
Frozen at heart, while speculation shines.
Awake, ye curious indagators! fond
Of knowing all, but what avails you, known;
If you would learn Death's character, attend.   755
All casts of conduct, all degrees of health,
All dies of fortune, and all dates of age,
Together shook in his impartial urn,
Come forth at random: Or, if choice is made,
The choice is quite sarcastic, and insults   760
All bold conjecture, and fond hopes of Man.
What countless multitudes not only leave,
But deeply disappoint us, by their deaths!
Though great our sorrow, greater our surprise.
Like other tyrants, Death delights to smite,   765
What smitten, most proclaims the pride of pow'r,
And arbitrary nod.   His joy supreme,
To bid the wretch survive the fortunate;
The feeble wrap th' athletic in his shroud;
And weeping fathers build their children's tomb; 770
Me, thine, NARCISSA!—What though short thy date?
Virtue, not rolling suns, the mind matures.
That life is long, which answers life's great end.
The time that bears no fruit, deserves no name;
The man of wisdom is the man of years.   775
In hoary youth METHUSALEMS may die;
O how misdated on their flatt'ring tombs!

NARCISSA's youth has lectur'd me thus far.
And can her gaiety give counsel too?
That, like the Jews' fam'd oracle of gems,   780
Sparkles instruction; such as throws new light,
And opens more the character of Death,
Ill known to thee, LORENZO! This thy vaunt:
" Give Death his due, the wretched and the old;
" Ev'n let him sweep his rubbish to the grave;   785
" Let him not violate kind Nature's laws,
" But own Man born to live as well as die."
Wretched and old thou giv'st him; young and gay
He takes; and plunder is a tyrant's joy.
What if I prove, " The farthest from the fear   790
" Are often nearest to the stroke of fate?"
    All, more than common, menaces an end.
A blaze betokens brevity of life:
As if bright embers should emit a flame,
Glad spirits sparkled from NARCISSA's eye,   795
And made youth younger, and taught life to live.
As Nature's opposites wage endless war,
For this offence, as treason to the deep
Inviolable stupor of his reign,
Where Lust, and turbulent Ambition, sleep,   800
Death took swift vengeance. As he life detests,
More life is still more odious; and, reduc'd
By conquest, aggrandizes more his pow'r.
But wherefore aggrandiz'd? By Heav'n's decree,
To plant the soul on her eternal guard,   805
In awful expectation of our end.
Thus runs Death's dread commission: " Strike, but so
" As most alarms the living by the dead."

Hence stratagem delights him, and surprise,
And cruel sport with Man's securities.   810
Not simple conquest, triumph is his aim;
And, where least fear'd, there conquest triumphs most:
This proves my bold assertion not too bold.
  What are his arts to lay our fears asleep?
Tiberian arts his purposes wrap up   815
In deep dissimulation's darkest night.
Like princes unconfest in foreign courts,
Who travel under cover, Death assumes
The name and look of Life, and dwells among us.
He takes all shapes that serve his black designs: 820
Though master of a wider empire far
Than that o'er which the ROMAN eagle flew;
Like NERO, he's a fiddler, charioteer,
Or drives his phaëton, in female guise;
Quite unsuspected, till, the wheel beneath,   825
His disarray'd oblation he devours.
  He most affects the forms least like himself,
His slender self.   Hence burly corpulence
Is his familiar wear, and sleek disguise.
Behind the rosy bloom he loves to lurk,   830
Or ambush in a smile; or wanton dive
In dimples deep; love's eddies, which draw in
Unwary hearts, and sink them in despair.
Such, on NARCISSA's couch, he loiter'd long
Unknown; and, when detected, still was seen   835
To smile; such peace has Innocence in death!
  Most happy they, whom least his arts deceive.
One eye on Death, and one full fix'd on Heav'n,
Becomes a mortal and immortal Man.

Q

Long on his wiles a piqu'd and jealous spy,   840
I've seen, or dreamt I saw, the tyrant dress;
Lay by his horrors, and put on his smiles.
Say, muse, for thou remember'st, call it back,
And shew LORENZO the surprising scene;
If 'twas a dream, his genius can explain.   845
    'Twas in a circle of the gay I stood.
Death would have enter'd; Nature push'd him back;
Supported by a doctor of renown,
His point he gain'd.   Then artfully dismist
The sage; for Death design'd to be conceal'd.   850
He gave an old vivacious usurer
His meagre aspect, and his naked bones;
In gratitude for plumping up his prey,
A pamper'd spendthrift; whose fantastic air,
Well-fashion'd figure, and cockaded brow,   855
He took in change, and underneath the pride
Of costly linen, tuck'd his filthy shroud.
His crooked bow he straiten'd to a cane;
And hid his deadly shafts in MYRA's eye.
    The dreadful masquerader, thus equipt,   860
Out-sallies on adventures.   Ask you where?
Where is he not? For his peculiar haunts,
Let this suffice; sure as night follows day,
Death treads in Pleasure's footsteps round the world,
When Pleasure treads the paths which Reason shuns.
When, against Reason, Riot shuts the door,   866
And Gaiety supplies the place of Sense,
Then, foremost at the banquet, and the ball,
Death leads the dance, or stamps the deadly die;
Nor ever fails the midnight bowl to crown.   870

_____ _____ __ __ _____ ___ _ he deepa her neach

_____ _____ ow pull, they start, despair expire

Published August 1st 1795 by T. Hopwrastall No 301 High Holborn

Gaily carousing to his gay compeers,
Inly he laughs, to see them laugh at him,
As absent far: And when the revel burns,
When fear is banish'd, and triumphant thought,
Calling for all the joys beneath the moon,   875
Against him turns the key, and bids him sup
With their progenitors—he drops his mask;
Frowns out at full; they start—despair—expire!
    Scarce with more sudden terror and surprise,
From his black masque of nitre, touch'd by fire, 880
He bursts, expands, roars, blazes, and devours.
And is not this triumphant treachery,
And more than simple conquest, in the fiend?
    And now, LORENZO, dost thou wrap thy soul
In soft security, because unknown   885
Which moment is commission'd to destroy?
In Death's uncertainty thy danger lies.
Is Death uncertain? Therefore thou be fixt;
Fixt as a centinel, all eye, all ear,
All expectation of the coming foe.   890
Rouse, stand in arms, nor lean against thy spear;
Lest slumber steal one moment o'er thy soul,
And Fate surprise thee nodding.   Watch, be strong;
Thus give each day the merit, and renown,
Of dying well; though doom'd but once to die. 895
Nor let Life's period hidden (as from most)
Hide too from thee the precious use of life.
    Early, not sudden, was NARCISSA's fate.
Soon, not surprising, Death his visit paid.
Her thought went forth to meet him on his way. 900
Nor Gaiety forgot it was to die:
Though Fortune too (our third and final theme,)

As an accomplice play'd her gaudy plumes,
And ev'ry glitt'ring gewgaw, on her sight,
To dazzle, and debauch it from its mark.   905
Death's dreadful advent is the mark of Man;
And ev'ry thought that misses it is blind.
Fortune, with Youth and Gaiety, conspir'd
To weave a triple wreath of happiness
(If happiness on earth) to crown her brow.   910
And could Death charge through such a shining shield?
    That shining shield invites the tyrant's spear,
As if to damp our elevated aims,
And strongly preach humility to Man.
O how portentous is prosperity!   915
How, comet-like, it threatens, while it shines!
Few years but yield us proof of Death's ambition,
To cull his victims from the fairest fold,
And sheath his shafts in all the pride of life.
When flooded with abundance, purpled o'er   920
With recent honours, bloom'd with ev'ry bliss,
Set up in ostentation, made the gaze,
The gaudy centre, of the public eye,
When Fortune thus has toss'd her child in air,
Snatch'd from the covert of an humble state,   925
How often have I seen him dropt at once,
Our morning's envy, and our ev'ning's sigh!
As if her bounties were the signal giv'n,
The flow'ry wreath to mark the sacrifice,
And call Death's arrows on the destin'd prey.   930
    High Fortune seems in cruel league with Fate.
Ask you for what? To give his war on Man
The deeper dread, and more illustrious spoil;
Thus to keep daring mortals more in awe.

And burns LORENZO still for the sublime 935
Of Life? to hang his airy nest on high,
On the slight timber of the topmost bough,
Rock'd at each breeze, and menacing a fall?
Granting grim Death at equal distance there;
Yet Peace begins just where Ambition ends. 940
What makes Man wretched? Happiness deny'd?
LORENZO! no: 'Tis Happiness disdain'd.
She comes too meanly drest to win our smile;
And calls herself Content, a homely name!
Our flame is Transport, and Content our scorn. 945
Ambition turns, and shuts the door against her,
And weds a Toil, a Tempest, in her stead;
A Tempest to warm Transport near a-kin.
Unknowing what our mortal state admits,
Life's modest joys we ruin, while we raise; 950
And all our ecstasies are wounds to peace:
Peace, the full portion of mankind below.

And since thy peace is dear, ambitious youth!
Of fortune fond, as thoughtless of thy fate!
As late I drew Death's picture, to stir up 955
Thy wholesome fears; now, drawn in contrast, see
Gay Fortune's, thy vain hopes to reprimand.
See, high in air, the sportive goddess hangs,
Unlocks her casket, spreads her glitt'ring ware,
And calls the giddy winds to puff abroad 960
Her random bounties o'er the gaping throng.
All rush rapacious; friends o'er trodden friends,
Sons o'er their fathers, subjects o'er their kings,
Priests o'er their gods, and lovers o'er the fair
(Still more ador'd,) to snatch the golden show'r. 965

Gold glitters most, where Virtue shines no more;
As stars from absent suns have leave to shine.
O what a precious pack of votaries,
Unkennell'd from the prisons, and the stews,
Pour in, all op'ning in their idol's praise!   970
All, ardent, eye each wafture of her hand,
And, wide expanding their voracious jaws,
Morsel on morsel swallow down unchew'd,
Untasted, through mad appetite for more;
Gorg'd to the throat, yet lean and rav'nous still.   975
Sagacious all, to trace the smallest game,
And bold to seize the greatest.   If (blest chance!)
Court-zephyrs sweetly breathe, they launch, they fly,
O'er just, o'er sacred all-forbidden ground,
Drunk with the burning scent of place or pow'r,   980
Staunch to the foot of lucre, till they die.
    Or, if for Men you take them, as I mark
Their manners, thou their various fates survey.
With aim mis-measur'd, and impetuous speed,
Some darting, strike their ardent wish far off,   985
Through fury to possess it: Some succeed,
But stumble, and let fall the taken prize;
From some, by sudden blasts, 'tis whirl'd away,
And lodg'd in bosoms that ne'er dream'd of gain;
To some it sticks so close, that, when torn off,   990
Torn is the man, and mortal is the wound.
Some, o'er-enamour'd of their bags, run mad,
Groan under gold, yet weep for want of bread.
Together some (unhappy rivals!) seize,
And rend abundance into poverty;   995
Loud croaks the raven of the law, and smiles:

Smiles too the goddess; but smiles most at those,
(Just victims of exorbitant desire!)
Who perish at their own request, and, whelm'd
Beneath her load of lavish grants, expire.   1000
Fortune is famous for her numbers slain.
The number small which happiness can bear.
Though various for awhile their fates; at last
One curse involves them all: At Death's approach,
All read their riches backward into loss,   1005
And mourn in just proportion to their store.

   And Death's approach (if orthodox my song)
Is hasten'd by the lure of Fortune's smiles.
And art thou still a glutton of bright gold?
And art thou still rapacious of thy ruin?   1010
Death loves a shining mark, a signal blow;
A blow, which, while it executes, alarms;
And startles thousands with a single fall.
As when some stately growth of oak, or pine,
Which nods aloft, and proudly spreads her shade, 1015
The sun's defiance, and the flocks defence;
By the strong strokes of lab'ring hinds subdu'd,
Loud groans her last, and, rushing from her height,
In cumbrous ruin, thunders to the ground:
The conscious forest trembles at the shock,   1020
And hill, and stream, and distant dale, resound.

   These high-aim'd darts of Death, and these alone,
Should I collect, my quiver would be full.
A quiver, which, suspended in mid air,
Or near Heav'n's Archer, in the zodiac, hung, 1025
(So could it be,) should draw the public eye,
The gaze and contemplation of mankind!
A constellation awful, yet benign,

To guide the gay through life's tempestuous wave,
Nor suffer them to strike the common rock;   1030
" From greater danger to grow more secure,
" And, wrapt in happiness, forget their fate."
    LYSANDER, happy past the common lot,
Was warn'd of danger, but too gay to fear.
He woo'd the fair ASPASIA: She was kind;   1035
In youth, form, fortune, fame, they both were blest:
All who knew envy'd; yet in envy lov'd:
Can fancy form more finish'd happiness!
Fixt was the nuptial hour.   Her stately dome
Rose on the sounding beach. The glitt'ring spires 1040
Float in the wave, and break against the shore:
So break those glitt'ring shadows, human joys.
The faithless morning smil'd: He takes his leave,
To re-embrace, in ecstasies, at eve.
The rising storm forbids.—The news arrives:— 1045
Untold, she saw it in her servant's eye.
She felt it seen (her heart was apt to feel;)
And, drown'd, without the furious ocean's aid,
In suffocating sorrows, shares his tomb.
Now, round the sumptuous, bridal monument, 1050
The guilty billows innocently roar;
And the rough sailor passing, drops a tear.
A tear! Can tears suffice?—But not for me.
How vain our efforts! and our arts, how vain!
The distant train of thought I took, to shun,   1055
Has thrown me on my fate—these died together;
Happy in ruin! undivorc'd by Death!
Or ne'er to meet, or ne'er to part, is peace—
NARCISSA! pity bleeds at thought of thee!
Yet thou wast only near me; not myself.   1060

Survive myself?—That cures all other woe.
NARCISSA lives; PHILANDER is forgot.
O the soft commerce! O the tender ties,
Close-twisted with the fibres of the heart!
Which, broken, break them; and drain off the soul
Of human joy; and make it pain to live—   1066
And is it then to live? When such friends part,
'Tis the survivor dies—My heart! no more.

PREFACE

TO

NIGHT THE SIXTH.

FEW ages have been deeper in dispute about Religion, than this. The dispute about Religion, and the practice of it, seldom go together. The shorter, therefore, the dispute, the better. I think it may be reduced to this single question—*Is Man immortal; or, Is he not?* If he be not, all our disputes are mere amusements, or trials of skill. In this case, *Truth, Reason, Religion,* which give our discourses such pomp and solemnity, are (as will be shewn) mere empty sounds, without any meaning in them. But, if *Man* be immortal, it will behove him to be very serious about eternal consequences; or, in other words, to be truly religious. And this great fundamental truth, unestablished, or unawakened in the minds of

men, is, I conceive, the real source and support of all
our infidelity; how remote soever the particular ob-
jections advanced may seem to be from it.

Sensible appearances affect most men much more
than abstract reasonings; and we daily see bodies
drop around us, but the soul is invisible. The power
which inclination has over the judgment, is greater
than can be well conceived by those that have not had
an experience of it; and of what numbers is it the sad
interest, that souls should not survive! The heathen
world confessed, that they rather hoped, than firmly
believed, immortality! and how many heathens have
we still amongst us! The sacred page assures us, that
life and immortality are brought to light by the gos-
pel: but by how many is the gospel rejected, or over-
looked! From these considerations, and from my
being, accidentally, privy to the sentiments of some
particular persons, I have been long persuaded, that
most, if not all our infidels (whatever name they
take, and whatever scheme, for argument's sake, and
to keep themselves in countenance, they patronize) are
supported in their deplorable error, by some doubt of
their immortality, at the bottom. And I am satis-

fied, that men once thoroughly convinced of their immortality, are not far from being Christians. For it is hard to conceive, that a man fully conscious eternal pain or happiness will certainly be his lot, should not earnestly and impartially inquire after, the surest means of escaping the one and securing the other: and of such an earnest and impartial enquiry, I well know the consequence.

Here, therefore, in proof of this most fundamental truth, some plain arguments are offered; arguments derived from principles which infidels admit in common with believers; arguments, which appear to me altogether irresistible; and such, as I am satisfied, will have great weight with all, who give themselves the small trouble of looking seriously into their own bosoms, and of observing, with any tolerable degree of attention, what daily passes round about them in the world. If some arguments shall, here, occur, which others have declined, they are submitted, with all deference, to better judgments in this, of all points, the most important. For, as to the being of a God, that is no longer disputed; but it is undisputed for this reason only; viz. Because where the least pretence to reason is admitted, it must for ever be indisputable. And of consequence no man can be betrayed into a dispute of that nature by vanity, which has a principal share in animating our modern combatants against other articles of our belief.

THE

COMPLAINT.

NIGHT VI.

THE INFIDEL RECLAIMED.

IN TWO PARTS.

CONTAINING

THE NATURE, PROOF, AND IMPORTANCE
OF IMMORTALITY.

PART THE FIRST.

SHE (for I know not yet her name in Heav'n)
Not early, like NARCISSA, left the scene;
Nor sudden, like PHILANDER.   What avails?
This seeming mitigation but inflames;
This fancy'd med'cine heightens the disease.   5
The longer known, the closer still she grew:
And gradual parting is a gradual death.

'Tis the grim tyrant's engine, which extorts
By tardy pressure's still-increasing weight,
From hardest hearts, confession of distress.   10
    O the long, dark approach, through years of pain,
Death's gall'ry! (might I dare to call it so,)
With dismal Doubt, and sable Terror, hung;
Sick Hope's pale lamp, its only glimm'ring ray:
There Fate my melancholy walk ordain'd,   15
Forbid self-love itself to flatter there.
How oft I gaz'd, prophetically sad!
How oft I saw her dead, while yet in smiles!
In smiles she sunk her grief, to lessen mine.
She spoke me comfort, and increas'd my pain.   20
Like pow'rful armies trenching at a town,
By slow, and silent, but resistless sap,
In his pale progress gently gaining ground,
Death urg'd his deadly siege in spite of art,
Of all the balmy blessings Nature lends   25
To succour frail humanity.   Ye stars!
(Not now first made familiar to my sight,)
And thou, O Moon! bear witness; many a night
He tore the pillow from beneath my head,
Ty'd down my sore attention to the shock,   30
By ceaseless depredations on a life
Dearer than that he left me.   Dreadful post
Of observation! darker ev'ry hour!
Less dread the day that drove me to the brink,
And pointed out eternity below;   35
When my soul shudder'd at futurity;
When, on a moment's point, th' important die
Of life and death, spun doubtful ere it fell,
And turn'd up Life; my title to more woe.

But why more woe? More comfort let it be.   40
Nothing is dead, but that which wish'd to die;
Nothing is dead, but Wretchedness and Pain;
Nothing is dead, but what incumber'd, gall'd,
Block'd up the pass, and barr'd from real life.
Where dwells that wish most ardent of the wise?   45
Too dark the sun to see it; highest stars,
Too low to reach it; Death, great Death alone,
O'er stars and sun, triumphant, lands us there.
Nor dreadful our transition; though the mind,
An artist at creating self-alarms,   50
Rich in expedients for inquietude,
Is prone to paint it dreadful.   Who can take
Death's portrait true? The tyrant never sat.
Our sketch all random strokes, conjecture all;
Close shuts the grave, nor tells one single tale.   55
Death, and his image, rising in the brain,
Bear faint resemblance; never are alike;
Fear shakes the pencil; Fancy loves excess;
Dark Ignorance is lavish of her shades:
And these the formidable picture draw.   60
     But grant the worst—'tis past—new prospects rise—
And drop a veil eternal o'er her tomb.
Far other views our contemplation claim,
Views that o'erpay the rigours of our life;
Views that suspend our agonies in death: 65
Wrapt in the thought of Immortality,
Wrapt in the single, the triumphant thought!
Long life might lapse, age unperceiv'd come on;
And find the soul unsated with her theme.
Its nature, proof, importance, fire my song.   70
O that my song could emulate my soul!

S

Like her, immortal.   No!—the soul disdains
A mark so mean; far nobler hope inflames;
If endless ages can outweigh an hour,
Let not the laurel, but the palm, inspire.   75
    Thy nature, Immortality! who knows?
And yet who knows it not? It is but life
In stronger thread of brighter colour spun,
And spun for ever; dipt by cruel Fate
In Stygian dye, how black, how brittle here!   80
How short our correspondence with the sun!
And while it lasts, inglorious! Our best deeds,
How wanting in their weight! Our highest joys,
Small cordials to support us in our pain,
And give us strength to suffer.   But how great   85
To mingle int'rests, converse, amities,
With all the sons of Reason, scatter'd wide
Through habitable space, wherever born,
Howe'er endow'd! to live free citizens
Of universal Nature; to lay hold   90
By more than feeble Faith on the SUPREME!
To call Heav'n's rich unfathomable mines
(Mines, which support archangels in their state)
Our own! to rise in science, as in bliss,
Initiate in the secrets of the skies!   95
To read creation; read its mighty plan
In the bare bosom of the Deity!
The plan, and execution, to collate!
To see, before each glance of piercing thought,
All cloud, all shadow, blown remote; and leave 100
No mystery—but that of love divine,
Which lifts us on the seraph's flaming wing,
From earth's Akeldama, this field of blood,

Of inward anguish, and of outward ill,
From darkness, and from dust, to such a scene!   105
Love's element, true joy's illustrious home!
From earth's sad contrast (now deplor'd) more fair,
What exquisite vicissitude of fate!
Blest absolution of our blackest hour!
   LORENZO, these are thoughts that make Man, Man,
The wise illumine, aggrandize the great.   111
How great (while yet we tread the kindred clod,
And ev'ry moment fear to sink beneath
The clod we tread; soon trodden by our sons,)
How great, in the wild whirl of Time's pursuits, 115
To stop, and pause, involv'd in high presage,
Through the long visto of a thousand years,
To stand contemplating our distant selves,
As in a magnifying mirror seen,
Enlarg'd, ennobled, elevate, divine!   120
To prophesy our own futurities!
To gaze in thought on what all thought transcends!
To talk, with fellow-candidates, of joys
As far beyond conception, as desert,
Ourselves th' astonish'd talkers, and the tale! 125
   LORENZO, swells thy bosom at the thought?
The swell becomes thee: 'Tis an honest pride.
Revere thyself;—and yet thyself despise.
His nature no man can o'er-rate; and none
Can under-rate his merit.   Take good heed,   130
Nor there be modest, where thou shouldst be proud;
That almost universal error shun.
How just our pride when we behold those heights,
Not those Ambition paints in air, but those
Reason points out, and ardent Virtue gains;   135

And angels emulate; our pride how just!
When mount we? When these shackles cast? When quit
This cell of the creation? This small nest,
Stuck in a corner of the universe,
Wrapt up in fleecy cloud, and fine-spun air?   140
Fine-spun to sense; but gross and feculent
To souls celestial; souls ordain'd to breathe
Ambrosial gales, and drink a purer sky;
Greatly triumphant on Time's farther shore,
Where Virtue reigns, enrich'd with full arrears;   145
While Pomp imperial begs an alms of Peace.

In empire high, or in proud science deep,
Ye born of earth! on what can you confer,
With half the dignity, with half the gain,
The gust, the glow of rational delight,   150
As on this theme, which angels praise and share!
Man's fates and favours are a theme in Heav'n.

What wretched repetition cloys us here!
What periodic potions for the sick!
Distemper'd bodies, and distemper'd minds!   155
In an eternity what scenes shall strike!
Adventures thicken! novelties surprise!
What webs of wonder shall unravel there!
What full day pour on all the paths of Heav'n,
And light th' ALMIGHTY's footsteps in the deep! 160
How shall the blessed day of our discharge
Unwind, at once, the labyrinths of fate,
And straighten its inextricable maze!

If inextinguishable thirst in Man
To know; how rich, how full, our banquet there! 165
There, not the moral world alone unfolds;
The world material, lately seen in shades,

And, in those shades, by fragments only seen,
And seen those fragments by the lab'ring eye,
Unbroken, then, illustrious, and entire, 170
Its ample sphere, its universal frame,
In full dimensions, swells to the survey;
And enters, at one glance, the ravish'd sight.
From some superior point, where, who can tell?
(Suffice it, 'tis a point where gods reside) 175
How shall the stranger Man's illumin'd eye,
In the vast ocean of unbounded space,
Behold an infinite of floating worlds
Divide the crystal waves of ether pure,
In endless voyage, without port? The least 180
Of these disseminated orbs, how great!
Great as they are, what numbers these surpass,
Huge, as Leviathan, to that small race,
Those twinkling multitudes of little life,
He swallows unperceiv'd! Stupendous these! 185
Yet what are these stupendous to the whole!
As particles, as atoms ill-perceiv'd;
As circulating globules in our veins;
So vast the plan! Fecundity divine!
Exub'rant Source! perhaps I wrong thee still. 190
    If admiration is a source of joy,
What transport hence! Yet this the least in Heav'n.
What this to that illustrious robe HE wears,
Who tost this mass of wonders from his hand,
A specimen, an earnest of his pow'r! 195
'Tis to that glory, whence all glory flows,
As the mead's meanest flow'ret to the sun,
Which gave it birth. But what this sun of Heav'n?
This bliss supreme of the supremely blest?

Death, only Death, the question can resolve.   200
By death, cheap bought th' ideas of our joy;
The bare ideas! Solid happiness
So distant from its shadow chas'd below.

  And chase we still the phantom through the fire,
O'er bog, and brake, and precipice, till death?   205
And toil we still for sublunary pay?
Defy the dangers of the field and flood,
Or, spider-like, spin out our precious all,
Our more than vitals spin (if no regard
To great futurity,) in curious webs   210
Of subtle thought, and exquisite design;
(Fine net-work of the brain!) to catch a fly?
The momentary buz of vain renown!
A name! a mortal immortality!

  Or (meaner still!) instead of grasping air,   215
For sordid lucre plunge we in the mire?
Drudge, sweat, through ev'ry shame, for ev'ry gain,
For vile contaminating trash; throw up
Our hope in Heav'n, or dignity with Man!
And deify the dirt, matur'd to gold!   220
Ambition, Av'rice; the two dæmons these,
Which goad through ev'ry slough our human herd,
Hard-travel'd from the cradle to the grave.
How low the wretches stoop! how steep they climb!
These dæmons burn mankind; but most possess   225
LORENZO's bosom, and turn out the skies.

  Is it in Time to hide Eternity?
And why not in an atom on the shore,
To cover ocean? or a mote, the sun?
Glory and Wealth have they this blinding pow'r?   230
What if to them I prove LORENZO blind?

Would it surprise thee? Be thou then surpris'd;
Thou, neither, know'st: Their nature learn from me.
    Mark well, as foreign as these subjects seem,
What close connection ties them to my theme.   235
First, what is true ambition? The pursuit
Of glory, nothing less than Man can share.
Were they as vain as gaudy-minded Man,
As flatulent with fumes of self-applause,
Their arts and conquest animals might boast,   240
And claim their laurel crowns, as well as we;
But not celestial.   Here we stand alone;
As in our form, distinct, pre-eminent;
If prone in thought, our stature is our shame;
And Man should blush, his forehead meets the skies.
The visible and present are for brutes,   246
A slender portion, and a narrow bound!
These, Reason, with an energy divine,
O'erleaps; and claims the future and unseen!
The vast unseen! the future fathomless!   250
When the great soul buoys up to this high point,
Leaving gross Nature's sediments below,
Then, and then only, ADAM's offspring quits
The sage and hero of the fields and woods,
Asserts his rank, and rises into Man.   255
This is ambition: This is human fire.
    Can Parts or Place (two bold pretenders!) make
LORENZO great, and pluck him from the throng?
    Genius and Art, Ambition's boasted wings,
Our boast but ill deserve.   A feeble aid!   260
Dedalian engin'ry! If these alone
Assist our flight, Fame's flight is Glory's fall.
Heart-merit wanting, mount we ne'er so high,

Our height is but the gibbet of our name.
A celebrated wretch when I behold,   265
When I behold a genius bright and base,
Of tow'ring talents and terrestrial aims;
Methinks I see, as torn from her high sphere,
The glorious fragments of a soul immortal,
With rubbish mix'd, and glitt'ring in the dust.   270
Struck at the splendid, melancholy sight,
At once Compassion soft, and Envy, rise—
But wherefore Envy? Talents angel-bright,
If wanting worth, are shining instruments
In false Ambition's hand, to finish faults   275
Illustrious, and give infamy renown.
    Great ill is an atchievement of great pow'rs.
Plain sense but rarely leads us far astray.
Reason the means, Affections chuse our end;
Means have no merit, if our end amiss.   280
If wrong our hearts, our heads are right in vain;
What is a PELHAM's head, to PELHAM's heart?
Hearts are proprietors of all applause.
Right ends, and means, make wisdom: Worldly wise
Is but half-witted, at its highest praise.   285
    Let Genius then despair to make thee great;
Nor flatter Station: What is Station high?
'Tis a proud mendicant; it boasts, and begs;
It begs an alms of homage from the throng,
And oft the throng denies its charity.   290
Monarchs, and ministers, are awful names:
Whoever wear them, challenge our devoir.
Religion, public order, both exact
External homage, and a supple knee,
To beings pompously set up, to serve   295

The meanest slave; all more is merit's due,
Her sacred and inviolable right:
Nor ever paid the monarch, but the man.
Our hearts ne'er bow but to superior worth;
Nor ever fail of their allegiance there.   300
Fools, indeed, drop the Man in their account,
And vote the mantle into majesty.
Let the small savage boast his silver fur;
His royal robe unborrow'd, and unbought,
His own, descending fairly from his sires.   305
Shall Man be proud to wear his livery,
And souls in ermine scorn a soul without?
Can place or lessen us, or aggrandize?
Pigmies are pigmies still, though perch'd on Alps;
And pyramids are pyramids in vales.   310
Each Man makes his own stature, builds himself:
Virtue alone out-builds the pyramids;
Her monuments shall last, when EGYPT's fall.
    Of these sure truths dost thou demand the cause?
The cause is lodg'd in Immortality.   315
Hear, and assent.   Thy bosom burns for pow'r—
What station charms thee? I'll instal thee there—
'Tis thine.   And art thou greater than before?
Then thou before wast something less than Man.
Has thy new post betray'd thee into pride?   320
That treach'rous pride betrays thy dignity;
That pride defames humanity, and calls
The being mean which staffs or strings can raise.
That pride, like hooded hawks, in darkness soars,
From blindness bold, and tow'ring to the skies.   325
'Tis born of Ignorance, which knows not Man:
An angel's second; nor his second long.

T

A NERO quitting his imperial throne,
And courting glory from the tinkling string,
But faintly shadows an immortal soul,   330
With Empire's self, to pride, or rapture, fir'd.
If nobler motives minister no cure,
Ev'n Vanity forbids thee to be vain.
    High worth is elevated place: 'Tis more—
It makes the post stand candidate for thee;   335
Makes more than monarchs, makes an honest man;
Though no exchequer it commands, 'tis wealth;
And though it wears no ribband, 'tis renown;
Renown, that would not quit thee, though disgrac'd,
Nor leave thee pendent on a master's smile.   340
Other ambition Nature interdicts;
Nature proclaims it most absurd in Man,
By pointing at his origin, and end;
Milk, and a swathe, at first, his whole demand;
His whole domain, at last, a turf or stone;   345
To whom, between, a world may seem too small.
    Souls, truly great, dart forward on the wing
Of just ambition, to the grand result,
The curtain's fall; there, see the buskin'd chief
Unshod behind this momentary scene;   350
Reduc'd to his own stature, low or high,
As Vice, or Virtue, sinks him, or sublimes;
And laugh at this fantastic mummery,
This antic prelude of grotesque events,
Where dwarfs are often stilted, and betray   355
A littleness of soul by worlds o'er run,
And nations laid in blood.   Dread sacrifice
To Christian pride! which had with horror shock'd
The darkest Pagans, offer'd to their gods.

O thou Most Christian enemy to peace! 360
Again in arms? Again provoking fate?
That prince, and that alone, is truly great,
Who draws the sword reluctant, gladly sheaths;
On empire builds what empire far outweighs,
And makes his throne a scaffold to the skies. 365
 Why this so rare? Because forgot of all
The day of death; that venerable day,
Which sits as judge; that day, which shall pronounce
On all our days, absolve them, or condemn.
LORENZO, never shut thy thought against it; 370
Be levees ne'er so full, afford it room,
And give it audience in the cabinet.
That friend consulted (flatteries apart)
Will tell thee fair, if thou art great or mean.
 To doat on aught may leave us, or be left, 375
Is that Ambition? Then let flames descend,
Point to the centre their inverted spires,
And learn humiliation from a soul
Which boasts her lineage from celestial fire.
Yet these are they the world pronounces wise; 380
The world, which cancels Nature's right and wrong,
And casts new wisdom: Ev'n the grave Man lends
His solemn face to countenance the coin.
Wisdom for parts is madness for the whole.
This stamps the paradox, and gives us leave 385
To call the wisest weak, the richest poor,
The most ambitious, unambitious, mean;
In triumph, mean; and abject, on a throne.
Nothing can make it less than mad in man,
To put forth all his ardour, all his art, 390
And give his soul her full unbounded flight,

But reaching HIM, who gave her wings to fly.
When blind Ambition quite mistakes her road,
And downward pores, for that which shines above,
Substantial happiness, and true renown;   395
Then, like an idiot, gazing on the brook,
We leap at stars, and fasten in the mud;
At glory grasp, and sink in infamy.
    Ambition! pow'rful source of good and ill!
Thy strength in Man, like length of wing in birds, 400
When disengag'd from earth, with greater ease,
And swifter flight, transports us to the skies:
By toys entangled, or in guilt bemir'd,
It turns a curse; it is our chain, and scourge,
In this dark dungeon, where confin'd we lie: 405
Close-grated by the sordid bars of sense;·
All prospect of eternity shut out;
And, but for execution, ne'er set free.
    With error in ambition justly charg'd,
Find we LORENZO wiser in his wealth?   410
What if thy rental I reform? And draw
An inventory new to set thee right?
Where, thy true treasure? Gold says, " Not in me:"
And, " Not in me," the di'mond.   Gold is poor;
INDIA's insolvent: Seek it in thyself,   415
Seek in thy naked self, and find it there;
In being so descended, form'd, endow'd;
Sky-born, sky-guided, sky-returning race!
Erect, immortal, rational, divine!
In senses, which inherit earth, and heav'ns;   420
Enjoy the various riches Nature yields;
Far nobler; give the riches they enjoy;
Give taste to fruits, and harmony to groves;

Their radiant beams to gold, and gold's bright sire:
Take in, at once, the landscape of the world,   425
At a small inlet, which a grain might close,
And half create the wondrous world they see.
Our senses, as our reason, are divine.
But for the magic organ's pow'rful charm,
Earth were a rude, uncolour'd chaos still.   430
Objects are but th' occasion; ours th' exploit;
Ours is the cloth, the pencil, and the paint,
Which Nature's admirable picture draws;
And beautifies creation's ample dome.
Like MILTON's EVE, when gazing on the lake,   435
Man makes the matchless image Man admires.
Say then, shall Man, his thoughts all sent abroad
(Superior wonders in himself forgot,)
His admiration waste on objects round,
When Heav'n makes him the soul of all he sees? 440
Absurd! not rare! so great, so mean, is Man!

     What wealth in senses such as these! what wealth
In Fancy, fir'd to form a fairer scene
Than sense surveys! In Mem'ry's firm record,
Which, should it perish, could this world recal   445
From the dark shadows of o'erwhelming years,
In colours fresh, originally bright,
Preserve its portrait, and report its fate!
What wealth in intellect, that sov'reign pow'r!
Which Sense, and Fancy, summon to the bar;   450
Interrogate, approve, or reprehend;
And from the mass those underlings import,
From their materials sifted, and refin'd,
And in Truth's balance accurately weigh'd,
Forms Art, and Science, Government, and Laws; 455

The solid basis, and the beauteous frame,
The vitals and the grace of civil life!
And manners (sad exception!) set aside,
Strikes out, with master-hand, a copy-fair
Of His idea, whose indulgent thought,   460
Long, long, ere chaos teem'd, plann'd human bliss.
    What wealth in souls that soar, dive, range around,
Disdaining limit, or from place, or time;
And hear at once, in thought extensive, hear
Th' Almighty Fiat, and the trumpet's sound;   465
Bold, on creation's outside walk, and view
What was, and is, and more than e'er shall be;
Commanding, with omnipotence of thought,
Creations new in Fancy's field to rise!
Souls, that can grasp whate'er th' ALMIGHTY made,
And wander wild through things impossible!   471
What wealth, in faculties of endless growth,
In quenchless passions violent to crave,
In liberty to chuse, in pow'r to reach,
And in duration (how thy riches rise!)   475
Duration to perpetuate—boundless bliss!
    Ask you, what pow'r resides in feeble Man
That bliss to gain? Is Virtue's, then, unknown?
Virtue, our present peace, our future prize.
Man's unprecarious, natural estate,   480
Improveable at will, in Virtue lies;
Its tenure sure; its income is divine.
    High-built abundance, heap on heap! for what?
To breed new wants, and beggar us the more;
Then, make a richer scramble for the throng.   485
Soon as this feeble pulse, which leaps so long
Almost by miracle, is tir'd with play,

Like rubbish from disploding engines thrown,
Our magazines of hoarded trifles fly;
Fly diverse; fly to foreigners, to foes;   490
New masters court, and call the former, fools
(How justly!) for dependence on their stay.
Wide scatter, first, our play-things; then, our dust.
    Dost court Abundance for the sake of peace?
Learn, and lament thy self-defeated scheme: 495
Riches enable to be richer still:
And, richer still, what mortal can resist?
Thus wealth (a cruel task-master!) injoins
New toils, succeeding toils, an endless train!
And murders Peace, which taught it first to shine. 500
The poor are half as wretched as the rich;
Whose proud and painful privilege it is,
At once, to bear a double load of woe;
To feel the stings of Envy and of Want,
Outrageous Want! both INDIES cannot cure.   505
    A competence is vital to content.
Much wealth is corpulence, if not disease;
Sick, or incumber'd, is our happiness.
A competence is all we can enjoy.
O be content, where Heav'n can give no more! 510
More, like a flash of water from a lock,
Quickens our spirit's movement for an hour;
But soon its force is spent, nor rise our joys
Above our native temper's common stream.
Hence disappointment lurks in ev'ry prize,   515
As bees in flow'rs; and stings us with success.
    The rich man, who denies it, proudly feigns;
Nor knows the wise are privy to the lie.
Much learning shews how little mortals know;

Much wealth, how little worldlings can enjoy: 520
At best, it babies us with endless toys,
And keeps us children till we drop to dust.
As monkeys at a mirror stand amaz'd,
They fail to find what they so plainly see;
Thus men, in shining riches, see the face   525
Of happiness, nor know it is a shade;
But gaze, and touch, and peep, and peep again,
And wish, and wonder it is absent still.

 How few can rescue opulence from want!
Who lives to Nature, rarely can be poor;   530
Who lives to Fancy, never can be rich.
Poor is the man in debt; the man of gold,
In debt to Fortune, trembles at her pow'r.
The Man of Reason, smiles at her, and Death.
O what a patrimony this! A being   535
Of such inherent strength and majesty,
Not worlds possest can raise it; worlds destroy'd
Can't injure; which holds on its glorious course,
When thine, O Nature! ends; too blest to mourn
Creation's obsequies. What treasure, this—   540
The Monarch is a beggar to the Man!

 Immortal! ages past, yet nothing gone!
Morn without eve! a race without a goal!
Unshorten'd by progression infinite!
Futurity for ever future! life   545
Beginning still, where computation ends!
'Tis the description of a Deity!
'Tis the description of the meanest slave:
The meanest slave dares then LORENZO scorn!
The meanest slave thy sov'reign glory shares.   550
Proud youth! fastidious of the lower world!

Man's lawful pride includes humility;
Stoops to the lowest; is too great to find
Inferiors: all immortal! brothers all!
Proprietors eternal of thy love!　　555
　　Immortal! what can strike the sense so strong,
As this the soul? It thunders to the thought;
Reason amazes; Gratitude o'erwhelms;
No more we slumber on the brink of fate;
Rous'd at the sound, th' exulting soul ascends,　　560
And breathes her native air; an air that feeds
Ambitions high, and fans ethereal fires;
Quick kindles all that is divine within us;
Nor leaves one loit'ring thought beneath the stars.
　　Has not LORENZO's bosom caught the flame?　565
Immortal! Were but one immortal, how
Would others envy! How would thrones adore!
Because 'tis common, is the blessing lost?
How this ties up the bounteous hand of Heav'n!
O vain, vain, vain! all else!—Eternity!　　570
A glorious, and a needful refuge, that,
From vile imprisonment in abject views.
'Tis Immortality, 'tis that alone,
Amid Life's pains, abasements, emptiness,
The soul can comfort, elevate, and fill.　　575
That only, and that amply, this performs;
Lifts us above Life's pains, her joys above;
Their terror those; and these their lustre lose;
Eternity depending covers all;
Eternity depending all atchieves;　　580
Sets Earth at distance; casts her into shades;
Blends her distinctions; abrogates her pow'rs;
The low, the lofty, joyous, and severe,

Fortune's dread frowns, and fascinating smiles,
Make one promiscuous and neglected heap,   585
The Man beneath; if I may call him Man,
Whom Immortality's full force inspires.
Nothing terrestrial touches his high thought;
Suns shine unseen, and thunders roll unheard,
By minds quite conscious of their high descent, 590
Their present province, and their future prize;
Divinely darting upward ev'ry wish,
Warm on the wing, in glorious absence lost!
    Doubt you this truth? Why labours your belief?
If Earth's whole orb, by some due-distant eye   595
Were seen at once, her tow'ring ALPS would sink,
And level'd ATLAS leave an even sphere.
Thus Earth, and all that earthly minds admire,
Is swallow'd in Eternity's vast round.
To that stupendous view, when souls awake,   600
So large of late, so mountainous to Man,
Time's toys subside; and equal all below.
    Enthusiastic, this? Then all are weak,
But rank enthusiasts. To this godlike height
Some souls have soar'd; or martyrs ne'er had bled. 605
And all may do what has by Man been done.
Who, beaten by these sublunary storms,
Boundless, interminable joys can weigh,
Unraptur'd, unexalted, uninflam'd?
What slave unblest, who from to-morrow's dawn 610
Expects an empire? He forgets his chain,
And, thron'd in thought, his absent sceptre waves.
    And what a sceptre waits us! what a throne!
Her own immense appointments to compute,
Or comprehend her high prerogatives,   615

In this her dark minority, how toils,
How vainly pants, the human soul divine!
Too great the bounty seems for earthly joy:
What heart but trembles at so strange a bliss?
  In spite of all the truths the Muse has sung,   620
Ne'er to be priz'd enough! enough resolv'd!
Are there who wrap the world so close about them,
They see no farther than the clouds? And dance
On heedless Vanity's fantastic toe,
Till, stumbling at a straw, in their career,   625
Headlong they plunge, where end both dance and song!
Are there, LORENZO? Is it possible?
Are there on earth (let me not call them men)
Who lodge a soul immortal in their breasts;
Unconscious as the mountain of its ore;   630
Or rock, of its inestimable gem?
When rocks shall melt, and mountains vanish, these
Shall know their treasure; treasure, then, no more.
  Are there (still more amazing!) who resist
The rising thought? Who smother, in its birth,   635
The glorious truth? Who struggle to be brutes?
Who through this bosom-barrier burst their way;
And, with revers'd ambition, strive to sink?
Who labour downwards through th' opposing pow'rs
Of instinct, reason, and the world against them,   640
To dismal hopes, and shelter in the shock
Of endless night? night darker than the grave!
Who fight the proofs of immortality?
With horrid zeal, and execrable arts,
Work all their engines, level their black fires,   645
To blot from Man this attribute divine

(Than vital blood far dearer to the wise,)
Blasphemers, and rank atheists to themselves?
　To contradict them, see all Nature rise!
What object, what event, the moon beneath,   650
But argues, or endears, an after-scene?
To Reason proves, or weds it to Desire?
All things proclaim it needful; some advance
One precious step beyond, and prove it sure.
A thousand arguments swarm round my pen,   655
From Heav'n, and Earth, and Man.　Indulge a few,
By Nature, as her common habit, worn;
So pressing Providence a truth to teach,
Which truth untaught, all other truths were vain.
　Thou! whose all-providential eye surveys,   660
Whose hand directs, whose Spirit fills and warms
Creation, and holds empire far beyond!
Eternity's inhabitant august!
Of two eternities amazing Lord!
One past, ere Man's, or Angel's, had begun;   665
Aid! while I rescue from the foe's assault
Thy glorious immortality in Man:
A theme for ever, and for all, of weight,
Of moment infinite! but relish'd most
By those who love Thee most, who most adore. 670
　Nature, thy daughter, ever-changing birth
Of Thee the great Immutable, to Man
Speaks wisdom; is his oracle supreme;
And he who most consults her, is most wise.
Lorenzo, to this heav'nly Delphos haste;   675
And come back all-immortal; all-divine:
Look Nature through, 'tis revolution all;

All change, no death. Day follows night; and night
The dying day; stars rise, and set, and rise;
Earth takes th' example. See the summer gay, 680
With her green chaplet, and ambrosial flow'rs,
Droops into pallid Autumn: Winter grey,
Horrid with frost, and turbulent with storm,
Blows Autumn, and his golden fruits, away:
Then melts into the Spring: Soft Spring, with breath
Favonian, from warm chambers of the south,   686
Recals the first.   All, to reflourish, fades.
As in a wheel, all sinks to re-ascend.
Emblems of Man, who passes, not expires!
    With this minute distinction, emblems just,   690
Nature revolves, but Man advances; both
Eternal, that a circle, this a line.
That gravitates, this soars.   Th' aspiring soul
Ardent, and tremulous, like flame, ascends;
Zeal, and Humility, her wings to Heav'n.   695
The world of matter, with its various forms,
All dies into new life.   Life born from Death
Rolls the vast mass, and shall for ever roll.
No single atom, once in being, lost,
With change of counsel charges the Most High. 700
    What hence infers Lorenzo? Can it be?
Matter immortal? And shall spirit die?
Above the nobler, shall less noble rise?
Shall Man alone, for whom all else revives,
No resurrection know? Shall Man alone,   705
Imperial Man, be sown in barren ground,
Less privileg'd than grain, on which he feeds?
Is Man, in whom alone is pow'r to prize
The bliss of being, or with previous pain

Deplore its period, by the spleen of Fate,   710
Severely doom'd Death's single unredeem'd?
   If Nature's revolution speaks aloud,
In her gradation, hear her louder still.
Look Nature through, 'tis neat gradation all.
By what minute degrees her scale ascends!   715
Each middle nature join'd at each extreme,
To that above it join'd, to that beneath.
Parts into parts reciprocally shot,
Abhor divorce: What love of union reigns!
Here, dormant matter waits a call to life;   720
Half-life, half-death, join there; here, Life and Sense;
There, Sense from Reason steals a glimm'ring ray;
Reason shines out in Man.   But how preserv'd
The chain unbroken upward, to the realms
Of incorporeal life? those realms of bliss,   725
Where Death hath no dominion! Grant a make
Half-mortal, half-immortal; earthy part;
And part ethereal; grant the soul of Man
Eternal; or in Man the series ends.
Wide yawns the gap; connection is no more;   730
Check'd Reason halts; her next step wants support;
Striving to climb, she tumbles from her scheme;
A scheme, analogy pronounc'd so true;
Analogy, Man's surest guide below.
   Thus far, all Nature calls on thy belief.   735
And will LORENZO, careless of the call,
False attestation on all Nature charge,
Rather than violate his league with Death?
Renounce his reason, rather than renounce
The dust belov'd, and run the risk of Heav'n?   740
O what indignity to deathless souls!

What treason to the majesty of Man!
Of Man immortal! Hear the lofty style:
" If so decreed, th' almighty will be done.
" Let earth dissolve, yon pond'rous orbs descend, 745
" And grind us into dust: The Soul is safe;
" The Man emerges; mounts above the wreck,
" As tow'ring flame from Nature's fun'ral pyre;
" O'er devastation, as a gainer, smiles;
" His charter, his inviolable rights,   750
" Well pleas'd to learn from thunder's impotence,
" Death's pointless darts, and Hell's defeated storms."
    But these chimeras touch not thee, LORENZO!
The glories of the world, thy sev'nfold shield.
Other ambition than of crowns in air,   755
And superlunary felicities,
Thy bosom warm.   I'll cool it, if I can;
And turn those glories that enchant, against thee.
What ties thee to this life, proclaims the next.
If wise, the cause that wounds thee is thy cure. 760
    Come, my ambitious! let us mount together
(To mount LORENZO never can refuse;)
And from the clouds, where Pride delights to dwell,
Look down on Earth—What seest thou? Wondrous
        things!
Terrestrial wonders, that eclipse the skies.   765
What lengths of labour'd lands! what loaded seas!
Loaded by men, for pleasure, wealth, or war!
Seas, winds, and planets, into service brought,
His art acknowledge, and promote his ends.
Nor can th' eternal rocks his will withstand;   770
What level'd mountains, and what lifted vales!
O'er vales and mountains sumptuous cities swell,

And gild our landscape with their glitt'ring spires.
Some mid the wand'ring waves majestic rise;
And NEPTUNE holds a mirror to their charms.   775
Far greater still! (what cannot mortal might?)
See, wide dominions ravish'd from the deep!
The narrow'd deep with indignation foams.
Or southward turn, to delicate, and grand;
The finer arts there ripen in the sun.   780
How the tall temples, as to meet their gods,
Ascend the skies! the proud triumphal arch
Shews us half Heav'n beneath its ample bend.
High through mid air, here, streams are taught to flow;
Whole rivers, there, laid by in basons, sleep.   785
Here, plains turn oceans; there, vast oceans join
Through kingdoms channel'd deep from shore to shore;
And chang'd creation takes its face from Man.
Beats thy brave breast for formidable scenes,
Where fame and empire wait upon the sword?   790
See fields in blood; hear naval thunders rise;
BRITANNIA's voice! that awes the world to peace.
How yon enormous mole, projecting, breaks
The mid-sea furious waves! their roar amidst,
Out-speaks the Deity, and says, " O main!   795
" Thus far, nor farther; new restraints obey."
Earth's disembowel'd! measur'd are the skies!
Stars are detected in their deep recess!
Creation widens! vanquish'd Nature yields!
Her secrets are extorted! Art prevails!   800
What monument of genius, spirit, pow'r!
   And now, LORENZO, raptur'd at this scene,
Whose glories render Heav'n superfluous! say,
Whose footsteps these?—Immortals have been here.

Could less than souls immortal this have done?   805
Earth's cover'd o'er with proofs of souls immortal;
And proofs of immortality forgot.
   To flatter thy grand foible, I confess,
These are Ambition's works: And these are great:
But this, the least immortal souls can do;   810
Transcend them all.—But what can these transcend?
Dost ask me, what?—One sigh for the distrest.
What then for infidels? A deeper sigh.
'Tis moral grandeur makes the mighty Man:
How little they, who think aught great below!   815
All our ambitions Death defeats, but one;
And that it crowns.—Here cease we: But, ere long,
More pow'rful proof shall take the field against thee,
Stronger than death, and smiling at the tomb.

X

PREFACE

NIGHT THE SEVENTH.

As we are at war with the power, it were well if we were at war with the manners, of France. *A land of levity is a land of guilt. A serious mind is the native soil of every virtue, and the single character that does true honour to mankind. The soul's immortality has been the favourite theme with the serious of all ages. Nor is it strange; it is a subject by far the most interesting, and important, that can enter the mind of Man. Of highest moment this subject always was, and always will be. Yet this its highest moment seems to admit of increase at this day; a sort of occasional importance is superadded to the natural weight of it; if that opinion, which is advanced in the Preface to the preceding Night, be just. It is there supposed, that all our infidels, whatever scheme,*

for argument's sake, and to keep themselves in coun-
tenance, they patronize, are betrayed into their deplo-
rable error, by some doubt of their immortality, at
the bottom. And the more I consider this point, the
more I am persuaded of the truth of that opinion.
Though the distrust of a futurity is a strange error;
yet it is an error into which bad men may naturally
be distressed. For it is impossible to bid defiance to
final ruin, without some refuge in imagination, some
presumption of escape. And what presumption is
there? There are but two in Nature; but two within
the compass of human thought. And these are—
That either GOD will not, or cannot, punish. Con-
sidering the divine attributes, the first is too gross to
be digested by our strongest wishes. And, since
Omnipotence is as much a divine attribute as Holi-
ness, that GOD cannot punish, is as absurd a suppo-
sition as the former. GOD certainly can punish, as
long as wicked men exist. In non-existence, there-
fore, is their only refuge; and, consequently, non-
existence is their strongest wish. And strong wishes
have a strange influence on our opinions; they bias
the judgment in a manner almost incredible. And
since on this member of their alternative, there are
some very small appearances in their favour, and
none at all on the other, they catch at this reed, they
lay hold on this chimera, to save themselves from the

shock and horror of an immediate and absolute des-
pair.

On reviewing my subject, by the light which this
argument, and others of like tendency, throw upon it,
I was more inclined than ever to pursue it, as it
appeared to me to strike directly at the main root of
all our infidelity. In the following pages, it is,
accordingly, pursued at large; and some arguments
for immortality, new (at least to me,) are ventured
on in them. There also the writer has made an
attempt to set the gross absurdities and horrors of
annihilation in a fuller and more affecting view, than
is (I think) to be met with elsewhere.

The gentlemen, for whose sake this attempt was
chiefly made, profess great admiration for the wisdom
of heathen antiquity: What pity it is, they are not
sincere! If they were sincere, how would it mortify
them to consider, with what contempt and abhorrence
their notions would have been received by those whom
they so much admire? What degree of contempt and
abhorrence would fall to their share, may be conjec-
tured by the following matter of fact (in my opinion)
extremely memorable. Of all their heathen worthies,
Socrates, (it is well known) was the most guarded,
dispassionate, and composed: Yet this great master of

temper was angry; and angry at his last hour; and angry with his friend; and angry for what deserved acknowledgement; angry, for a right and tender instance of true friendship towards him. Is not this surprising? What could be the cause? The cause was for his honour; it was a truly noble, though, perhaps, a too punctilious regard for immortality: For his friend, asking him, with such an affectionate concern, as became a friend, " Where he should " deposit his remains?" it was resented by Socrates, as implying a dishonourable supposition, that he could be so mean, as to have regard for any thing, even in himself, that was not immortal.

This fact, well considered, would make our infidels withdraw their admiration from Socrates; or make them endeavour, by their imitation of this illustrious example, to share his glory: And, consequently, it would incline them to peruse the following pages with candour and impartiality: Which is all I desire; and that, for their sakes: For I am persuaded, that an unprejudiced infidel must necessarily receive some advantageous impressions from them.

JULY 7, 1744.

COMPLAINT.

NIGHT VII.

THE INFIDEL RECLAIMED.

PART THE SECOND.

HEAV'N gives the needful, but neglected, call.
What day, what hour, but knocks at human hearts,
To wake the soul to sense of future scenes!
Deaths stand, like Mercuries, in ev'ry way;
And kindly point us to our journey's end.   5
POPE, who couldst make immortals; art thou dead?
I give thee joy: Nor will I take my leave;
So soon to follow.   Man but dives in death;
Dives from the sun, in fairer day to rise;
The grave, his subterranean road to bliss.   10
Yes, infinite indulgence plann'd it so:
Through various parts our glorious story runs;
Time gives the preface, endless age unrolls
The volume (ne'er unroll'd) of human fate.

This, earth and skies already have proclaim'd.   15
The world's a prophesy of worlds to come;
And who, what GOD foretels (who speaks in things
Still louder than in words) shall dare deny?
If Nature's arguments appear too weak,
Turn a new leaf, and stronger read in Man.   20
If Man sleeps on, untaught by what he sees,
Can he prove infidel to what he feels?
He, whose blind thought Futurity denies,
Unconscious bears, BELLEROPHON! like thee,
His own indictment; he condemns himself: 25
Who reads his bosom, reads immortal life;
Or, Nature, there, imposing on her sons,
Has written fables; Man was made a lie.
    Why discontent for ever harbour'd there:
Incurable consumption of our peace!   30
Resolve me, why the cottager and king,
He whom sea-sever'd realms obey, and he
Who steals his whole dominion from the waste,
Repelling winter blasts with mud and straw,
Disquieted alike, draw sigh for sigh,   35
In fate so distant, in complaint so near?
    Is it, that things terrestrial can't content?
Deep in rich pasture, will thy flocks complain?
Not so; but to their master is deny'd
To share their sweet serene. · Man, ill at ease, 40
In this, not his own place, this foreign field,
Where Nature fodders him with other food,
Than was ordain'd his cravings to suffice,
Poor in abundance, famish'd at a feast,
Sigh on for something more, when most enjoy'd.   45
Is Heav'n then kinder to thy flocks than thee?

Not so; thy pasture richer, but remote;
In part, remote; for that remoter part
Man bleats from instinct, though, perhaps, debauch'd
By Sense, his Reason sleeps, nor dreams the cause. 50
The cause how obvious, when his Reason wakes!
His grief is but his grandeur in disguise;
And discontent is immortality.

Shall sons of æther, shall the blood of Heav'n,
Set up their hopes on earth, and stable here   55
With brutal acquiescence in the mire?
LORENZO! no! they shall be nobly pain'd;
The glorious foreigners, distrest, shall sigh
On thrones; and thou congratulate the sigh:
Man's misery declares him born for bliss;   60
His anxious heart asserts the truth I sing,
And gives the sceptic in his head the lie.

Our heads, our hearts, our passions, and our pow'rs,
Speak the same language; call us to the skies:
Unripen'd these in this inclement clime,   65
Scarce rise above conjecture and mistake;
And for this land of trifles those too strong
Tumultuous rise, and tempest human life:
What prize on earth can pay us for the storm?
Meet objects for our passions Heav'n ordain'd,   70
Objects that challenge all their fire, and leave
No fault, but in defect: Blest Heav'n! avert
A bounded ardour for unbounded bliss;
O for a bliss unbounded! Far beneath
A soul immortal, is a mortal joy.   75
Nor are our pow'rs to perish immature;
But, after feeble effort here, beneath
A brighter sun, and in a nobler soil,

Y

Transplanted from this sublunary bed,
Shall flourish fair, and put forth all their bloom.   80
    Reason progressive, Instinct is complete;
Swift Instinct leaps; slow Reason feebly climbs.
Brutes soon their zenith reach; their little all
Flows in at once; in ages they no more
Could know, or do, or covet, or enjoy.   85
Were Man to live coëval with the sun,
The patriarch pupil would be learning still;
Yet, dying, leave his lesson half-unlearnt.
Men perish in advance, as if the sun
Should set ere noon, in eastern oceans drown'd;   90
(If fit, with dim, illustrious to compare,
The sun's meridian with the soul of Man.)
To Man, Why, step-dame Nature so severe?
Why thrown aside thy master-piece half-wrought,
While meaner efforts thy last hand enjoy?   95
Or, if abortively, poor Man must die,
Nor reach, what reach he might, why die in dread?
Why curst with foresight? Wise to misery?
Why of his proud prerogative the prey?
Why less pre-eminent in rank, than pain?   100
His immortality alone can tell;
Full ample fund to balance all amiss,
And turn the scale in favour of the just!
    His immortality alone can solve
That darkest of enigmas, human hope;   105
Of all the darkest, if at death we die.
Hope, eager Hope, th' assassin of our joy,
All present blessings treading under foot,
Is scarce a milder tyrant than Despair.
With no past toils content, still planning new,   110

Hope cages less the apassion of our joy,
All present blessings treading underfoot.

Young 205

Hope turns us o'er to Death alone for ease.
Possession, why, more tasteless than Pursuit?
Why is a wish far dearer than a crown?
That wish accomplish'd, why, the grave of bliss?
Because, in the great future bury'd deep,   115
Beyond our plans of empire, and renown,
Lies all that Man with ardour should pursue;
And HE who made him, bent him to the right.
   Man's heart th' ALMIGHTY to the future sets,
By secret and inviolable springs;   120
And makes his hope his sublunary joy.
Man's heart eats all things, and is hungry still;
" More, more!" the glutton cries: For something new
So rages appetite, if Man can't mount,
He will descend.   He starves on the possest.   125
Hence, the world's master, from ambition's spire,
In CAPREA plung'd; and div'd beneath the brute.
In that rank sty why wallow'd empire's son
Supreme? Because he could no higher fly;
His riot was ambition in despair.   130
   Old ROME consulted birds; LORENZO! thou,
With more success, the flight of Hope survey;
Of restless Hope, for ever on the wing.
High-perch'd o'er ev'ry thought, that falcon sits,
To fly at all that rises in her sight;   135
And, never stooping, but to mount again
Next moment, she betrays her aim's mistake,
And owns her quarry lodg'd beyond the grave.
   There should it fail us (it must fail us there,
If being fails,) more mournful riddles rise,   140
And Virtue vies with Hope in mystery.
Why Virtue? Where its praise, its being, fled?
Virtue is true self-interest pursu'd:

What true self-interest of quite-mortal Man
To close with all that makes him happy here!   145
If Vice (as sometimes) is our friend on earth,
Then Vice is Virtue; 'tis our sov'reign good.
In self-applause is Virtue's golden prize;
No self-applause attends it on thy scheme:
Whence self-applause? From conscience of the right.
And what is right, but means of happiness?   151
No means of happiness when Virtue yields;
That basis failing, falls the building too,
And lays in ruin every virtuous joy.

The rigid guardian of a blameless heart,   155
So long rever'd, so long reputed wise,
Is weak; with rank knight-errantries o'er-run.
Why beats thy bosom with illustrious dreams
Of self-exposure, laudable and great?
Of gallant enterprise, and glorious death?   160
Die for thy country—Thou romantic fool!
Seize, seize the plank thyself, and let her sink:
Thy country!—what to thee!—The Godhead, what!
(I speak with awe!) though HE should bid thee bleed?
If, with thy blood, thy final hope is spilt,   165
Nor can Omnipotence reward the blow;
Be deaf—preserve thy being—disobey.

Nor is it disobedience: Know, LORENZO!
Whate'er th'ALMIGHTY's subsequent command,
His first command is this:—" Man, love thyself." 170
In this alone, free-agents are not free.
Existence is the basis, bliss the prize;
If Virtue costs existence, 'tis a crime;
Bold violation of our law supreme,
Black suicide; though nations, which consult   175
Their gain, at thy expence, resound applause.

Since Virtue's recompence is doubtful, here,
If Man dies wholly, well may we demand,
Why is Man suffer'd to be good in vain?
Why to be good in vain, is Man injoin'd?   180
Why to be good in vain, is Man betray'd?
Betray'd by traitors lodg'd in his own breast,
By sweet complacencies from Virtue felt?
Why whispers Nature lies on Virtue's part?
Or if blind Instinct (which assumes the name   185
Of sacred Conscience) plays the fool in Man,
Why Reason made accomplice in the cheat?
Why are the wisest loudest in her praise?
Can Man by Reason's beam be led astray?
Or, at his peril, imitate his GOD?   190
Since Virtue sometimes ruins us on earth,
Or both are true; or Man survives the grave.
    Or Man survives the grave, or own, LORENZO,
Thy boast supreme, a wild absurdity.
Dauntless thy spirit; cowards are thy scorn.   195
Grant Man immortal, and thy scorn is just.
The Man immortal, rationally brave,
Dares rush on Death—because he cannot die.
But if Man loses all, when life is lost,
He lives a coward, or a fool expires.   200
A daring infidel (and such there are,
From pride, example, lucre, rage, revenge,
Or pure heroical defect of thought,)
Of all Earth's madmen, most deserves a chain.
    When to the grave we follow the renown'd   205
For valour, virtue, science, all we love,
And all we praise; for worth, whose noon-tide beam,
Enabling us to think in higher style,

Mends our ideas of ethereal pow'rs;
Dream we, that lustre of the moral world   210
Goes out in stench, and rottenness the close?
Why was he wise to know, and warm to praise,
And strenuous to transcribe in human life,
The Mind Almighty? Could it be, that Fate,
Just when the lineaments began to shine,   215
And dawn the Deity, should snatch the draught,
With night eternal blot it out, and give
The skies alarm, lest angels too might die?
    If human souls, why not angelic too
Extinguish'd? and a solitary God,   220
O'er ghastly ruin, frowning from his throne?
Shall we this moment gaze on GOD in Man?
The next, lose Man for ever in the dust?
From dust we disengage, or Man mistakes;
And there, where least his judgment fears a flaw. 225
Wisdom and worth, how boldly he commends!
Wisdom and worth are sacred names; rever'd,
Where not embrac'd; applauded! deify'd!
Why not compassion'd too? If spirits die,
Both are calamities, inflicted both   230
To make us but more wretched: Wisdom's eye
Acute, for what? To spy more miseries;
And worth so recompens'd, new points their stings.
Or Man surmounts the grave, or gain is loss,
And worth exalted humbles us the more.   235
Thou wilt not patronize a scheme that makes
Weakness, and Vice, the refuge of Mankind.
    " Has Virtue then no joys?"—Yes, joys dear-bought;
Talk ne'er so long, in this imperfect state,
Virtue, and Vice, are at eternal war.   240

Virtue's a combat; and who fights for nought?
Or for precarious, or for small reward?
Who Virtue's self-reward so loud resound,
Would take degrees angelic here below,
And Virtue, while they compliment, betray,   245
By feeble motives, and unfaithful guards.
The crown, th' unfading crown, her soul inspires:
'Tis that, and that alone, can countervail
The body's treach'ries, and the world's assaults:
On Earth's poor pay our famish'd virtue dies.   250
Truth incontestable! in spite of all
A BAYLE has preach'd, or a V——E believ'd.
   In Man the more we dive, the more we see
Heav'n's signet stamping an immortal make.
Dive to the bottom of his soul, the base   255
Sustaining all; what find we? Knowledge, Love.
As light, and heat, essential to the sun,
These to the soul. And why, if souls expire?
How little lovely here? How little known?
Small knowledge we dig up with endless toil!   260
And love unfeign'd may purchase perfect hate.
Why starv'd on earth, our angel-appetites;
While brutal are indulg'd their fulsome fill?
Were then capacities divine conferr'd
As a mock-diadem, in savage sport,   265
Rank insult of our pompous poverty,
Which reaps but pain, from seeming claims so fair?
In future age lies no redress! And shuts
Eternity the door on our complaint?
If so, for what strange ends were mortals made!   270
The worst to wallow, and the best to weep;

The Man who merits most, must most complain.
Can we conceive a disregard in Heav'n,
What the worst perpetrate, or best endure?
    This cannot be. To love, and know, in Man 275
Is boundless appetite, and boundless pow'r;
And these demonstrate boundless objects too.
Objects, pow'rs, appetites, Heav'n suits in all;
Nor, Nature through, e'er violates this sweet,
Eternal concord, on her tuneful string.   280
Is Man the sole exception from her laws?
Eternity struck off from human hope
(I speak with truth, but veneration too,)
Man is a monster, the reproach of Heav'n,
A stain, a dark impenetrable cloud   285
On Nature's beauteous aspect; and deforms,
(Amazing blot!) deforms her with her Lord.
If such is Man's allotment, what is Heav'n?
Or own the soul immortal, or blaspheme.
    Or own the soul immortal, or invert   290
All order. Go, mock-majesty! go, Man!
And bow to thy superiors of the stall;
Through ev'ry scene of Sense superior far:
They graze the turf untill'd; they drink the stream
Unbrew'd, and ever full, and un-embitter'd   295
With doubts, fears, fruitless hopes, regrets, despairs;
Mankind's peculiar! Reason's precious dow'r!
No foreign clime they ransack for their robes;
Nor brothers cite to the litigious bar;
Their good is good entire, unmix'd, unmarr'd;   300
They find a paradise in ev'ry field,
On boughs forbidden where no curses hang:

Their ill, no more than strikes the sense; unstretch'd
By previous dread, or murmur in the rear;
When the worst comes, it comes unfear'd; one stroke
Begins, and ends, their woe: They die but once; 306
Blest, incommunicable privilege! for which
Proud Man, who rules the globe, and reads the stars,
Philosopher, or hero, sighs in vain.
　　Account for this prerogative in brutes.　　　　310
No day, no glimpse of day, to solve the knot,
But what beams on it from Eternity.
O sole and sweet solution! that unties
The difficult, and softens the severe;
The cloud on Nature's beauteous face dispels;　　315
Restores bright order; casts the brute beneath;
And re-inthrones us in supremacy
Of joy, ev'n here: Admit immortal life,
And Virtue is knight-errantry no more;
Each Virtue brings in hand a golden dow'r,　　320
Far richer in reversion: Hope exults;
And though much bitter in our cup is thrown,
Predominates, and gives the taste of Heav'n.
O wherefore is the DEITY so kind?
Astonishing beyond astonishment!　　　　325
Heav'n our reward—for Heav'n enjoy'd below.
　　Still unsubdu'd thy stubborn heart?—For there
The traitor lurks, who doubts the truth I sing.
Reason is guiltless; Will alone rebels.
What, in that stubborn heart, if I should find　　330
New, unexpected witnesses against thee?
Ambition, Pleasure, and the Love of Gain!
Canst thou suspect that these, which make the soul
The slave of Earth, should own her heir of Heav'n?

z

Canst thou suspect what makes us disbelieve   335
Our immortality, should prove it sure?
   First, then, Ambition summon to the bar.
Ambition's shame, extravagance, disgust,
And inextinguishable nature, speak.
Each much deposes; hear them in their turn.   340
   Thy soul, how passionately fond of fame!
How anxious, that fond passion to conceal!
We blush, detected in designs on praise,
Though for best deeds, and from the best of men;
And why? Because immortal.   Art divine   345
Has made the body tutor to the soul:
Heav'n kindly gives our blood a moral flow;
Bids it ascend the glowing cheek, and there
Upbraid that little heart's inglorious aim,
Which stoops to court a character from Man;   350
While o'er us, in tremendous judgment sit
Far more than Man, with endless praise and blame.
   Ambition's boundless appetite out-speaks
The verdict of its shame.   When souls take fire
At high presumptions of their own desert,   355
One age is poor applause; the mighty shout,
The thunder by the living few begun,
Late time must echo; worlds unborn, resound.
We wish our names eternally to live:
Wild dream! which ne'er had haunted human thought,
Had not our natures been eternal too.   361
Instinct points out an int'rest in hereafter;
But our blind reason sees not where it lies;
Or, seeing, gives the substance for the shade.
   Fame is the shade of immortality,   365
And in itself a shadow.   Soon as caught,

Contemn'd; it shrinks to nothing in the grasp.
Consult th' ambitious, 'tis ambition's cure.
" And is this all!" cry'd CÆSAR at his height,
Disgusted.   This third proof Ambition brings   370
Of immortality.   The first in fame—
Observe him near—your envy will abate:
Sham'd at the disproportion vast, between
The passion and the purchase, he will sigh
At such success, and blush at his renown.   375
And why? Because far richer prize invites
His heart; far more illustrious glory calls;
It calls in whispers, yet the deafest hear.
    And can Ambition a fourth proof supply?
It can, and stronger than the former three;   380
Yet quite o'erlook'd by some reputed wise.
Though disappointments in ambition pain,
And though success disgusts; yet still, LORENZO!
In vain we strive to pluck it from our hearts;
By Nature planted for the noblest ends.   385
Absurd the fam'd advice to PYRRHUS giv'n,
More prais'd, than ponder'd; specious, but unsound:
Sooner that hero's sword the world had quell'd,
Than reason, his ambition.   Man must soar.
An obstinate activity within,   390
An insuppressive spring, will toss him up
In spite of Fortune's load.   Not kings alone,
Each villager has his ambition too;
No sultan prouder than his fetter'd slave:
Slaves build their little Babylons of straw,   395
Echo the proud Assyrian, in their hearts,
And cry—" Behold the wonders of my might!"
And why? Because immortal as their lord;

And souls immortal must for ever heave
At something great; the glitter, or the gold;   400
The praise of mortals, or the praise of Heav'n.
    Nor absolutely vain is human praise,
When human is supported by divine.
I'll introduce LORENZO to himself:
Pleasure and Pride (bad masters!) share our hearts. 405
As love of pleasure is ordain'd to guard
And feed our bodies, and extend our race;
The love of praise is planted to protect
And propagate the glories of the mind.
What is it, but the love of praise, inspires,   410
Matures, refines, embellishes, exalts,
Earth's happiness? From that, the delicate,
The grand, the marvellous, of civil life.
Want and Convenience, under workers, lay
The basis, on which love of glory builds.   415
Nor is thy life, O Virtue! less in debt
To Praise, thy secret stimulating friend.
Were men not proud, what merit should we miss!
Pride made the virtues of the Pagan world.
Praise is the salt that seasons right to Man,   420
And whets his appetite for moral good.
Thirst of applause is Virtue's second guard;
Reason, her first; but Reason wants an aid;
Our private reason is a flatterer;
Thirst of applause calls public judgment in,   425
To poise our own, to keep an even scale,
And give endanger'd virtue fairer play.
    Here a fifth proof arises, stronger still:
Why this so nice construction of our hearts;
These delicate moralities of sense;   430

This constitutional reserve of aid
To succour Virtue, when our reason fails;
If Virtue, kept alive by care and toil,
And of the mark of injuries on earth,
When labour'd to maturity (its bill   435
Of disciplines, and pain, unpaid) must die?
Why freighted rich to dash against a rock?
Were Man to perish when most fit to live,
O how mis-spent were all these stratagems,
By skill divine inwoven in our frame?   440
Where are Heav'n's holiness and mercy fled?
Laughs Heav'n, at once, at Virtue, and at Man?
If not, why that discourag'd, this destroy'd?
      Thus far Ambition.   What says Avarice?
This her chief maxim which has long been thine: 445
" The wise and wealthy are the same."—I grant it.
To store up treasure with incessant toil,
This is Man's province, this his highest praise.
To this great end keen Instinct stings him on.
To guide that Instinct, Reason! is thy charge;   450
'Tis thine to tell us where true treasure lies:
But, Reason failing to discharge her trust,
Or to the deaf discharging it in vain,
A blunder follows; and blind Industry,
Gall'd by the spur, but stranger to the course   455
(The course where stakes of more than gold are won,)
O'erloading, with the cares of distant age,
The jaded spirsts of the present hour,
Provides for an eternity below.
      " Thou shalt not covet," is a wise command; 460
But bounded to the wealth the sun surveys:
Look farther, the command stands quite revers'd,

And Av'rice is a virtue most divine.
Is Faith a refuge for our happiness?
Most sure: And is it not for Reason too?   465
Nothing this world unriddles, but the next.
Whence inextinguishable thirst of gain?
From inextinguishable life in Man:
Man, if not meant, by worth to reach the skies,
Had wanted wing to fly so far in guilt.   470
Sour grapes, I grant, Ambition, Avarice:
Yet still their root is Immortality.
These its wild growths so bitter, and so base,
(Pain, and reproach!) Religion can reclaim,
Refine, exalt, throw down their pois'nous lee,   475
And make them sparkle in the bowl of bliss.
    See the third witness laughs at bliss remote,
And falsely promises an EDEN here:
Truth she shall speak for once, though prone to lie,
A common cheat, and Pleasure is her name.   480
To Pleasure never was LORENZO deaf;
Then hear her now, now first thy real friend.
    Since Nature made us not more fond than proud
Of happiness (whence hypocrites in joy,
Makers of mirth, artificers of smiles,)   485
Why should the joy most poignant Sense affords,
Burn us with blushes, and rebuke our pride?—
Those heav'n-born blushes tell us Man descends,
Ev'n in the zenith of his earthly bliss:
Should Reason take her infidel repose,   490
This honest Instinct speaks our lineage high;
This Instinct calls on darkness to conceal
Our rapturous relation to the stalls.
Our glory covers us with noble shame,

And he that's unconfounded, is unmann'd: 495
The Man that blushes is not quite a brute.
Thus far with thee, LORENZO! will I close;
Pleasure is good, and Man for pleasure made;
But pleasure full of glory, and of joy;
Pleasure, which neither blushes, nor expires. 500
    The witnesses are heard; the cause is o'er;
Let Conscience file the sentence in her court,
Dearer than deeds that half a realm convey:
Thus, seal'd by Truth, th' authentic record runs:
    " Know, all! know, infidels—unapt to know! 505
" 'Tis Immortality your nature solves;
" 'Tis Immortality decyphers Man,
" And opens all the myst'ries of his make.
" Without it, half his instincts are a riddle;
" Without it, all his virtues are a dream. 510
" His very crimes attest his dignity;
" His sateless thirst of pleasure, gold, and fame,
" Declares him born for blessings infinite:
" What less than infinite, makes un-absurd
" Passions, which all on earth but more inflames? 515
" Fierce passions, so mis-measur'd to this scene,
" Stretch'd out, like eagles' wings, beyond our nest,
" Far, far beyond the worth of all below;
" For Earth too large, presage a nobler flight,
" And evidence our title to the skies." 520
    Ye gentle theologues of calmer kind!
Whose constitution dictates to your pen,
Who, cold yourselves, think ardour comes from hell!
Think not our passions from corruption sprung,
Though to corruption now they lend their wings; 525

That is their mistress, not their mother.　All
(And justly) reason deem divine: I see,
I feel a grandeur in the passions too,
Which speaks their high descent, and glorious end;
Which speaks them rays of an eternal fire.　　　　530
In paradise itself they burnt as strong,
Ere ADAM fell; though wiser in their aim.
Like the proud Eastern, struck by Providence,
What though our passions are run mad, and stoop
With low, terrestrial appetite, to graze　　　　535
On trash, on toys, dethron'd from high desire?
Yet, still, through their disgrace a feeble ray
Of greatness shines, and tells us whence they fell:
But these (like that fall'n monarch when reclaim'd,)
When Reason moderates the rein aright,　　　　540
Shall re-ascend, remount their former sphere,
Where once they soar'd illustrious; ere seduc'd
By wanton EVE's debauch, to stroll on earth,
And set the sublunary world on fire.

　　But grant their frenzy lasts; their frenzy fails　545
To disappoint one providential end,
For which Heav'n blew up ardour in our hearts:
Were Reason silent, boundless Passion speaks
A future scene of boundless objects too,
And brings glad tidings of eternal day.　　　　550
Eternal day! 'Tis that enlightens all:
And all, by that enlighten'd, proves it sure.
Consider Man as an immortal being,
Intelligible all; and all is great;
A crystalline transparency prevails,　　　　555
And strikes full lustre through the human sphere:

Consider Man as mortal, all is dark,
And wretched; Reason weeps at the survey.
    The learn'd LORENZO cries, " And let her weep, .
" Weak, modern Reason! Ancient times were wise.
" Authority, that venerable guide,   561
" Stands on my part; the fam'd Athenian Porch
" (And who for wisdom so renown'd as they?)
" Deny'd this immortality to Man."
I grant it; but affirm, they prov'd it too.   565
A riddle this!—Have patience; I'll explain.
    What noble vanities, what moral flights,
Glitt'ring through their romantic wisdom's page,
Make us, at once, despise them, and admire!
Fable is flat to these high-season'd sires;   570
They leave th' extravagance of song below.
" Flesh shall not feel; or, feeling, shall enjoy
" The dagger or the rack; to them, alike
" A bed of roses, or the burning bull."
In men exploding all beyond the grave,   575
Strange doctrine, this!—As doctrine, it was strange;
But not, as prophesy; for such it prov'd,
And, to their own amazement, was fulfill'd:
They feign'd a firmness Christians need not feign.
The Christian truly triumph'd in the flame: 580
The Stoic saw, in double wonder lost,
Wonder at them, and wonder at himself,
To find the bold adventures of his thought
Not bold, and that he strove to lie in vain.
    Whence, then, those thoughts? those tow'ring
        thoughts, that flew   585
Such monstrous heights?—From Instinct, and from
        Pride.

The glorious instinct of a deathless soul,
Confus'dly conscious of her dignity,
Suggested truths they could not understand.
In Lust's dominion, and in Passion's storm,   590
Truth's system broken, scatter'd fragments lay
(As light in chaos, glimm'ring through the gloom:)
Smit with the pomp of lofty sentiments,
Pleas'd Pride proclaim'd what Reason disbeliev'd.
Pride, like the DELPHIC priestess, with a swell,   595
Rav'd nonsense, destin'd to be future sense,
When life immortal in full day should shine;
And Death's dark shadows fly the Gospel sun.
They spoke what nothing but immortal souls
Could speak; and thus the truth they question'd, prov'd.
    Can then absurdities, as well as crimes,   601
Speak Man immortal? All things speak him so.
Much has been urg'd; and dost thou call for more?
Call; and with endless questions be distrest,
All unresolvable, if earth is all.   605
    " Why life, a moment? infinite, desire?
    " Our wish, eternity? Our home, the grave?
    " Heav'n's promise dormant lies in human hope;
    " Who wishes life immortal, proves it too.
    " Why happiness pursu'd, though never found? 610
    " Man's thirst of happiness declares it is
    " (For Nature never gravitates to nought,)
    " That thirst unquench'd declares it is not here.
    " My LUCIA, thy CLARISSA call to thought:
    " Why cordial friendship rivetted so deep,   615
    " As hearts to pierce at first, at parting, rend,
    " If friend, and friendship, vanish in an hour?
    " Is not this torment in the mask of joy?

" Why by reflection marr'd the joys of sense?
" Why past, and future, preying on our hearts, 620
" And putting all our present joys to death?
" Why labours Reason? Instinct were as well;
" Instinct, far better; what can chuse, can err:
" O how infallible the thoughtless brute!
" 'Twere well his Holiness were half as sure.   625
" Reason with inclination why at war?
" Why sense of guilt? Why conscience up in arms?"
    Conscience of guilt is prophesy of pain,
And bosom-counsel to decline the blow.
Reason with inclination ne'er had jarr'd,   630
If nothing future paid forbearance here.
Thus on—these, and a thousand pleas uncall'd,
All promise, some ensure, a second scene;
Which, were it doubtful, would be dearer far
Than all things else most certain; were it false, 635
What truth on earth so precious as the lie?
This world it gives us, let what will ensue;
This world it gives, in that high cordial, Hope:
The future of the present is the soul:
How this life groans, when sever'd from the next! 640
Poor, mutilated wretch, that disbelieves!
By dark distrust his being cut in two,
In both parts perishes; life void of joy,
Sad prelude of eternity in pain!
    Couldst thou persuade me, the next life could fail 645
Our ardent wishes; how should I pour out
My bleeding heart in anguish, new, as deep!
Oh! with what thoughts, thy hope, and my despair,
Abhorr'd Annihilation, blasts the soul,
And wide extends the bounds of human woe!   650

Could I believe LORENZO's system true,
In this black channel would my ravings run:
   " Grief from the future borrow'd peace, ere-while.
" The future vanish'd! and the present pain'd!
" Strange import of unprecedented ill!   655
" Fall, how profound! like LUCIFER's, the fall!
" Unequal fate! his fall, without his guilt!
" From where fond Hope built her pavilion high,
" The gods among, hurl'd headlong, hurl'd at once
" To night! to nothing! darker still than night. 660
" If 'twas a dream, why wake me, my worst foe?
" LORENZO! boastful of the name of friend!
" O for delusion! O for error still!
" Could vengeance strike much stronger than to plant
" A thinking being in a world like this,   665
" Not over-rich before, now beggar'd quite;
" More curst than at the fall?—The sun goes out!
" The thorns shoot up! What thorns in every thought!
" Why sense of better? It embitters worse.
" Why sense? Why life? If but to sigh, then sink 670
" To what I was? Twice nothing! and much woe!
" Woe, from Heav'n's bounties! woe, from what was
    " wont
" To flatter most, high intellectual pow'rs!
   " Thought, virtue, knowledge! blessings, by thy
    " scheme,
" All poison'd into pains. First, knowledge, once 675
" My soul's ambition, now her greatest dread.
" To know myself, true wisdom?—No, to shun
" That shocking science. Parent of despair!
" Avert thy mirror: If I see, I die.
   " Know, my Creator? Climb his blest abode 680

" By painful speculation, pierce the veil,
" Dive in his nature, read his attributes,
" And gaze in admiration—on a foe,
" Obtruding life, with-holding happiness!
" From the full rivers that surround his throne,   685
" Not letting fall one drop of joy on Man;
" (Man gasping for one drop, that he might cease
" To curse his birth, nor envy reptiles more!)
" Ye sable clouds! ye darkest shades of night!
" Hide him, for ever hide him, from my thought,   690
" Once all my comfort; source, and soul of joy!
" Now leagu'd with furies, and with thee, against me.
   " Know his atchievements? Study his renown?
" Contemplate this amazing universe,
" Dropt from his hand, with miracles replete!   695
" For what? 'Mid miracles of nobler name,
" To find one miracle of misery?
" To find the being, which alone can know
" And praise his works, a blemish on his praise?
" Through Nature's ample range, in thought to stroll,
" And start at Man, the single mourner there,   701
" Breathing high hope! chain'd down to pangs and
      " death?
      " Knowing is suff'ring: And shall Virtue share
" The sigh of Knowledge?—Virtue shares the sigh.
" By straining up the steep of excellent,   705
" By battles fought, and, from temptation, won,
" What gains she, but the pang of seeing worth,
" Angelic worth, soon shuffled in the dark
" With ev'ry vice, and swept to brutal dust?
" Merit is madness; virtue is a crime;   710
" A crime to Reason, if it costs us pain

" Unpaid: What pain, amidst a thousand more,
" To think the most abandon'd, after days
" Of triumph o'er their betters, find in death
" As soft a pillow, nor make fouler clay!   715
  " Duty! Religion!—These, our duty done,
" Imply reward.   Religion is mistake.
" Duty!—There's none, but to repel the cheat.
" Ye cheats! away! ye daughters of my pride!
" Who feign yourselves the fav'rites of the skies: 720
" Ye tow'ring hopes! abortive energies!
" That toss, and struggle, in my lying breast,
" To scale the skies, and build presumptions there,
" As I were heir of an eternity;
" Vain, vain ambitions! trouble me no more.   725
" Why travel far in quest of sure defeat?
" As bounded as my being, be my wish.
" All is inverted, Wisdom is a fool.
" Sense, take the rein; blind Passion, drive us on;
" And, Ignorance, befriend us on our way;   730
" Ye new, but truest patrons of our peace!
" Yes; give the pulse full empire; live the brute,
" Since, as the brute, we die.   The sum of Man,
" Of godlike Man! to revel, and to rot.
  " But not on equal terms with other brutes: 735
" Their revels a more poignant relish yield,
" And safer too; they never poisons chuse.
" Instinct, than Reason, makes more wholesome meals,
" And sends all-marring murmur far away.
" For sensual life they best philosophise;   740
" Theirs, that serene, the sages sought in vain:
" 'Tis Man alone expostulates with Heav'n;
" His, all the pow'r, and all the cause to mourn.

" Shall human eyes alone dissolve in tears?
" And bleed, in anguish, none but human hearts? 745
" The wide-stretch'd realm of intellectual woe,
" Surpassing sensual far, is all our own.
" In life so fatally distinguish'd, why
" Cast in one lot, confounded, lump'd, in death?
   " Ere yet in being, was mankind in guilt?   750
" Why thunder'd this peculiar clause against us?
" All-mortal, and all-wretched!—Have the skies
" Reasons of state, their subjects may not scan,
" Nor humbly reason, when they sorely sigh?
" All-mortal, and all-wretched!—'Tis too much; 755
" Unparallel'd in nature: 'Tis too much;
" On being unrequested at thy hands,
" Omnipotent! for I see nought but pow'r.
   " And why see that? Why thought? To toil, and eat,
" Then make our bed in darkness, needs no thought.
" What superfluities are reasoning souls!   761
" Oh give eternity! or thought destroy.
" But without thought our curse were half unfelt;
" Its blunted edge would spare the throbbing heart;
" And, therefore, 'tis bestow'd. I thank thee, Reason!
" For aiding life's too small calamities,   766
" And giving being to the dread of death.
" Such are thy bounties!—Was it then too much
" For me, to trespass on the brutal rights?
" Too much for Heav'n to make one emmet more? 770
" Too much for chaos to permit my mass
" A longer stay with essences unwrought,
" Unfashion'd, untormented into Man?
" Wretched preferment to this round of pains!
" Wretched capacity of frenzy, Thought!   775

" Wretched capacity of dying, Life!

" Life, Thought, Worth, Wisdom, all (O foul revolt!)

" Once friends to peace, gone over to the foe.

 " Death, then, has chang'd its nature too: O Death!

" Come to my bosom, thou best gift of Heav'n! 780

" Best friend of Man! since Man is Man no more.

" Why in this thorny wilderness so long,

" Since there's no promis'd land's ambrosial bow'r,

" To pay me with its honey for my stings?

" If needful to the selfish schemes of Heav'n 785

" To sting us sore, why mock'd our misery?

" Why this so sumptuous insult o'er our heads?

" Why this illustrious canopy display'd?

" Why so magnificently lodg'd despair?

" At stated periods, sure-returning, roll 790

" These glorious orbs, that mortals may compute

" Their length of labours, and of pains; nor lose

" Their misery's full measure?—Smiles with flow'rs,

" And fruits, promiscuous, ever-teeming earth,

" That Man may languish in luxurious scenes, 795

" And in an EDEN mourn his wither'd joys?

" Claim earth and skies Man's admiration, due

" For such delights! Blest animals! too wise

" To wonder; and too happy to complain!

 " Our doom decreed demands a mournful scene:

" Why not a dungeon dark, for the condemn'd? 801

" Why not the dragon's subterraneous den,

" For Man to howl in? Why not his abode

" Of the same dismal colour with his fate?

" A THEBES, a BABYLON, a vast expence 805

" Of time, toil, treasure, art, for owls and adders,

" As congruous, as, for Man, this lofty dome,

" Which prompts proud thought, and kindles high
  " desire;
" If, from her humble chamber in the dust,
" While proud thought swells, and high desire inflames,
" The poor worm calls us for her inmates there; 811
" And, round us, Death's inexorable hand
" Draws the dark curtain close; undrawn no more.
  " Undrawn no more!—Behind the cloud of Death,
" Once I beheld a sun; a sun which gilt   815
" That sable cloud, and turn'd it all to gold:
" How the grave's alter'd! fathomless, as hell!
" A real hell to those who dreamt of heav'n.
" Annihilation! how it yawns before me!
" Next moment I may drop from thought, from sense,
" The privilege of angels, and of worms,   821
" An outcast from existence! and this spirit,
" This all-pervading, this all-conscious soul,
" This particle of energy divine,
" Which travels Nature, flies from star to star, 825
" And visits gods, and emulates their pow'rs,
" For ever is extinguish'd.   Horror! Death!
" Death of that death I fearless once survey'd!
" When horror universal shall descend,
" And Heav'n's dark concave urn all human race,
" On that enormous, unrefunding tomb,   831
" How just this verse! this monumental sigh!"
    Beneath the lumber of demolish'd worlds,
    Deep in the rubbish of the gen'ral wreck,
    Swept ignominious to the common mass   835
    Of matter, never dignify'd with life,
    Here lie proud rationals; the sons of heav'n!
    The lords of earth! the property of worms!

Beings of yesterday, and no to-morrow!
Who liv'd in terror, and in pangs expir'd!   840
All gone to rot in chaos; or, to make
Their happy transit into blocks or brutes;
Nor longer sully their CREATOR's Name.
    LORENZO! hear, pause, ponder, and pronounce.
Just is this history! If such is Man,   845
Mankind's historian, though divine, might weep.
And dares LORENZO smile?—I know thee proud:
For once let pride befriend thee; pride looks pale
At such a scene, and sighs for something more.
Amid thy boasts, presumptions, and displays,   850
And art thou then a shadow? Less than shade?
A nothing? Less than nothing? To have been,
And not to be, is lower than unborn.
Art thou ambitious? Why then make the worm
Thine equal? Runs thy taste of pleasure high?   855
Why patronize sure death of ev'ry joy?
Charm riches? Why chuse begg'ry in the grave,
Of ev'ry hope a bankrupt! and for ever?
Ambition, Pleasure, Avarice, persuade thee
To make that world of glory, rapture, wealth,   860
They lately prov'd, thy soul's supreme desire.
    What art thou made of? rather, How unmade?
Great Nature's master-appetite destroy'd!
Is endless life, and happiness despis'd?
Or both wish'd here, where neither can be found?   865
Such Man's perverse, eternal war with Heav'n!
Dar'st thou persist? And is there nought on earth,
But a long train of transitory forms,
Rising, and breaking, millions in an hour?
Bubbles of a fantastic Deity, blown up   870

In sport, and then in cruelty destroy'd?
Oh! for what crime, unmerciful LORENZO!
Destroys thy scheme the whole of human race?
Kind is fell LUCIFER, compar'd to thee:
Oh! spare this waste of being half-divine;   875
And vindicate th' œconomy of Heav'n.
   Heav'n is all love; all joy in giving joy:
It never had created but to bless:
And shall it, then, strike off the list of life,
A being blest, or worthy so to be?   880
Heav'n starts at an annihilating God.
Is that, all Nature starts at, thy desire?
Art such a clod to wish thyself all clay?
What is that dreadful wish?—The dying groan
Of Nature, murder'd by the blackest guilt.   885
What deadly poison has thy nature drank?
To Nature undebauch'd no shock so great;
Nature's first wish is endless happiness;
Annihilation is an after-thought,
A monstrous wish, unborn till virtue dies.   890
And, oh! what depth of horror lies inclos'd!
For non-existence no man ever wish'd,
But, first, he wish'd the DEITY destroy'd.
   If so; what words are dark enough to draw
Thy picture true? The darkest are too fair.   895
Beneath what baleful planet, in what hour
Of desperation, by what fury's aid,
In what infernal posture of the soul,
All hell invited, and all hell in joy
At such a birth, a birth so near of kin,   900
Did thy foul fancy whelp so black a scheme

Of hopes abortive, faculties half-blown,
And deities begun, reduc'd to dust?
  There's nought (thou say'st) but one eternal flux
Of feeble essences, tumultuous driv'n   905
Through Time's rough billows into Night's abyss.
Say, in this rapid tide of human ruin,
Is there no rock, on which Man's tossing thought
Can rest from terror, dare his fate survey,
And boldly think it something to be born?   910
Amid such hourly wrecks of being fair,
Is there no central, all sustaining base,
All-realizing, all-connecting Pow'r,
Which, as it call'd forth all things, can recall,
And force Destruction to refund her spoil?   915
Command the grave restore her taken prey?
Bid Death's dark vale its human harvest yield,
And earth, and ocean, pay their debt of Man,
True to the grand deposit trusted there?
Is there no potentate, whose out-stretch'd arm   920
When rip'ning time calls forth th' appointed hour,
Pluck'd from foul Devastation's famish'd maw,
Binds present, past, and future, to his throne?
His throne, how glorious, thus divinely grac'd,
By germinating beings clust'ring round!   925
A garland worthy the Divinity!
A throne, by Heav'n's omnipotence in smiles,
Built (like a PHAROS tow'ring in the waves)
Amidst immense effusions of his love!
An ocean of communicated bliss!   930
  An all-prolific, all-preserving God!
This were a God indeed.—And such is Man,

As here presum'd: He rises from his fall.
Think'st thou Omnipotence a naked root,
Each blossom fair of Deity destroy'd?   935
Nothing is dead; nay, nothing sleeps; each soul,
That ever animated human clay,
Now wakes; is on the wing: And where, O where,
Will the swarm settle?—When the trumpet's call,
As sounding brass, collects us, round Heav'n's throne
Conglob'd, we bask in everlasting day,   941
(Paternal splendour!) and adhere for ever.
Had not the soul this outlet to the skies,
In this vast vessel of the universe,
How should we gasp, as in an empty void!   945
How in the pangs of famish'd hope expire!
     How bright my prospect shines! how gloomy thine!
A trembling world! and a devouring God!
Earth, but the shambles of Omnipotence!
Heav'n's face all stain'd with causeless massacres 950
Of countless millions, born to feel the pang
Of being lost.   LORENZO! can it be?
This bids us shudder at the thoughts of life.
Who would be born to such a phantom world,
Where nought substantial, but our misery?   955
Where joy (if joy) but heightens our distress,
So soon to perish, and revive no more?
The greater such a joy, the more it pains.
A world, so far from great, (and yet how great
It shines to thee!) there's nothing real in it;   960
Being, a shadow! Consciousness, a dream!
A dream, how dreadful! Universal blank
Before it, and behind! Poor Man, a spark
From non-existence struck by wrath divine,

Glitt'ring a moment, nor that moment sure,   965
'Midst upper, nether, and surrounding night,
His sad, sure, sudden, and eternal tomb!
     LORENZO! dost thou feel these arguments?
Or is there nought but vengeance can be felt?
How hast thou dar'd the DEITY dethrone?   970
How dar'd indict him of a world like this?
If such the world, creation was a crime;
For what is crime, but cause of misery?
Retract, blasphemer! and unriddle this,
Of endless arguments above, below,   975
Without us, and within, the short result—
" If Man's immortal, there's a GOD in Heav'n."
     But wherefore such redundancy? Such waste
Of argument? One sets my soul at rest;
One obvious, and at hand, and, oh!—at heart.   980
So just the skies, PHILANDER's life so pain'd,
His heart so pure; that or succeeding scenes
Have palms to give, or ne'er had he been born.
     " What an old tale is this!" LORENZO cries.—
I grant this argument is old; but truth   985
No years impair; and had not this been true,
Thou never hadst despis'd it for its age.
Truth is immortal as thy soul; and fable
As fleeting as thy joys: Be wise, nor make
Heav'n's highest blessing, vengeance; O be wise; 990
Nor make a curse of immortality!
     Say, know'st thou what it is? Or what thou art?
Know'st thou th' importance of a soul immortal?
Behold this midnight glory: Worlds on worlds!
Amazing pomp! Redouble this amaze;   995
Ten thousand add; add twice ten thousand more;

Then weigh the whole; one soul outweighs them all;
And calls th' astonishing magnificence
Of unintelligent creation poor.
  For this, believe not me; no man believe;   1000
Trust not in words, but deeds; and deeds no less
Than those of the SUPREME; nor his, a few;
Consult them all; consulted, all proclaim
Thy soul's importance.: Tremble at thyself!
For whom Omnipotence has wak'd so long: 1005
Has wak'd, and work'd, for ages; from the birth
Of Nature to this unbelieving hour.
  In this small province of his vast domain
(All Nature bow, while I pronounce his name!)
What has GOD done, and not for this sole end, 1010
To rescue souls from death? The soul's high price
Is writ in all the conduct of the skies.
The soul's high price is the creation's key,
Unlocks its mysteries, and naked lays
The genuine cause of ev'ry deed divine: 1015
That, is the chain of ages, which maintains
Their obvious correspondence, and unites
Most distant periods in one blest design:
That, is the mighty hinge, on which have turn'd
All revolutions, whether we regard   1020
The nat'ral, civil, or religious, world;
The former two, but servants to the third;
To that their duty done, they both expire,
Their mass new-cast, forgot their deeps renown'd;
And angels ask, " Where once they shone so fair?"
  To lift us from this abject, to sublime;   1026
This flux, to permanent; this dark, to day;
This foul, to pure; this turbid, to serene;

This mean, to mighty! for this glorious end
Th'Almighty, rising, his long sabbath broke;   1030
The world was made; was ruin'd; was restor'd;
Laws from the skies were publish'd; were repeal'd;
On earth, kings, kingdoms, rose; kings, kingdoms, fell;
Fam'd sages lighted up the Pagan world;
Prophets from Sion darted a keen glance   1035
Through distant age; saints travell'd; martyrs bled;
By wonders sacred Nature stood controll'd;
The living were translated; dead were rais'd;
Angels, more than angels, came from Heav'n;
And, oh! for this, descended lower still;   1040
Gilt was hell's gloom; astonish'd at his guest,
For one short moment Lucifer ador'd:
Lorenzo! and wilt thou do less?—For this,
That hallow'd page, fools scoff at, was inspir'd,
Of all these truths, thrice-venerable code!   1045
Deists! perform your quarantine; and then
Fall prostrate, ere you touch it, lest you die.
    Nor less intensely bent infernal pow'rs
To mar, than those of light, this end to gain.
O what a scene is here!—Lorenzo! wake,   1050
Rise to the thought; exert, expand thy soul
To take the vast idea: It denies
All else the name of great.   Two warring worlds,
Not Europe against Afric; warring worlds,
Of more than mortal! mounted on the wing!   1055
On ardent wings of energy, and zeal,
High-hov'ring o'er this little brand of strife!
This sublunary ball—but strife, for what?
In their own cause conflicting? No; in thine,
In Man's.   His single int'rest blows the flame;   1060

His the sole stake; his fate the trumpet sounds,
Which kindles war immortal. How it burns!
Tumultuous swarms of deities in arms!
Force, force opposing, till the waves run high,
And tempest Nature's universal sphere.   1065
Such opposites eternal, stedfast, stern,
Such foes implacable, are good, and ill;
Yet Man, vain Man, would mediate peace between them.
    Think not this fiction. "There was war in heav'n."
From heav'n's high crystal mountain, where it hung,
Th' ALMIGHTY's out-stretcht arm took down his bow,
And shot his indignation at the deep:
Re-thunder'd Hell, and darted all her fires.—
And seems the stake of little moment still?
And slumbers Man, who singly caus'd the storm? 1075
He sleeps.—And art thou shock'd at mysteries?
The greatest, thou. How dreadful to reflect,
What ardour, care, and counsel, mortals cause
In breasts divine! How little in their own!
    Where'er I turn, how new proofs pour upon me!
How happily this wondrous view supports   1081
My former argument! How strongly strikes
Immortal life's full demonstration, here!
Why this exertion? Why this strange regard
From Heav'n's Omnipotent indulg'd to Man?   1085
Because, in Man, the glorious, dreadful pow'r,
Extremely to be pain'd, or blest, for ever.
Duration gives importance; swells the price.
An angel, if a creature of a day,
What would he be? A trifle of no weight;   1090
Or stand, or fall; no matter which; he's gone.
Because immortal, therefore is indulg'd

C C

This strange regard of deities to dust.
Hence, Heav'n looks down on Earth with all her eyes:
Hence, the soul's mighty moment in her sight: 1095
Hence, ev'ry soul has partizans above,
And ev'ry thought a critic in the skies:
Hence, clay, vile clay! has angels for its guard,
And ev'ry guard a passion for his charge:
Hence, from all age, the cabinet divine   1100
Has held high counsel o'er the fate of Man.
    Nor have the clouds those gracious counsels hid.
Angels undrew the curtain of the throne,
And PROVIDENCE came forth to meet mankind;
In various modes of emphasis and awe,   1105
He spoke his will, and trembling Nature heard;
He spoke it loud, in thunder, and in storm.
Witness, thou SINAI! whose cloud-cover'd height,
And shaken basis, own'd the present GOD:
Witness, ye billows! whose-returning tide,   1110
Breaking the chain that fasten'd it in air,
Swept EGYPT, and her menaces, to hell:
Witness, ye flames! th' ASSYRIAN tyrant blew
To sev'nfold rage, as impotent, as strong:
And thou, Earth! witness, whose expanding jaws 1115
Clos'd o'er presumption's sacrilegious sons:
Has not each element, in turn, subscrib'd
The soul's high price, and sworn it to the wise?
Has not flame, ocean, æther, earthquake, strove
To strike this truth through adamantine Man?   1120
If not all-adamant, LORENZO! hear;
All is delusion, Nature is wrapt up
In tenfold night, from Reason's keenest eye:
There's no consistence, meaning, plan, or end,

In all beneath the sun, in all above   1125
(As far as Man can penetrate,) or heav'n
Is an immense, inestimable prize;
Or all is nothing, or that prize is all.—
And shall each toy be still a match for heav'n?
And full equivalent for groans below?   1130
Who would not give a trifle to prevent
What he would give a thousand worlds to cure?

   Lorenzo! thou hast seen (if thine to see)
All Nature, and her God (by Nature's course,
And Nature's course controll'd,) declare for me: 1135
The skies above proclaim " Immortal Man!"
And " Man immortal!" all below resounds.
The world's a system of theology,
Read, by the greatest strangers to the schools;
If honest, learn'd; and sages o'er a plough.   1140
Is not, Lorenzo! then, impos'd on thee
This hard alternative; or, to renounce
Thy reason, and thy sense; or, to believe?
What then is unbelief? 'Tis an exploit;
A strenuous enterprise: To gain it, Man   1145
Must burst through ev'ry bar of common sense,
Of common shame, magnanimously wrong.
And what rewards the sturdy combatant?
His prize, repentance; infamy, his crown.

   But wherefore infamy?—For want of faith,   1150
Down the steep precipice of wrong he slides;
There's nothing to support him in the right.
Faith in the future wanting, is, at least
In embryo, ev'ry weakness, ev'ry guilt;
And strong temptation ripens it to birth.   1155
If this life's gain invites him to the deed,

Why not his country sold, his father slain?
'Tis virtue to pursue our good supreme;
And his supreme, his only good is here.
Ambition, Av'rice, by the wise disdain'd, 1160
Is perfect wisdom, while mankind are fools,
And think a turf, or tombstone, covers all: •
These find employment, and provide for sense
A richer pasture, and a larger range:
And sense by right divine ascends the throne, 1165
When Virtue's prize and prospect are no more;
Virtue no more we think the will of Heav'n.
Would Heav'n quite beggar Virtue, if belov'd?

 " Has Virtue charms?" I grant her heav'nly fair;
But if unportion'd, all will Int'rest wed; 1170
Though that our admiration, this our choice.
The Virtues grow on Immortality;
That root destroy'd, they wither and expire.
A DEITY believ'd, will nought avail;
Rewards and punishments make GOD ador'd; 1175
And hopes and fears give Conscience all her pow'r.
As in the dying parent dies the child,
Virtue, with Immortality, expires.
Who tells me he denies his soul immortal,
Whate'er his boast, has told me, he's a knave. 1180
His duty 'tis, to love himself alone;
Nor care though mankind perish, if he smiles.
Who thinks ere long the Man shall wholly die,
Is dead already; nought but brute survives.

 And are there such?—Such candidates there are
For more than death; for utter loss of being, 1186
Being, the basis of the DEITY!
Ask you the cause?—The cause they will not tell:

Nor need they: Oh the sorceries of sense!
They work this transformation on the soul,   1190
Dismount her like the serpent at the fall,
Dismount her from her native wing (which soar'd
Erewhile ethereal heights,) and throw her down,
To lick the dust, and crawl, in such a thought.

    Is it in words to paint you? O ye fall'n!   1195
Fall'n from the wings of reason, and of hope!
Erect in stature, prone in appetite!
Patrons of pleasure, posting into pain!
Lovers of argument, averse to sense!
Boasters of liberty, fast-bound in chains!   1200
Lords of the wide creation, and the shame!
More senseless than th' irrationals you scorn!
More base than those you rule! than those you pity,
Far more undone! O ye most infamous
Of beings, from superior dignity!   1205
Deepest in woe from means of boundless bliss!
Ye curst by blessings infinite! because
Most highly favour'd, most profoundly lost!
Ye motley mass of contradiction strong!
And are you, too, convinc'd, your souls fly off   1210
In exhalation soft, and die in air,
From the full flood of evidence against you?
In the coarse drudgeries and sinks of sense,
Your souls have quite worn out the make of heav'n,
By vice new-cast, and creatures of your own: 1215
But though you can deform, you can't destroy;
To curse, not uncreate, is all your pow'r.

    LORENZO! this black brotherhood renounce;
Renounce ST. EVREMONT, and read ST. PAUL.
Ere rapt by miracle, by reason wing'd,   1220

His mounting mind made long abode in heav'n.
This is freethinking, unconfin'd to parts,
To send the soul, on curious travel bent,
Through all the provinces of human thought;
To dart her flight through the whole sphere of Man;
Of this vast universe to make the tour;   1226
In each recess of space, and time, at home;
Familiar with their wonders; diving deep;
And like a prince of boundless int'rests there,
Still most ambitious of the most remote;   1230
To look on truth unbroken, and entire;
Truth in the system, the full orb; where truths,
By truths enlighten'd, and sustain'd, afford
An arch-like, strong foundation, to support
The incumbent weight of absolute, complete   1235
Conviction; here, the more we press, we stand
More firm; who most examine most believe.
Parts, like half-sentences, confound; the whole
Conveys the sense, and GOD is understood;
Who not in fragments writes to human race: 1240
Read his whole volume, sceptic! then reply.
    This, this, is thinking free, a thought that grasps
Beyond a grain, and looks beyond an hour.
Turn up thine eye, survey this midnight scene;
What are earth's kingdoms to yon boundless orbs,
Of human souls one day the destin'd range?   1246
And what yon boundless orbs to godlike Man?
Those num'rous worlds that throng the firmament,
And ask more space in heav'n, can roll at large
In Man's capacious thought, and still leave room 1250
For ampler orbs; for new creations, there.
Can such a soul contract itself, to gripe

A point of no dimension, of no weight?
It can; it does: The world is such a point:
And, of that point, how small a part enslaves!   1255
   How small a part!—of nothing, shall I say?
Why not?—Friends, our chief treasure! how they drop!
LUCIA, NARCISSA fair, PHILANDER, gone!
The grave, like fabled CERBERUS, has op'd
A triple mouth; and, in an awful voice,   1260
Loud calls my soul, and utters all I sing.
How the world falls to pieces round about us!
And leaves us in a ruin of our joy!
What says this transportation of my friends?
It bids me love the place where now they dwell, 1265
And scorn this wretched spot, they leave so poor.
Eternity's vast ocean lays before thee;
There, there, LORENZO! thy CLARISSA sails.
Give thy mind sea-room; keep it wide of earth,
That rock of souls immortal; cut thy cord;   1270
Weigh anchor; spread thy sails; call ev'ry wind;
Eye thy great Pole-star; make the land of life.
   Two kinds of life has double-natur'd Man,
And two of death; the last far more severe.
Life animal is nurtur'd by the sun;   1275
Thrives on his bounties, triumphs in his beams.
Life rational subsists on higher food,
Triumphant in his beams who made the day.
When we leave that sun, and are left by this
(The fate of all who die in stubborn guilt,)   1280
'Tis utter darkness; strictly double death.
We sink by no judicial stroke of Heav'n,
But Nature's course; as sure as plummets fall.
Since GOD, or Man, must alter, ere they meet

(Since light and darkness blend not in one sphere,)
'Tis manifest, LORENZO! who must change.   1286
    If, then, that double death should prove thy lot,
Blame not the bowels of the DEITY;
Man shall be blest, as far as Man permits.
Not Man alone, all rationals, Heav'n arms   1290
With an illustrious, but tremendous pow'r
To counteract its own most gracious ends;
And this, of strict necessity, not choice:
That pow'r deny'd, men, angels were no more,
But passive engines, void of praise, or blame.   1295
A nature rational implies the pow'r
Of being blest, or wretched, as we please;
Else idle Reason would have nought to do;
And he that would be barr'd capacity
Of pain, courts incapacity of bliss.   1300
Heav'n wills our happiness, allows our doom;
Invites us ardently, but not compels;
Heav'n but persuades, almighty Man decrees;
Man is the maker of immortal fates.
Man falls by Man, if finally he falls;   1305
And fall he must, who learns from Death alone
The dreadful secret—that he lives for ever.
    Why this to thee? Thee yet, perhaps, in doubt
Of second life! But wherefore doubtful still?
Eternal life is Nature's ardent wish: 1310
What ardently we wish, we soon believe;
Thy tardy faith declares that wish destroy'd:
What has destroy'd it?   Shall I tell thee, what?
When fear'd the future, 'tis no longer wish'd;
And, when unwish'd, we strive to disbelieve.   1315
" Thus Infidelity our guilt betrays."

Nor that the sole detection! Blush, LORENZO!
Blush for hypocrisy, if not for guilt.
The future fear'd?   An infidel! and fear!—
Fear what? A dream! A fable!   How thy dread, 1320
Unwilling evidence, and therefore strong,
Affords my cause an undesign'd support!
How disbelief affirms, what it denies!
" It, unawares, asserts immortal life."
Surprising! Infidelity turns out   1325
A creed, and a confession of our sins:
Apostates, thus, are orthodox divines.
     LORENZO! with LORENZO clash no more:
Nor longer a transparent vizor wear.
Think'st thou, Religion only has the mask?   1330
Our infidels are SATAN's hypocrites,
Pretend the worst, and, at the bottom, fail.
When visited by thought (thought will intrude,)
Like him they serve, they tremble, and believe.
Is there hypocrisy so foul as this?   1335
So fatal to the welfare of the world?
What detestation, what contempt, their due!
And, if unpaid, be thank'd for their escape
That Christian candour they strive hard to scorn.
If not for that asylum, they might find   1340
A hell on earth; nor 'scape a worse below.
     With insolence, and impotence of thought,
Instead of racking fancy, to refute,
Reform thy manners, and the truth enjoy.
But shall I dare confess the dire result?   1345
Can thy proud Reason brook so black a brand?
From purer manners, to sublimer faith,

Is Nature's unavoidable ascent;
An honest deist, where the gospel shines,
Matur'd to nobler, in the Christian ends.   1350
When that blest change arrives, e'en cast aside
This song superfluous; life immortal strikes
Conviction, in a flood of light divine.
A Christian dwells, like URIEL, in the sun.
Meridian evidence puts Doubt to flight;   1355
And ardent Hope anticipates the skies.
Of that bright sun, LORENZO! scale the sphere;
'Tis easy; it invites thee; it descends
From heav'n to woo, and waft thee whence it came:
Read and revere the sacred page; a page   1360
Where triumphs immortality; a page
Which not the whole creation could produce;
Which not the conflagration shall destroy;
In Nature's ruins not one letter lost:
'Tis printed in the mind of gods for ever.   1365
     In proud disdain of what e'en gods adore,
Dost smile? Poor wretch! thy guardian angel weeps.
Angels, and Men, assent to what I sing;
Wits smile, and thank me for my midnight dream.
How vicious hearts fume phrenzy to the brain! 1370
Parts push us on to pride, and pride to shame;
Pert Infidelity is Wit's cockade,
To grace the brazen brow that braves the skies,
By loss of being, dreadfully secure.
LORENZO! if thy doctrine wins the day,   1375
And drives my dreams, defeated, from the field;
If this is all, if earth's the final scene,
Take heed; stand fast; be sure to be a knave;

A knave in grain! ne'er deviate to the right:
Shouldst thou be good—how infinite thy loss!   1380
Guilt only makes annihilation gain.
Blest scheme! which life deprives of comfort, death
Of hope; and which Vice only recommends.
If so; where, infidels! your bait thrown out
To catch weak converts? Where your lofty boast 1385
Of zeal for Virtue, and of love to Man?
Annihilation! I confess, in these.

    What can reclaim you? Dare I hope profound
Philosophers the converts of a song?
Yet know, its title flatters you, not me;   1390
Yours be the praise to make my title good;
Mine, to bless Heav'n, and triumph in your praise.
But since so pestilential your disease,
Though sov'reign is the medicine I prescribe,
As yet, I'll neither triumph, nor despair: 1395
But hope, ere long, my midnight dream will wake
Your hearts, and teach your wisdom—to be wise:
For why should souls immortal, made for bliss,
E'er wish (and wish in vain!) that souls could die?
What ne'er can die, oh! grant to live; and crown
The wish, and aim, and labour of the skies;   1401
Increase, and enter on the joys of heav'n:
Thus shall my title pass a sacred seal,
Receive an imprimatur from above,
While angels shout—An Infidel reclaim'd!   1405
    To close, LORENZO! spite of all my pains,
Still seems it strange, that thou shouldst live for ever?
Is it less strange that thou shouldst live at all?
This is a miracle; and that no more.
Who gave beginning, can exclude an end.   1410

Deny thou art: Then, doubt if thou shalt be.
A miracle with miracles inclos'd,
Is Man: And starts his faith at what is strange?
What less than wonders, from the Wonderful?
What less than miracles from GOD can flow?   1415
Admit a GOD—that mystery supreme!
That Cause uncaus'd! All other wonders cease;
Nothing is marvellous for him to do:
Deny him—all is mystery besides;
Millions of mysteries! each darker far,   1420
Than that thy wisdom would, unwisely,shun.
If weak thy faith, why chuse the harder side?
We nothing know, but what is marvellous;
Yet what is marvellous, we can't believe.
So weak our reason, and so great our GOD,   1425
What most surprises in the sacred page,
Or full as strange, or stranger, must be true.
Faith is not Reason's labour, but repose.
    To Faith, and Virtue, why so backward Man?
From hence: The present strongly strikes us all; 1430
The future, faintly: Can we, then, be Men?
If Men, LORENZO! the reverse is right.
Reason is Man's peculiar: Sense, the brute's.
The present is the scanty realm of Sense;
The future, Reason's empire unconfin'd: 1435
On that expending all her godlike pow'r,
She plans, provides, expatiates, triumphs, there;
There builds her blessings; there expects her praise;
And nothing asks of Fortune, or of Men.
And what is Reason? Be she thus defin'd: 1440
Reason is upright stature in the soul.
Oh! be a Man;—and strive to be a God.

" For what? (thou say'st :(To damp the joys of life?"
No; to give heart and substance to thy joys.
That tyrant Hope, mark, how she domineers;   1445
She bids us quit realities, for dreams;
Safety and peace, for hazard and alarm;
That tyrant o'er the tyrants of the soul,
She bids Ambition quit its taken prize,
Spurn the luxuriant branch on which it sits,   1450
Though bearing crowns, to spring at distant game;
And plunge in toils and dangers—for repose.
If hope precarious, and if things, when gain'd,
Of little moment, and as little stay,
Can sweeten toils and dangers into joys;   1455
What then, that hope, which nothing can defeat,
Our leave unask'd? Rich hope of boundless bliss!
Bliss, past Man's pow'r to paint it; Time's, to close!
    This hope is earth's most estimable prize:
This is Man's portion, while no more than Man:
Hope, of all passions, most befriends us here;   1461
Passions of prouder name befriend us less.
Joy has her tears; and Transport has her death;
Hope, like a cordial, innocent though strong,
Man's heart, at once, inspirits and serenes;   1465
Nor makes him pay his wisdom for his joys;
'Tis all our present state can safely bear,
Health to the frame! and vigour to the mind!
A joy attemper'd! a chastis'd delight!
Like the fair summer-ev'ning, mild, and sweet! 1470
'Tis Man's full cup; his paradise below!
    A blest hereafter, then, or hop'd, or gain'd,
Is all; our whole of happiness: Full proof,
I chose no trivial or inglorious theme.

And know, ye foes to song! (well-meaning Men, 1475
Though quite forgotten half your Bible's praise!)
Important truths, in spite of verse, may please:
Grave minds you praise; nor can you praise too much:
If there is weight in an eternity,
Let the grave listen; and be graver still.   1480

THE

COMPLAINT.

NIGHT VIII.

VIRTUE's APOLOGY;

OR, THE

MAN OF THE WORLD ANSWERED.

IN WHICH ARE CONSIDERED,

THE LOVE OF THIS LIFE; THE AMBITION AND PLEASURE,
WITH THE WIT AND WISDOM, OF THE WORLD.

AND has all Nature, then, espous'd my part?
Have I brib'd heav'n, and earth, to plead against thee?
And is thy soul immortal?—What remains?
All, all, LORENZO; make immortal, blest.
Unblest immortals! what can shock us more?   5
And yet LORENZO still affects the world;
There, stows his treasure; thence, his title draws,
Man of the World! (for such wouldst thou be call'd;)
And art thou proud of that inglorious style?

Proud of reproach? For a reproach it was,   10
In ancient days; and Christian—in an age,
When men were men, and not asham'd of heav'n—
Fir'd their ambition, as it crown'd their joy.
Sprinkled with dews from the CASTALIAN font,
Fain would I re-baptize thee, and confer   15
A purer spirit, and a nobler name.
    Thy fond attachments fatal, and inflam'd,
Point out my path, and dictate to my song:
To thee, the world how fair! how strongly strikes
Ambition! and gay Pleasure stronger still!   20
Thy triple bane! the triple bolt, that lays
Thy virtue dead! be these my triple theme;
Nor shall thy wit or wisdom be forgot.
    Common the theme; not so the song; if she
My song invokes, URANIA, deigns to smile.   25
The charm that chains us to the world, her foe,
If she dissolves, the man of earth, at once,
Starts from his trance, and sighs for other scenes;
Scenes, where these sparks of night, these stars, shall
        shine
Unnumber'd suns (for all things, as they are,   30
The blest behold;) and, in one glory, pour
Their blended blaze on Man's astonish'd sight;
A blaze—the least illustrious object there.
    LORENZO! since eternal is at hand,
To swallow Time's ambitions; as the vast   35
Leviathan, the bubbles vain, that ride
High on the foaming billow; what avail
High titles, high descent, attainments high,
If unattain'd our highest? O LORENZO!
What lofty thoughts, these elements above,   40

What tow'ring hopes, what sallies from the sun,
What grand surveys of destiny divine,
And pompous presage of unfathom'd fate,
Should roll in bosoms where a spirit burns,
Bound for eternity! in bosoms read   45
By HIM, who foibles in archangels sees!
On human hearts HE bends a jealous eye,
And marks, and in heav'n's register inrolls,
The rise, and progress, of each option there;
Sacred to doomsday! That the page unfolds,   50
And spreads us to the gaze of gods and men.
    And what an option, O LORENZO, thine!
This world! and this, unrivall'd by the skies!
A world, where lust of Pleasure, Grandeur, Gold,
Three dæmons that divide its realms between them, 55
With strokes alternate buffet to and fro
Man's restless heart, their sport, their flying ball;
Till, with the giddy circle sick and tir'd,
It pants for peace, and drops into despair.
Such is the world LORENZO sets above   60
That glorious promise, angels were esteem'd
Too mean to bring; a promise, their ADOR'D
Descended to communicate, and press,
By counsel, miracle, life, death, on Man.
Such is the world LORENZO's wisdom woos,   65
And on its thorny pillow seeks repose;
A pillow, which, like opiates ill-prepar'd,
Intoxicates, but not composes; fills
The visionary mind with gay chimeras,   .   .
All the wild trash of sleep, without the rest;   70
What unfeign'd travel, and what dreams of joy!
                    E E

How frail, men, things! how momentary both!
Fantastic chase, of shadows hunting shades!
The gay, the busy, equal, though unlike;
Equal in wisdom, differently wise!   75
Through flow'ry meadows, and through dreary wastes,
One bustling, and one dancing, into death.
There's not a day, but to the man of thought,
Betrays some secret, that throws new reproach
On life, and makes him sick of seeing more.   80
The scenes of business tell us—" what are men;"
The scenes of pleasure—" what is all beside:"
There, others we despise; and here, ourselves.
Amid disgust eternal, dwells delight?
'Tis approbation strikes the string of joy.   85
      What wondrous prize has kindled this career,
Stuns with the din, and choaks us with the dust,
On life's gay stage, one inch above the grave?
The proud run up and down in quest of eyes;
The sensual, in pursuit of something worse;   90
The grave, of gold; the politic, of pow'r;
And all, of other butterflies, as vain!
As eddies draw things frivolous, and light,
How is Man's heart by vanity drawn in!
On the swift circle of returning toys,   95
Whirl'd, straw-like, round and round, and then in-
            gulph'd,
Where gay delusion darkens to despair!
      " This is a beaten track."   Is this a track
Should not be beaten? Never beat enough,
Till enough learnt the truths it would inspire,   100
Shall Truth be silent, because Folly frowns?

Turn the world's history; what find we there,
But Fortune's sports, or Nature's cruel claims,
Or Woman's artifice, or Man's revenge,
And endless inhumanities on Man?   105
Fame's trumpet seldom sounds, but, like the knell,
It brings bad tidings! How it hourly blows
Man's misadventures round the list'ning world!
Man is the tale of narrative old Time;
Sad tale! which high as Paradise begins;   110
As if, the toil of travel to delude,
From stage to stage, in his eternal round,
The Days, his daughters, as they spin our hours
On Fortune's wheel, where accident unthought,
Oft, in a moment, snaps life's strongest thread,   115
Each, in her turn, some tragic story tells,
With, now and then, a wretched farce between;
And fills his chronicle with human woes.

Time's daughters, true as those of men, deceive us;
Not one, but puts some cheat on all mankind: 120
While in their father's bosom, not yet ours,
They flatter our fond hopes; and promise much
Of amiable; but hold him not o'erwise,
Who dares to trust them? and laugh round the year,
At still-confiding, still-confounded Man;   125
Confiding, though confounded; hoping on,
Untaught by trial, unconvinc'd by proof,
And ever looking for the never-seen:
Life to the last, like harden'd felons, lies;
Nor owns itself a cheat, till it expires.   130
Its little joys go out by one and one,
And leave poor Man, at length, in perfect night;
Night, darker than what, now, involves the pole.

O Thou, who dost permit these ills to fall,
For gracious ends, and wouldst that Man should mourn!
O Thou, whose hand this goodly fabric fram'd, 136
Who know'st it best, and wouldst that Man should know!
What is this sublunary world? A vapour!
A vapour all it holds; itself a vapour, .
From the damp bed of chaos, by thy beam 140
Exhal'd, ordain'd to swim its destin'd hour
In ambient air, then melt, and disappear.
Earth's days are number'd, nor remote her doom;
As mortal, though less transient, than her sons;
Yet they doat on her, as the world and they 145
Were both eternal, solid; Thou! a dream.

They doat—on what? Immortal views apart,
A region of outsides! a land of shadows!
A fruitful field of flow'ry promises!
A wilderness of joys perplex'd with doubts, 150
And sharp with thorns! a troubled ocean, spread
With bold adventurers, their all on board;
No second hope, if here their fortune frowns;
Frown soon it must. Of various rates they sail,
Of ensigns various; all alike in this, 155
All restless, anxious; tost with hopes and fears,
In calmest skies; obnoxious all to storm!
And stormy the most general blast of life:
All bound for Happiness; yet few provide
The chart of Knowledge, pointing where it lies; 160
Or Virtue's helm, to shape the course design'd:
All, more or less, capricious fate lament,
Now lifted by the tide, and now resorb'd,
And farther from their wishes than before:
All, more or less, against each other dash, 165

To mutual hurt, by gusts of passion driv'n,
And suff'ring more from folly than from fate.
   Ocean! thou dreadful and tumultuous home
Of dangers, at eternal war with Man!
Death's capital, where most he domineers,   170
With all his chosen terrors frowning round
(Though lately feasted high at ALBION's cost,)
Wide-op'ning, and loud-roaring still for more!
Too faithful mirror; how dost thou reflect
The melancholy face of human life!   175
The strong resemblance tempts me farther still:
And, haply, BRITAIN may be deeper struck
By moral truth, in such a mirror seen,
Which Nature holds for ever at her eye.
   Self-flatter'd, unexperienc'd, high in hope,   180
When young, with sanguine cheer, and streamers gay,
We cut our cable, launch into the world,
And fondly dream each wind and star our friend;
All, in some darling enterprise embark'd:
But where is he can fathom its event?   185
Amid a multitude of artless hands,
Ruin's sure perquisite, her lawful prize,
Some steer aright; but the black blast blows hard,
And puffs them wide of hope: With hearts of proof,
Full against wind and tide, some win their way; 190
And when strong effort has deserv'd the port,
And tugg'd it into view, 'tis won! 'tis lost!
Though strong their oar, still stronger is their fate:
They strike; and while they triumph, they expire.
In stress of weather, most; some sink outright;   195
O'er them, and o'er their names, the billows close;
To-morrow knows not they were ever born,

Others a short memorial leave behind,
Like a flag floating, when the bark's ingulph'd;
It floats a moment, and is seen no more: 200
One CÆSAR lives; a thousand are forgot.
How few, beneath auspicious planets born,
(Darlings of Providence! fond Fate's elect!)
With swelling sails make good the promis'd port,
With all their wishes freighted! Yet ev'n these, 205
Freighted with all their wishes, soon complain;
Free from misfortune, not from nature free,
They still are Men; and when is Man secure?
As fatal time as storm! the rush of years
Beats down their strength; their numberless escapes 210
In ruin end: And, now, their proud success
But plants new terrors on the victor's brow;
What pain to quit the world, just made their own,
Their nest so deeply down'd, and built so high!
Too low they build, who build beneath the stars. 215
    Woe then apart (if woe apart can be
From mortal Man,) and fortune at our nod,
The gay, rich, great, triumphant, and august,
What are they?—The most happy (strange to say!)
Convince me most of human misery: 220
What are they? Smiling wretches of to-morrow!
More wretched, then, than e'er their slave can be;
Their treach'rous blessings, at the day of need,
Like other faithless friends, unmask, and sting:
Then, what provoking indigence in wealth!   225
What aggravated impotence in power!
High titles, then, what insult of their pain!
If that sole anchor, equal to the waves,
Immortal Hope! defies not the rude storm,

Takes comfort from the foaming billow's rage,   230
And makes a welcome harbour of the tomb.
   Is this a sketch of what thy soul admires?
" But here (thou say'st) the miseries of life
" Are huddled in a group.   A more distinct
" Survey, perhaps, might bring thee better news." 235
Look on life's stages: They speak plainer still;
The plainer they, the deeper wilt thou sigh.
Look on thy lovely boy; in him behold
The best that can befal the best on earth;
The boy has virtue by his mother's side: 240
Yes, on FLORELLO look: A father's heart
Is tender, though the man's is made of stone;
The truth, through such a medium seen, may make
Impression deep, and fondness prove thy friend.
   FLORELLO, lately cast on this rude coast   245
A helpless infant; now a heedless child;
To poor CLARISSA's throes, thy care succeeds:
Care full of love, and yet severe as hate!
O'er thy soul's joy how oft thy fondness frowns!
Needful austerities his will restrain;   250
As thorns fence in the tender plant from harm.
As yet, his reason cannot go alone;
But asks a sterner nurse to lead it on.
His little heart is often terrify'd;
The blush of morning, in his cheek, turns pale; 255
Its pearly dew-drop trembles in his eye;
His harmless eye! and drowns an angel there.
Ah! what avails his innocence? The task
Injoin'd must discipline his early pow'rs;
He learns to sigh, ere he is known to sin;   260
Guiltless, and sad! a wretch before the fall!

How cruel this! more cruel to forbear.
Our nature such, with necessary pains
We purchase prospects of precarious peace:
Though not a father, this might steal a sigh.   265
　　Suppose him disciplin'd aright (if not,
'Twill sink our poor account to poorer still;)
Ripe from the tutor, proud of liberty,
He leaps inclosure, bounds into the world;
The world is taken, after ten years toil,   270
Like ancient TROY, and all its joys his own.
Alas! the world's a tutor more severe;
Its lesson's hard, and ill deserves his pains;
Unteaching all his virtuous nature taught,
Or books (fair Virtue's advocates) inspir'd.   275
　　For who receives him into public life?
Men of the world, the terræ-filial breed,
Welcome the modest stranger to their sphere
(Which glitter'd long, at distance, in his sight,)
And, in their hospitable arms, inclose: 280
Men, who think nought so strong of the romance,
So rank knight-errant, as a real friend:
Men, that act up to Reason's golden rule,
All weakness of affection quite subdu'd:
Men, that would blush at being thought sincere, 285
And feign, for glory, the few faults they want;
That love a lie, where truth would pay as well;
As if, to them, Vice shone her own reward.
　　LORENZO! canst thou bear a shocking sight!
Such, for FLORELLO's sake, 'twill now appear: 290
See, the steel'd files of season'd veterans,
Train'd to the world, in burnish'd falsehood bright;
Deep in the fatal stratagems of peace;

All soft sensation, in the throng, rubb'd off;
All their keen purpose, in politeness, sheath'd;   295
His friends eternal—during interest;
His foes implacable—when worth their while;
At war with ev'ry welfare, but their own;
As wise as LUCIFER; and half as good;
And by whom none, but LUCIFER, can gain—   300
Naked, through these (so common fate ordains,)
Naked of heart, his cruel course he runs,
Stung out of all most amiable in life,
Prompt truth, and open thought, and smiles unfeign'd;
Affection, as his species, wide diffus'd;   305
Noble presumptions to mankind's renown;
Ingenuous trust, and confidence of love.
    These claims to joy (if mortals joy might claim)
Will cost him many a sigh; till time, and pains,
From the slow mistress of this school, Experience, 310
And her assistant, pausing, pale, Distrust,
Purchase a dear-bought clue, to lead his youth
Through serpentine obliquities of life,
And the dark labyrinth of human hearts.
And happy! if the clue shall come so cheap;   315
For, while we learn to fence with public guilt,
Full oft we feel its foul contagion too,
If less than heav'nly Virtue is our guard.
Thus, a strange kind of curst necessity
Brings down the sterling temper of his soul,   320
By base alloy, to bear the current stamp,
Below call'd wisdom; sinks him into safety;
And brands him into credit with the world;
Where specious titles dignify disgrace;
And Nature's injuries are arts of life;   325

F F

Where brighter reason prompts to bolder crimes;
And heav'nly talents make infernal hearts;
That unsurmountable extreme of guilt!
  Poor MACHIAVEL! who labour'd hard his plan,
Forgot, that Genius need not go to school;   330
Forgot, that Man, without a tutor wise,
His plan had practis'd, long before 'twas writ.
The world's all title-page, there's no contents;
The world's all face; the man who shews his heart,
Is hooted for his nudities, and scorn'd.   335
A man I knew, who liv'd upon a smile;
And well it fed him; he look'd plump and fair;
While rankest venom foam'd through every vein.
LORENZO! what I tell thee, take not ill:
Living, he fawn'd on ev'ry fool alive;   340
And, dying, curst the friend on whom he liv'd.
To such proficients thou art half a saint.
In foreign realms (for thou has travell'd far)
How curious to contemplate two state-rooks,
Studious their nests to feather in a trice,   345
With all the necromantics of their art,
Playing the game of faces on each other,
Making court sweetmeats of their latent gall,
In foolish hope, to steal each other's trust;
Both cheating, both exulting, both deceiv'd;   350
And, sometimes, both (let Earth rejoice) undone!
Their parts we doubt not; but be that their shame;
Shall men of talents, fit to rule mankind,
Stoop to mean wiles, that would disgrace a fool!
And lose the thanks of those few friends they serve?
For who can thank the man he cannot see?   356
Why so much cover? It defeats itself.

Ye that know all things! know ye not mens' hearts
Are therefore known, because they are conceal'd?
For why conceal'd?—The cause they need not tell.
I give him joy, that's awkward at a lie;   361
Whose feeble nature truth keeps still in awe;
His incapacity is his renown.
    'Tis great, 'tis manly, to disdain disguise;
It shews our spirit, or it proves our strength.   365
Thou say'st, 'tis needful: Is it therefore right?
Howe'er, I grant it some small sign of grace,
To strain at an excuse: And wouldst thou then
Escape that cruel need? Thou may'st, with ease;
Think no post needful that demands a knave.   370
When late our civil helm was shifting hands,
So P——— thought: Think better, if you can.
    But this, how rare! the public path of life
Is dirty:—Yet, allow that dirt its due,
It makes the noble mind more noble still: 375
The world's no neuter; it will wound, or save;
Our virtue quench, or indignation fire.
You say, the world, well-known, will make a man:—
The world, well-known, will give our hearts to Heav'n,
Or make us dæmons, long before we die.   380
    To shew how fair the world (thy mistress) shines,
Take either part, sure ills attend the choice;
Sure, though not equal, detriment ensues.
Not Virtue's self is deify'd on earth;
Virtue has her relapses, conflicts, foes;   385
Foes, that ne'er fail to make her feel their hate.
Virtue has her peculiar set of pains.
True; friends to Virtue, last, and least, complain;
But if they sigh, can others hope to smile?

If Wisdom has her miseries to mourn,   390
How can poor Folly lead a happy life?
And if both suffer, what has Earth to boast,
Where he's most happy, who the least laments?
Where much, much patience, the most envy'd state,
And some forgiveness, needs, the best of friends? 395
For friend, or happy life, who looks not higher,
Of neither shall he find the shadow here.
 The world's sworn advocate, without a fee,
LORENZO smartly, with a smile replies:
" Thus far my song is right; and all must own, 400
" Virtue has her peculiar set of pains.—
" And joys peculiar who to Vice denies?
" If vice it is, with nature to comply:
" If pride, and sense, are so predominant,
" To check, not overcome them, makes a saint; 405
" Can Nature in a plainer voice proclaim
" Pleasure, and glory, the chief good of Man?"
 Can Pride, and Sensuality, rejoice?
From purity of thought, all pleasure springs;
And, from an humble spirit, all our peace.   410
Ambition—Pleasure—let us talk of these:
Of these, the Porch and Academy talk'd;
Of these, each following age had much to say;
Yet unexhausted, still, the needful theme.
Who talks of these, to mankind all at once   415
He talks; for where's the saint from either free?
Are these thy refuge?—No; these rush upon thee;
Thy vitals seize, and, vulture-like, devour:
I'll try, if I can pluck thee from thy rock,
PROMETHEUS! from this barren ball of earth,   420
If Reason can unchain thee—thou art free.

And, first, thy CAUCASUS, Ambition calls;
Mountain of torments! eminence of woes!
Of courted woes! and courted through mistake!
'Tis not Ambition charms thee; 'tis a cheat   425
Will make thee start, as H———— at his Moor.
Dost grasp at greatness? First, know what it is:
Think'st thou thy greatness in distinction lies?
Not in the feather, wave it e'er so high,
By Fortune stuck, to mark us from the throng,   430
Is glory lodg'd: 'Tis lodg'd in the reverse;
In that which joins, in that which equals all,
The monarch and his slave;—" a deathless soul,
" Unbounded prospect, and immortal kin,
" A father GOD, and brothers in the skies."   435
Elder, indeed, in time; but less remote
In excellence, perhaps, than thought by Man;
Why greater what can fall, than what can rise?
    If still delirious, now, LORENZO! go;
And with thy full-blown brothers of the world,   440
Throw scorn around thee; cast it on thy slaves;
Thy slaves, and equals: How scorn cast on them
Rebounds on thee! If Man be mean as Man,
Art thou a God? If Fortune make him so,
Beware the consequence: a maxim that,   445
Which draws a monstrous picture of mankind,
Where, in the drapery, the man is lost;
Externals flutt'ring, and the soul forgot.
Thy greatest glory, when dispos'd to boast,
Boast that aloud, in which thy servants share.   450
    We wisely strip the steed we mean to buy:
Judge we, in their caparisons, of men?
It nought avails thee, where, but what, thou art;

All the distinctions of this little life
Are quite cutaneous, foreign to the man.　　455
When, through Death's streights, Earth's subtle ser-
　　pents creep,
Which wriggle into wealth, or climb renown,
As crooked Satan the forbidden tree;
They leave their party-colour'd robe behind,
All that now glitters, while they rear aloft　　460
Their brazen crests, and hiss at us below.
Of Fortune's fucus strip them, yet alive;
Strip them of body too; nay, closer still,
Away with all, but moral, in their minds,
And let, what then remains, impose their name; 465
Pronounce them weak, or worthy; great, or mean;
How mean that snuff of glory Fortune lights,
And Death puts out! Dost thou demand a test
(A test, at once, infallible and short)
Of real greatness? That man greatly lives,　　470
Whate'er his fate, or fame, who greatly dies;
High-flush'd with hope, where heroes shall despair.
If this a true criterion, many courts
Illustrious, might afford but few grandees.

　　Th'ALMIGHTY, from his throne, on earth surveys
Nought greater than an honest, humble heart;　476
An humble heart, his residence! pronounc'd
His second seat; and rival to the skies.
The private path, the secret acts of men,
If noble, far the noblest of our lives!　　480
How far above LORENZO's glory sits
Th' illustrious master of a name unknown;
Whose worth unrivall'd, and unwitness'd, loves
Life's sacred shades, where gods converse with men;

And peace, beyond the world's conception, smiles! 485
As thou (now dark) before we part, shalt see.
But thy great soul this skulking glory scorns.
LORENZO's sick, but when LORENZO's seen;
And, when he shrugs at public bus'ness, lies;
Deny'd the public eye, the public voice,   490
As if he liv'd on others' breath, he dies.
Fain would he make the world his pedestal;
Mankind, the gazers, the sole figure, he.
Knows he, that mankind praise against their will,
And mix as much detraction as they can?   495
Knows he, that faithless Fame her whisper has,
As well as trumpet? That his vanity
Is so much tickled from not hearing all?
Knows this all-knower, that from itch of praise,
Or, from an itch more sordid, when he shines,   500
Taking his country by five hundred ears,
Senates at once admire him, and despise,
With modest laughter lining loud applause,
Which makes the smile more mortal to his fame?
His fame, which (like the mighty CÆSAR,) crown'd
With laurels, in full senate, greatly falls,   506
By seeming friends, that honour, and destroy.
We rise in glory, as we sink in pride;
Where boasting ends, there dignity begins;
And yet, mistaken beyond all mistake,   510
The blind LORENZO's proud—of being proud;
And dreams himself ascending in his fall.
    An eminence, though fancy'd, turns the brain;
All vice wants hellebore; but of all vice,
Pride loudest calls, and for the largest bowl;   515
Because, all other vice unlike, it flies,

In fact, the point, in fancy most pursu'd.
Who court applause, oblige the world in this;
They gratify Man's passion to refuse.
Superior honour, when assum'd, is lost;   520
Ev'n good men turn banditti, and rejoice,
Like KOULI KHAN, in plunder of the proud.
    Though somewhat disconcerted, steady still
To the world's cause, with half a face of joy,
LORENZO cries—" Be, then, Ambition cast;   525
" Ambition's dearer far stands unimpeach'd,
" Gay Pleasure! Proud Ambition is her slave;
" For her, he soars at great, and hazards ill;
" For her, he fights, and bleeds, or overcomes;
" And paves his way, with crowns, to reach her smile:
" Who can resist her charms?"—Or should, LORENZO?
What mortal shall resist, where angels yield?   531
Pleasure's the mistress of ethereal pow'rs;
For her contend the rival gods above;
Pleasure's the mistress of the world below;   535
And well it is for Man, that Pleasure charms;
How would all stagnate, but for Pleasure's ray!
How would the frozen stream of action cease!
What is the pulse of this so busy world?
The love of Pleasure: That, through every vein, 540
Throws motion, warmth; and shuts out death from life.
    Though various are the tempers of mankind,
Pleasure's gay family holds all in chains:
Some most affect the black; and some the fair;
Some honest pleasures court; and some, obscene. 545
Pleasures obscene are various, as the throng
Of passions, that can err in human hearts;
Mistake their objects, or transgress their bounds.

Think you there's but one whoredom? Whoredom, all,
But when our Reason licenses delight.   550
Dost doubt, LORENZO? Thou shalt doubt no more.
Thy father chides thy gallantries; yet hugs
An ugly, common harlot in the dark;
A rank adulterer with others' gold;
And that hag, Vengeance, in a corner, charms.   555
Hatred her brothel has, as well as Love,
Where horrid epicures debauch in blood.
Whate'er the motive, Pleasure is the mark:
For her, the black assassin draws his sword;
For her, dark statesmen trim their midnight lamp, 560
To which no single sacrifice may fall;
For her, the saint abstains; the miser starves;
The stoic proud, for Pleasure, Pleasure scorn'd;
For her, Affliction's daughters grief indulge,
And find, or hope, a luxury in tears;   565
For her, guilt, shame, toil, danger, we defy;
And, with an aim voluptuous, rush on death.
Thus universal her despotic pow'r.
    And as her empire wide, her praise is just.
Patron of pleasure! doter on delight!   570
I am thy rival; Pleasure I profess;
Pleasure's the purpose of my gloomy song.
Pleasure is nought but Virtue's gayer name;
I wrong her still, I rate her worth too low;
Virtue the root, and Pleasure is the flow'r;   575
And honest EPICURUS' foes were fools.
    But this sounds harsh, and gives the wise offence;
If o'erstrain'd wisdom still retains the name.
How knits Austerity her cloudy brow,
And blames, as bold, and hazardous, the praise   580

G G

Of Pleasure, to mankind, unprais'd, too dear!
Ye modern stoics! hear my soft reply:—
Their senses men will trust: We can't impose;
Or, if we could, is imposition right?
Own honey sweet; but, owning, add this sting;   585
" When mix'd with poison, it is deadly too,"
Truth never was indebted to a lie.
Is nought but Virtue to be prais'd, as good?
Why then is health preferr'd before disease?
What Nature loves is good, without our leave.   590
And where no future drawback cries, " Beware,"
Pleasure, though not from Virtue, should prevail.
'Tis balm to life, and gratitude to Heav'n;
How cold our thanks for bounties unenjoy'd!
The Love of Pleasure is Man's eldest-born,   595
Born in his cradle, living to his tomb;
Wisdom, her younger sister, though more grave,
Was meant to minister, and not to mar,
Imperial Pleasure, queen of human hearts.

LORENZO! thou her majesty's renown'd,   600
Though uncoift counsel, learned in the world!
Who think'st thyself a MURRAY, with disdain
May'st look on me.   Yet, my DEMOSTHENES!
Canst thou plead Pleasure's cause as well as I?
Know'st thou her nature, purpose, parentage?   605
Attend my song, and thou shalt know them all;
And know thyself; and know thyself to be
(Strange truth!) the most abstemious man alive.
Tell not CALISTA; she will laugh thee dead;
Or send thee to her hermitage with L———:   610
Absurd presumption! thou, who never knew'st
A serious thought! shalt thou dare dream of joy?

No man e'er found a happy life by chance;
Or yawn'd it into being, with a wish;
Or, with the snout of grov'ling Appetite,   615
E'er smelt it out, and grubb'd it from the dirt.
An art it is, and must be learnt; and learnt
With unremitting effort, or be lost;
And leave us perfect blockheads in our bliss.
The clouds may drop down titles and estates;   620
Wealth may seek us; but Wisdom must be sought;
Sought before all; but (how unlike all else
We seek on earth!) 'tis never sought in vain.

    First, Pleasure's birth, rise, strength, and grandeur, see:
Brought forth by Wisdom, nurst by Discipline,   625
By Patience taught, by Perseverance crown'd,
She rears her head majestic; round her throne,
Erected in the bosom of the just,
Each Virtue, listed, forms her manly guard.
For what are Virtues? (formidable name!)   630
What, but the fountain, or defence, of joy?
Why, then, commanded? Need mankind commands,
At once to merit, and to make, their bliss?—
Great Legislator! scarce so great, as kind!
If men are rational, and love delight,   635
Thy gracious law but flatters human choice;
In the transgression lies the penalty;
And they the most indulge, who most obey.

    Of Pleasure, next, the final cause explore;
Its mighty purpose, its important end.   640
Not to turn human, brutal, but to build
Divine on human, Pleasure came from Heav'n.
In aid to Reason was the goddess sent;

To call up all its strength by such a charm.
Pleasure, first, succours Virtue; in return,　　645
Virtue gives Pleasure an eternal reign.
What, but the pleasure of food, friendship, faith,
Supports life nat'ral, civil, and divine?
'Tis from the pleasure of repast, we live;
'Tis from the pleasure of applause, we please;　　650
'Tis from the pleasure of belief, we pray;
(All pray'r would cease, if unbeliev'd the prize:)
It serves ourselves, our species, and our God;
And to serve more, is past the sphere of Man.
Glide then, for ever, Pleasure's sacred stream!　　655
Through EDEN, as EUPHRATES ran, it runs,
And fosters ev'ry growth of happy life;
Makes a new EDEN where it flows—but such
As must be lost, LORENZO! by thy fall.

　　" What mean I by thy fall?"—Thou'lt shortly see,
While Pleasure's nature is at large display'd;　　661
Already sung her origin and ends.
Those glorious ends, by kind, or by degree,
When Pleasure violates, 'tis then a vice,
And vengeance too; it hastens into pain:　　665
From due refreshment, life, health, reason, joy;
From wild excess, pain, grief, distraction, death;
Heav'n's justice this proclaims; and that, her love.
What greater evil can I wish my foe,
Than his full draught of pleasure, from a cask　　670
Unbroach'd by just authority, ungaug'd
By Temperance, by Reason unrefin'd?
A thousand dæmons lurk within the lee.
Heav'n, others, and ourselves! uninjur'd these,

Drink deep; the deeper, then, the more divine; 675
Angels are angels from indulgence there;
'Tis unrepenting pleasure makes a god.
   Dost think thyself a god from other joys?
A victim rather! shortly sure to bleed.
The wrong must mourn: Can Heav'n's appointments
     fail? 680
Can Man outwit Omnipotence? Strike out
A self-wrought happiness unmeant by Him
Who made us, and the world we should enjoy?
Who forms an instrument, ordains from whence
Its dissonance, or harmony, shall rise. 685
Heav'n bid the soul this mortal frame inspire;
Bid Virtue's ray divine inspire the soul
With unprecarious flows of vital joy;
And, without breathing, Man as well might hope
For life, as, without piety, for peace. 690
   " Is Virtue, then, and Piety the same?"—
No: Piety is more; 'tis Virtue's source;
Mother of ev'ry worth, as that, of joy.
Men of the world this doctrine ill digest;
They smile at Piety; yet boast aloud 695
Good-will to men; nor know they strive to part
What Nature joins; and thus confute themselves.
With Piety begins all good on earth;
'Tis the first born of Rationality.
Conscience, her first law broken, wounded lies; 700
Enfeebled, lifeless, impotent to good;
A feign'd affection bounds her utmost pow'r.
Some we can't love, but for th'Almighty's sake;
A foe to God was ne'er true friend to Man:

Some sinister intent taints all he does;   705
And, in his kindest actions, he's unkind.
   On Piety, humanity is built;
And, on humanity, much happiness;
And yet still more on Piety itself.
A soul in commerce with her GOD, is heav'n;   710
Feels not the tumults and the shocks of life;
The whirls of passions, and the strokes of heart.
A Deity believ'd, is joy begun;
A Deity ador'd, is joy advanc'd;
A Deity belov'd, is joy matur'd.   715
Each branch of Piety delight inspires;
Faith builds a bridge from this world to the next,
O'er Death's dark gulph, and all its horror hides;
Praise, the sweet exhalation of our joy,
That joy exalts, and makes it sweeter still;   720
Pray'r ardent opens heav'n, lets down a stream
Of glory on the consecrated hour
Of Man, in audience with the Deity.
Who worships the great GOD, that instant joins
The first in heav'n, and sets his foot on hell.   725
   LORENZO! when wast thou at church before?
Thou think'st the service long: But is it just?
Though just, unwelcome: Thou hadst rather tread
Unhallow'd ground; the muse, to win thine ear,
Must take an air less solemn. She complies.   730
Good conscience! at the sound the world retires;
Verse disaffects it, and LORENZO smiles;
Yet has she her scraglio full of charms;
And such as age shall heighten, not impair.
Art thou dejected? Is thy mind o'ercast?   735

Published by R. Ackermann R.A. delin.   Engraved by J. Saunders.

Prayr ardent opens heaven, lets down a stream,
Of Glory on the consecrated hour
Of Man, in audience with the Deity   Page 280

London Published Nov.r 6.th 1797, by I.Heptinstall, 304 Holborn.

Amid her fair ones, thou the fairest chuse,
To chase thy gloom.—" Go, fix some weighty truth;
" Chain down some passion; do some gen'rous good;
" Teach Ignorance to see, or Grief to smile;
" Correct thy friend; befriend thy greatest foe;   740
" Or with warm heart, and confidence divine,
" Spring up, and lay strong hold on HIM who made
        " thee."
—Thy gloom is scatter'd, sprightly spirits flow:
Though wither'd is thy vine, and harp unstrung.
    Dost call the bowl, the viol, and the dance,   745
Loud mirth, mad laughter? Wretched comforters!
Physicians! more than half of thy disease.
Laughter, though never censur'd yet as sin
(Pardon a thought that only seems severe,)
Is half-immoral: Is it much indulg'd?   750
By venting spleen, or dissipating thought,
It shews a scorner, or it makes a fool;
And sins, as hurting others, or ourselves.
'Tis pride, or emptiness, applies the straw,
That tickles little minds to mirth effuse;   755
Of grief approaching, the portentous sign!
The house of laughter makes a house of woe.
A Man triumphant is a monstrous sight;
A Man dejected is a sight as mean.
What cause for triumph, where such ills abound? 760
What for dejection, where presides a Pow'r,
Who call'd us into being to be blest?
So grieve, as conscious grief may rise to joy;
So joy, as conscious joy to grief may fall.
Most true, a wise man never will be sad;   765
But neither will sonorous, bubbling mirth,

A shallow stream of happiness betray:
Too happy to be sportive, he's serene.

    Yet wouldst thou laugh (but at thy own expence,)
This counsel strange should I presume to give— 770
" Retire, and read thy Bible, to be gay."
There truths abound of sov'reign aid to peace;
Ah! do not prize them less, because inspir'd,
As thou, and thine, are apt and proud to do.
If not inspir'd, that pregnant page had stood,   775
Time's treasure, and the wonder of the wise!
Thou think'st, perhaps, thy soul alone at stake;
Alas!—should men mistake thee for a fool;—
What man of taste for genius, wisdom, truth,
Though tender of thy fame, could interpose?   780
Believe me, Sense here acts a double part,
And the true critic is a Christian too.
But these, thou think'st, are gloomy paths to joy.—
True joy in sunshine ne'er was found at first;
They, first, themselves offend, who greatly please;
And travel only gives us sound repose.   786
Heav'n sells all pleasure; effort is the price;
The joys of conquest, are the joys of Man;
And Glory the victorious laurel spreads
O'er Pleasure's pure, perpetual, placid stream.   790
    There is a time, when toil must be preferr'd,
Or joy, by mis-tim'd fondness, is undone.
A man of pleasure is a man of pains.
Thou wilt not take the trouble to be blest.
False joys, indeed, are born from want of thought; 795
From thought's full bent, and energy, the true;
And that demands a mind in equal poise,
Remote from gloomy grief, and glaring joy.

Much joy not only speaks small happiness,
But happiness that shortly must expire.　　　　800
Can joy, unbottom'd in reflection, stand?
And, in a tempest, can reflection live?
Can joy, like thine, secure itself an hour?
Can joy, like thine, meet accident unshock'd?
Or ope the door to honest Poverty?　　　　805
Or talk with threat'ning Death, and not turn pale?
In such a world, and such a nature, these
Are needful fundamentals of delight:
These fundamentals give delight indeed;
Delight, pure, delicate, and durable;　　　　810
Delight, unshaken, masculine, divine;
A constant, and a sound, but serious joy.
　　Is Joy the daughter of Severity?
It is:—Yet far my doctrine from severe.
" Rejoice for ever:" It becomes a Man;　　　　815
Exalts, and sets him nearer to the gods.
" Rejoice for ever:" Nature cries, " Rejoice;"
And drinks to Man in her nectareous cup,
Mix'd up of delicates for ev'ry sense;
To the great Founder of the bounteous feast,　　　　820
Drinks glory, gratitude, eternal praise;
And he that will not pledge her, is a churl.
Ill firmly to support, good fully taste,
Is the whole science of felicity:
Yet sparing pledge: Her bowl is not the best　　　　825
Mankind can boast.—" A rational repast;
" Exertion, vigilance, a mind in arms,
" A military discipline of thought,
" To foil temptation in the doubtful field;
" And ever-waking ardour for the right;"　　　　830

'Tis these, first give, then guard, a cheerful heart.
Nought that is right, think little; well aware,
What Reason bids, GOD bids; by his command
How aggrandiz'd the smallest thing we do!
Thus, nothing is insipid, to the wise;   835
To thee, insipid all, but what is mad;
Joys season'd high, and tasting strong of guilt.
  " Mad!—(thou reply'st, with indignation fir'd;)
" Of ancient sages proud to tread the steps,
" I follow Nature."—Follow Nature still,   840
But look it be thine own: Is Conscience, then,
No part of Nature? Is she not supreme?
Thou regicide! O raise her from the dead!
Then, follow Nature; and resemble GOD.
  When, spite of Conscience, Pleasure is pursu'd, 845
Man's nature is unnaturally pleas'd:
And what's unnatural, is painful too
At intervals, and must disgust ev'n thee!
The fact thou know'st; but not, perhaps, the cause.
Virtue's foundations with the world's were laid; 850
Heav'n mix'd her with our make, and twisted close
Her sacred int'rests with the strings of life.
Who breaks her awful mandate, shocks himself,
His better self: And is it greater pain,
Our soul should murmur, or our dust repine?   855
And one, in their eternal war, must bleed.
  If one must suffer, which should least be spar'd?
The pains of mind surpass the pains of sense.
Ask, then, the gout, what torment is in guilt.
The joys of sense to mental joys are mean: 860
Sense on the present only feeds; the soul
On past, and future, forages for joy.

'Tis her's, by retrospect, through time to range;
And forward time's great sequel to survey.
Could human courts take vengeance on the mind, 865
Axes might rust, and racks, and gibbets, fall:
Guard, then, thy mind, and leave the rest to fate.
    LORENZO! wilt thou never be a Man?
The man is dead, who for the body lives,
Lur'd, by the beating of his pulse, to list   870
With ev'ry lust, that wars against his peace;
And sets him quite at variance with himself.
Thyself, first know; then love: A self there is
Of Virtue fond, that kindles at her charms.
A self there is, as fond of ev'ry vice,   875
While ev'ry virtue wounds it to the heart;
Humility degrades it, Justice robs,
Blest Bounty beggars it, fair Truth betrays,
And godlike Magnanimity destroys.
This self, when rival to the former, scorn;   880
When not in competition, kindly treat,
Defend it, feed it:—But when Virtue bids,
Toss it, or to the fowls, or to the flames.
And why? 'Tis love of pleasure bids thee bleed;
Comply, or own self-love extinct, or blind.   885
    For what is Vice? Self-love in a mistake;
A poor blind merchant buying joys too dear.
And Virtue, what? 'Tis Self-love in her wits,
Quite skilful in the market of delight.
Self-love's good sense is love of that dread Pow'r, 890
From whom she springs, and all she can enjoy.
Other self-love, is but disguis'd self-hate;
More mortal than the malice of our foes;
A self-hate, now, scarce felt; then felt full-sore,

When being curst, extinction loud-implor'd;   895
And every thing preferr'd to what we are.
   Yet this self-love LORENZO makes his choice;
And, in this choice triumphant, boasts of joy.
How is his want of happiness betray'd,
By disaffection to the present hour!   900
Imagination wanders far a-field:
The future pleases: Why? The present pains.—
" But that's a secret."—Yes, which all men know;
And know from thee, discover'd unawares.
Thy ceaseless agitation restless rolls   905
From cheat to cheat, impatient of a pause;
What is it?—'Tis the cradle of the soul,
From Instinct sent, to rock her in disease,
Which her physician, Reason, will not cure.
A poor expedient! yet thy best; and while   910
It mitigates thy pain, it owns it too.
   Such are LORENZO's wretched remedies!
The weak have remedies; the wise have joys.
Superior wisdom is superior bliss.
And what sure mark distinguishes the wise?   915
Consistent wisdom ever wills the same;
Thy fickle wish is ever on the wing.
Sick of herself, is Folly's character;
As Wisdom's is, a modest self-applause.
A change of evils is thy good supreme;   920
Nor, but in motion, canst thou find thy rest.
Man's greatest strength is shewn in standing still.
The first sure symptom of a mind in health,
Is rest at heart, and pleasure felt at home.
False Pleasure from abroad her joys imports;   925
Rich from within, and self-sustain'd, the true.

The true is fix'd, and solid as a rock;
Slipp'ry the false, and tossing as the wave.
This, a wild wanderer on earth, like CAIN;
That, like the fabled, self-enamour'd boy,   930
Home-contemplation her supreme delight;
She dreads an interruption from without,
Smit with her own condition; and the more
Intense she gazes, still it charms the more.

      No man is happy, till he thinks, on earth   935
There breathes not a more happy than himself:
Then envy dies, and love o'erflows on all;
And love o'erflowing makes an angel here.
Such angels all, entitled to repose
On HIM who governs fate: Tho' tempest frowns, 940
Though Nature shakes, how soft to lean on Heav'n!
To lean on HIM, on whom archangels lean!
With inward eyes, and silent as the grave,
They stand collecting ev'ry beam of thought,
Till their hearts kindle with divine delight;   945
For all their thoughts, like angels, seen of old
In ISRAEL'S dream, come from, and go to heav'n:
Hence, are they studious of sequest'red scenes;
While noise, and dissipation, comfort thee.

      Were all men happy, revellings would cease, 950
That opiate for inquietude within.
LORENZO! never man was truly blest,
But it compos'd, and gave him such a cast,
As Folly might mistake for want of joy.
A cast, unlike the triumph of the proud;   955
A modest aspect, and a smile at heart.
O for a joy from thy PHILANDER's spring!
A spring perennial, rising in the breast,

And permanent, as pure! no turbid stream
Of rapt'rous exultation, swelling high;   960
Which, like land-floods, impetuous pour awhile,
Then sink at once, and leave us in the mire.
What does the man, who transient joy prefers?
What, but prefer the bubbles to the stream?
   Vain are all sudden sallies of delight;   965
Convulsions of a weak distemper'd joy.
Joy's a fix'd state; a tenure, not a start.
Bliss there is none, but unprecarious bliss:
That is the gem: Sell all, and purchase that.
Why go a-begging to contingencies,   970
Not gain'd with ease, nor safely lov'd, if gain'd?
At good fortuitous, draw back, and pause;
Suspect it; what thou canst ensure, enjoy;
And nought but what thou giv'st thyself, is sure.
Reason perpetuates joy that reason gives,   975
And makes it as immortal as herself:
To mortals, nought immortal, but their worth.
   Worth, conscious worth! should absolutely reign;
And other joys ask leave for their approach;
Nor, unexamin'd, ever leave obtain.   980
Thou art all anarchy; a mob of joys
Wage war, and perish in intestine broils;
Not the least promise of internal peace!
No bosom-comfort! or unborrow'd bliss!
Thy thoughts are vagabonds: All outward-bound, 985
'Mid sands, and rocks, and storms, to cruise for pleasure;
If gain'd, dear-bought; and better miss'd than gain'd.
Much pain must expiate what much pain procur'd.
Fancy, and Sense, from an infected shore,
Thy cargo bring; and pestilence the prize.   990

Then, such thy thirst, (insatiable thirst!
By fond indulgence but inflam'd the more!)
Fancy still cruises, when poor Sense is tir'd.
    Imagination is the Paphian shop,
Where feeble Happiness, like VULCAN, lame,   995
Bids foul ideas, in their dark recess,
And hot as hell (which kindled the black fires,)
With wanton art, those fatal arrows form,
Which murder all thy time, health, wealth, and fame.
Wouldst thou receive them, other thoughts there are,
On angel-wing, descending from above,   1001
Which these, with art divine, would counterwork,
And form celestial armour for thy peace.
    In this is seen Imagination's guilt;
But who can count her follies? She betrays thee, 1005
To think in grandeur there is something great.
For works of curious art, and ancient fame,
Thy genius hungers, elegantly pain'd;
And foreign climes must cater for thy taste.
Hence, what disaster!—tho' the price was paid, 1010
That persecuting priest, the Turk of ROME,
Whose foot (ye gods!) though cloven, must be kiss'd,
Detain'd thy dinner on the Latian shore;
(Such is the fate of honest Protestants!)
And poor Magnificence is starv'd to death.   1015
Hence just resentment, indignation, ire!—
Be pacify'd; if outward things are great,
'Tis magnanimity great things to scorn;
Pompous expences, and parades august,
And courts; that insalubrious soil to peace.   1020
True happiness ne'er enter'd at an eye;
True happiness resides in things unseen.

No smiles of Fortune ever blest the bad,
Nor can her frowns rob Innocence of joys;
That jewel wanting, triple crowns are poor: 1025
So tell his Holiness, and be reveng'd.
    Pleasure, we both agree, is Man's chief good;
Our only contest, what deserves the name
Give Pleasure's name to nought, but what has pass'd
Th' authentic seal of Reason (which, like YORKE,
Demurs on what it passes,) and defies   1031
The tooth of Time; when past, a pleasure still;
Dearer on trial, lovelier for its age,
And doubly to be priz'd, as it promotes
Our future, while it forms our present, joy.   1035
Some joys the future overcast; and some
Throw all their beams that way, and gild the tomb.
Some joys endear eternity; some give
Abhorr'd annihilation dreadful charms.
Are rival joys contending for thy choice?   1040
Consult thy whole existence, and be safe;
That oracle will put all doubt to flight.
Short is the lesson, though my lecture long,
Be good—and let Heav'n answer for the rest.
    Yet, with a sigh o'er all mankind, I grant,   1045
In this our day of proof, our land of hope,
The good man has his clouds that intervene;
Clouds, that obscure his sublunary day,
But never conquer: Ev'n the best must own,
Patience, and Resignation, are the pillars   1050
Of human peace on earth. The pillars, these:
But those of SETH not more remote from thee,
Till this heroic lesson thou hast learnt;
To frown at pleasure, and to smile in pain.

Fir'd at the prospect of unclouded bliss, 1055
Heav'n, in reversion, like the sun, as yet
Beneath th' horizon, cheers us in this world;
It sheds, on souls susceptible of light,
The glorious dawn of our eternal day.
    " This (says LORENZO) is a fair harangue: 1060
" But can harangues blow back strong Nature's stream?
" Or stem the tide Heav'n pushes through our veins,
" Which sweeps away Man's impotent resolves,
" And lays his labour level with the world?" 1064
    Themselves men make their comment on mankind;
And think nought is, but what they find at home:
Thus, weakness to chimera turns the truth.
Nothing romantic has the muse prescrib'd.
Above, LORENZO saw the Man of earth,
The mortal Man; and wretched was the sight. 1070
To balance that, to comfort, and exalt,
Now see the Man immortal: Him, I mean,
Who lives as such; whose heart, full bent on Heav'n,
Leans all that way, his bias to the stars.
The world's dark shades, in contrast set, shall raise
His lustre more; though bright without a foil: 1076
Observe his awful portrait, and admire;
Nor stop at wonder; imitate, and live.
    Some angel guide my pencil, while I draw,
What nothing less than angel can exceed, 1080
A man on earth devoted to the skies;
Like ships at sea, while in, above the world.
    With aspect mild, and elevated eye,
Behold him seated on a mount serene,
Above the fogs of Sense, and Passion's storm; 1085
All the black cares, and tumults, of this life

(Like harmless thunders, breaking at his feet,)
Excite his pity, not impair his peace.
Earth's genuine sons, the scepter'd, and the slave,
A mingled mob! a wand'ring herd! he sees,   1090
Bewilder'd in the vale; in all unlike!
His full reverse in all! What higher praise!
What stronger demonstration of the right!

   The present all their care; the future, his.
When public welfare calls, or private want,   1095
They give to fame; his bounty he conceals.
Their virtues varnish Nature; his, exalt.
Mankind's esteem they court: and he, his own.
Theirs, the wild chase of false felicities;
His, the compos'd possession of the true.   1100
Alike throughout is his consistent piece,
All of one colour, and an even thread;
While party-colour'd shreds of happiness,
With hideous gaps between, patch up for them
A madman's robe; each puff of fortune blows   1105
The tatters by, and shews their nakedness.

   He sees with other eyes than theirs: Where they
Behold a sun, he spies a Deity;
What makes them only smile, makes him adore.
Where they see mountains, he but atoms sees;   1110
An empire, in his balance, weighs a grain.
They things terrestrial worship, as divine;
His hopes immortal, blow them by, as dust,
That dims his sight, and shortens his survey,
Which longs, in infinite, to lose all bound.   1115
Titles and honours (if they prove his fate)
He lays aside to find his dignity;
No dignity they find in aught besides.

They triumph in externals (which conceal
Man's real glory,) proud of an eclipse.　　　　1120
Himself too much he prizes to be proud,
And nothing thinks so great in Man, as Man.
Too dear he holds his int'rest, to neglect
Another's welfare, or his right invade;
Their int'rest, like a lion, lives on prey.　　　1125
They kindle at the shadow of a wrong;
Wrong he sustains with temper, looks on Heav'n,
Nor stoops to think his injurer his foe;
Nought, but what wounds his virtue, wounds his peace.
A cover'd heart their character defends;　　　1130
A cover'd heart denies him half his praise.
With nakedness his innocence agrees;
While their broad foliage testifies their fall.
Their no-joys end, where his full feast begins:
His joys create, theirs murder, future bliss.　　1135
To triumph in existence, his alone;
And his alone, triumphantly to think
His true existence is not yet begun.
His glorious course was, yesterday, complete;
Death, then, was welcome; yet life still is sweet. 1140
　　But nothing charms LORENZO, like the firm,
Undaunted breast—and whose is that high praise?
They yield to pleasure, though they danger brave,
And shew no fortitude, but in the field;
If there they shew it, 'tis for glory shewn;　　1145
Nor will that cordial always man their hearts.
A cordial his sustains, that cannot fail:
By pleasure unsubdu'd, unbroke by pain,
He shares in that Omnipotence he trusts,
All-bearing, all-attempting, till he falls;　　　1150

And when he falls, writes VICI on his shield.
From magnanimity, all fear above;
From nobler recompense, above applause;
Which owes to Man's short out-look all its charms.
    Backward to credit what he never felt,   1155
LORENZO cries—" Where shines this miracle?
" From what root rises this immortal Man?"
A root that grows not in LORENZO's ground;
The root dissect, nor wonder at the flower.
    He follows Nature, (not like thee!) and shews us
An uninverted system of a Man.   1161
His appetite wears Reason's golden chain,
And finds, in due restraint, its luxury.
His passion, like an eagle well-reclaim'd,
Is taught to fly at nought, but infinite.   1165
Patient his hope, unanxious is his care,
His caution fearless, and his grief (if grief
The gods ordain) a stranger to despair.
And why?—Because affection, more than meet,
His wisdom leaves not disengag'd from Heav'n. 1170
Those secondary goods that smile on earth,
He, loving, in proportion, loves in peace.
They most the world enjoy, who least admire.
His understanding 'scapes the common cloud
Of fumes, arising from a boiling breast.   1175
His head is clear, because his heart is cool,
By worldly competitions uninflam'd.
The mod'rate movements of his soul admit
Distinct ideas, and matur'd debate,
An eye impartial, and an even scale;   1180
Whence judgment sound, and unrepenting choice.
Thus, in a double sense, the good are wise;

On its own dunghill, wiser than the world.
What, then, the world? It must be doubly weak;
Strange truth! as soon would they believe the creed!
     Yet thus it is; nor otherwise can be;   1186
So far from aught romantic what I sing.
Bliss has no being, Virtue has no strength,
But from the prospect of immortal life.
Who thinks earth all, or (what weighs just the same)
Who cares no farther, must prize what it yields; 1191
Fond of its fancies, proud of its parades.
Who thinks earth nothing, can't its charms admire;
He can't a foe, though most malignant, hate,
Because that hate would prove his greater foe. 1195
'Tis hard for them (yet who so loudly boast
Good-will to Men?) to love their dearest friend;
For may not he invade their good supreme,
Where the least jealousy turns love to gall?
All shines to them, that for a season shines.   1200
Each act, each thought, he questions, " what its weight,
" Its colour what, a thousand ages, hence?"
And what it there appears, he deems it now.
Hence, pure are the recesses of his soul.
The godlike Man has nothing to conceal.   1205
His virtue, constitutionally deep,
Has habit's firmness, and affection's flame;
Angels, ally'd, descend to feed their fire;
And Death, which others slays, makes him a god.
     And now, LORENZO! bigot of the world!   1210
Wont to disdain poor bigots caught by Heav'n!
Stand by thy scorn, and be reduc'd to nought:
For what art thou?—Thou boaster! while thy glare,
Thy gaudy grandeur, and mere worldly worth,

Like a broad mist, at distance strikes us most;   1215
And, like a mist, is nothing when at hand;
His merit, like a mountain, on approach,
Swells more, and rises nearer to the skies,
By promise, now, and, by possession, soon
(Too soon, too much, it cannot be) his own.   1220
    From this thy just annihilation rise,
LORENZO! rise to something, by reply.
The world, thy client, listens, and expects;
And longs to crown thee with immortal praise.
Canst thou be silent? No; for Wit is thine;   1225
And Wit talks most, when least she has to say,
And Reason interrupts not her career.
She'll say—That mists above the mountains rise;
And, with a thousand pleasantries, amuse:
She'll sparkle, puzzle, flutter, raise a dust,   1230
And fly conviction, in the dust she rais'd.
    Wit, how delicious to Man's dainty taste!
'Tis precious, as the vehicle of Sense;
But, as its substitute, a dire disease.
Pernicious talent! flatter'd by the world,   1235
By the blind world, which thinks the talent rare.
Wisdom is rare, LORENZO! Wit abounds;
Passion can give it; sometimes wine inspires
The lucky flash: And madness rarely fails.
Whatever cause the spirit strongly stirs,   1240
Confers the bays, and rivals thy renown.
For thy renown, 'twere well, was this the worst;
Chance often hits it, and, to pique thee more,
See Dulness, blund'ring on vivacities,
Shakes her sage head at the calamity,   1245
Which has expos'd, and let her down to thee.

But Wisdom, awful Wisdom! which inspects,
Discerns, compares, weighs, separates, infers,
Seizes the right, and holds it to the last;
How rare! in senates, synods, sought in vain; 1250
Or if there found, 'tis sacred to the few;
While a lewd prostitute to multitudes,
Frequent, as fatal, Wit; In civil life,
Wit makes an enterpriser; Sense a Man.
Wit hates authority; commotion loves, 1255
And thinks herself the lightning of the storm.
In states, 'tis dangerous; in religion, death:
Shall Wit turn Christian, when the dull believe?
Sense is our helmet, Wit is but the plume;
The plume exposes, 'tis our helmet saves. 1260
Sense is the di'mond, weighty, solid, sound;
When cut by Wit, it casts a brighter beam;
Yet, Wit apart, it is a di'mond still.
Wit, widow'd of Good Sense, is worse than nought;
It hoists more sail to run against a rock. 1265
Thus, a half CHESTERFIELD is quite a fool;
Whom dull fools scorn, and bless their want of wit.
    How ruinous the rock I warn thee shun,
Where sirens sit, to sing thee to thy fate!
A joy, in which our reason bears no part, 1270
Is but a sorrow tickling, ere it stings.
Let not the cooings of the world allure thee;
Which of her lovers ever found her true?
Happy! of this bad world who little know!—
And yet, we much must know her, to be safe. 1275
To know the world, not love her, is thy point;
She gives but little, nor that little, long.

There is, I grant, a triumph of the pulse;
A dance of spirits, a mere froth of joy,
Our thoughtless agitation's idle child,   1280
That mantles high, that sparkles, and expires,
Leaving the soul more vapid than before.
An animal ovation! such as holds
No commerce with our reason, but subsists
On juices, through the well-ton'd tubes well-strain'd;
A nice machine! scarce ever tun'd aright;   1286
And when it jars—thy sirens sing no more;
Thy dance is done; the Demi-god is thrown
(Short apotheosis!) beneath the Man,
In coward gloom immers'd, or fell despair.   1290
      Art thou yet dull enough despair to dread,
And startle at destruction? If thou art,
Accept a buckler, take it to the field;
(A field of battle is this mortal life!)
When danger threatens, lay it on thy heart;   1295
A single sentence proof against the world.
" Soul, body, fortune! ev'ry good pertains
" To one of these; but prize not all alike;
" The goods of fortune to thy body's health,
" Body to soul, and soul submit to GOD."   1300
Wouldst thou build lasting happiness? Do this;
Th' inverted pyramid can never stand.
      Is this truth doubtful? It outshines the sun;
Nay, the sun shines not, but to shew us this,
The single lesson of Mankind on earth.   1305
And yet—yet, what? No news! Mankind is mad;
Such mighty numbers list against the right,
(And what can't numbers, when bewitch'd, atchieve?)

They talk themselves to something like belief,
That all earth's joys are theirs: As ATHENS' fool
Grinn'd from the port, on ev'ry sail his own.		1311
    They grin; but wherefore, and how long the laugh?
Half ignorance, their mirth; and half, a lie;
To cheat the world, and cheat themselves, they smile.
Hard either task! The most abandon'd own,		1315
That others, if abandon'd, are undone:
Then, for themselves, the moment Reason wakes
(And Providence denies it long repose,)
O how laborious is their gaiety!
They scarce can swallow their ebullient spleen, 1320
Scarce muster patience to support the farce,
And pump sad laughter, till the curtain falls.
Scarce, did I say? Some cannot sit it out;
Oft their own daring hands the curtain draw,
And shew us what their joy, by their despair.		1325
    The clotted hair! gor'd breast! blaspheming eye!
Its impious fury still alive in death!—
Shut, shut the shocking scene.—But Heav'n denies
A cover to such guilt; and so should Man.
Look round, LORENZO! see the reeking blade, 1330
Th' invenom'd phial, and the fatal ball;
The strangling cord, and suffocating stream;
The loathsome rottenness, and foul decays
From raging riot, (slower suicides!)
And pride in these, more execrable still!—		1335
How horrid all to thought!—But horrors, these,
That vouch the truth; and aid my feeble song.
    From Vice, Sense, Fancy, no man can be blest;
Bliss is too great to lodge within an hour;
When an immortal being aims at bliss,		1340

Duration is essential to the name.
O for a joy from Reason! joy from that
Which makes Man Man; and, exercis'd aright,
Will make him more: A bounteous joy! that gives,
And promises; that weaves, with art divine,   1345
The richest prospect into present peace;
A joy ambitious! joy in common held
With thrones ethereal, and their greater far:
A joy high-privileg'd from chance, time, death!
A joy, which death shall double! judgment crown!
Crown'd higher, and still higher at each stage,   1351
Through blest eternity's long day; yet still,
Not more remote from sorrow, than from HIM,
Whose lavish hand, whose love, stupendous, pours
So much of Deity on guilty dust.   1355
There, O my LUCIA! may I meet thee there,
Where not thy presence can improve my bliss!
    Affects not this the sages of the world?
Can nought affect them, but what fools them too?
Eternity, depending on an hour,   1360
Makes serious thought Man's wisdom, joy, and praise.
Nor need you blush (though sometimes your designs
May shun the light) at your designs on Heav'n:
Sole point! where over-bashful is your blame.
Are you not wise?—You know you are: Yet hear 1365
One truth, amid your num'rous schemes, mislaid,
Or overlook'd, or thrown aside, if seen;
" Our schemes to plan by this world, or the next,
" Is the sole difference between wise and fool."
All worthy men will weigh you in this scale;   1370
What wonder, then, if they pronounce you light?
Is their esteem alone not worth your care?

Accept my simple scheme of common sense:
Thus, save your fame, and make two worlds your own.
The world replies not; but the world persists;   1375
And puts the cause off to the longest day,
Planning evasions for the day of doom.
So far, at that re-hearing, from redress,
They then turn witnesses against themselves.
Hear that, LORENZO! nor be wise to-morrow.   1380
Haste, haste! a Man, by nature, is in haste;
For who shall answer for another hour?
'Tis highly prudent to make one sure friend;
And that thou canst not do, this side the skies.

 Ye sons of earth! nor willing to be more!   1385
Since verse you think from priestcraft somewhat free,
Thus, in an age so gay, the muse plain truths
(Truths, which at church you might have heard in
       prose)
Has ventur'd into light; well-pleas'd the verse
Should be forgot, if you the truths retain;   1390
And crown her with your welfare, not your praise.
But praise she need not fear: I see my fate:
And headlong leap, like CURTIUS, down the gulph.
Since many an ample volume, mighty tome,
Must die; and die unwept; O thou minute,   1395
Devoted page! go forth among thy foes;
Go, nobly proud of martyrdom for truth,
And die a double death: Mankind, incens'd,
Denies thee long to live: Nor shalt thou rest,
When thou art dead; in Stygian shades arraign'd 1400
By LUCIFER, as traitor to his throne:
And bold blasphemer of his friend—the World;
The World, whose legions cost him slender pay,

And volunteers around his banner swarm;
Prudent, as PRUSSIA, in her zeal for GAUL.   1405
    " Are all, then, fools?" LORENZO cries.—Yes, all,
But such as hold this doctrine (new to thee;)
    " The mother of true wisdom is the will;"
The noblest intellect, a fool without it.
World-wisdom much has done, and more may do, 1410
In arts and sciences, in wars and peace;
But art and science, like thy wealth, will leave thee,
And make thee twice a beggar at thy death.
This is the most indulgence can afford;
    " Thy wisdom all can do, but—make thee wise."
Nor think this censure is severe on thee;   1416
SATAN, thy master, I dare call a dunce.

CONSOLATION.

NIGHT IX.

CONTAINING, AMONG OTHER THINGS,

I. A MORAL SURVEY OF THE NOCTURNAL HEAVENS.
II. A NIGHT ADDRESS TO THE DEITY.

——— Fatis contraria fata rependens.

VIRGIL.

As when a traveller, a long day past
In painful search of what he cannot find,
At night's approach, content with the next cot,
There ruminates, awhile, his labour lost;
Then cheers his heart with what his fate affords,   5
And chants his sonnet to deceive the time,
Till the due season calls him to repose:
Thus I, long travell'd in the ways of men,
And dancing, with the rest, the giddy maze,
Where Disappointment smiles at Hope's career;   10
Warn'd by the languor of Life's ev'ning ray,
At length have hous'd me in an humble shed;

Where, future wand'ring banish'd from my thought,
And waiting, patient, the sweet hour of rest;
I chase the moments with a serious song.   15
Song sooths our pains; and age has pains to sooth.
   When age, care, crime, and friends embrac'd at
      heart,
Torn from my bleeding breast, and Death's dark shade,
Which hovers o'er me, quench th' ethereal fire;
Canst thou, O Night! indulge one labour more?   20
One labour more indulge! Then sleep, my strain!
Till, haply wak'd by RAPHAEL's golden lyre,
Where night, death, age, care, crime, and sorrow, cease;
To bear a part in everlasting lays;
Though far, far higher set, in aim, I trust,   25
Symphonious to this humble prelude here.
Has not the muse asserted pleasures pure,
Like those above; exploding other joys?
Weigh what was urg'd, LORENZO! fairly weigh;
And tell me, hast thou cause to triumph still?   30
I think thou wilt forbear a boast so bold.
But if, beneath the favour of mistake,
Thy smile's sincere; not more sincere can be
LORENZO's smile than my compassion for him.
The sick in body call for aid; the sick   35
In mind are covetous of more disease;
And when at worst, they dream themselves quite well.
To know ourselves diseas'd, is half our cure.
When Nature's blush by custom is wip'd off,
And conscience deaden'd by repeated strokes,   40
Has into manners naturaliz'd our crimes;
The curse of curses is, our curse to love;
To triumph in the blackness of our guilt

(As Indians glory in the deepest jet;)
And throw aside our senses with our peace.   45
    But, grant no guilt, no shame, no least alloy;
Grant joy and glory, quite unsully'd, shone;
Yet, still, it ill deserves LORENZO's heart.
No joy, no glory, glitters in thy sight,
But, through the thin partition of an hour,   50
I see its sables wove by Destiny;
And that in sorrow bury'd; this in shame;
While howling furies ring the doleful knell;
And Conscience, now so soft thou scarce canst hear
Her whisper, echoes her eternal peal.   55
    Where the prime actors of the last year's scene;
Their port so proud, their buskin, and their plume?
How many sleep, who kept the world awake
With lustre, and with noise! Has Death proclaim'd
A truce, and hung his sated lance on high?   60
'Tis brandish'd still, nor shall the present year
Be more tenacious of her human leaf,
Or spread of feeble life a thinner fall.
    But needless monuments to wake the thought;
Life's gayest scenes speak Man's mortality;   65
Though in a style more florid, full as plain,
As mausoleums, pyramids, and tombs.
What are our noblest ornaments, but deaths
Turn'd flatterers of life, in paint or marble,
The well-stain'd canvas, or the featur'd stone?   70
Our fathers grace, or rather haunt, the scene.
Joy peoples her pavilion from the dead.
    " Profest diversions! cannot these escape?"—
Far from it: These present us with a shroud;

And talk of Death, like garlands o'er a grave.　75
As some bold plunderers, for bury'd wealth,
We ransack tombs for pastime; from the dust
Call up the sleeping hero; bid him tread
The scene for our amusement: How like gods
We sit; and, wrapt in immortality,　80
Shed gen'rous tears on wretches born to die;
Their fate deploring, to forget our own!

What, all the pomps and triumphs of our lives,
But legacies in blossom? Our lean soil,
Luxuriant grown, and rank in vanities,　85
From friends interr'd beneath; a rich manure!
Like other worms, we banquet on the dead;
Like other worms, shall we crawl on, nor know
Our present frailties, or approaching fate?

Lorenzo! such the glories of the world!　90
What is the world itself? Thy world?—A grave.
Where is the dust that has not been alive?
The spade, the plough, disturb our ancestors;
From human mould we reap our daily bread.
The globe around earth's hollow surface shakes,　95
And is the ceiling of her sleeping sons.
O'er devastation we blind revels keep;
Whole bury'd towns support the dancer's heel.
The moist of human frame the sun exhales;
Winds scatter, through the mighty void, the dry; 100
Earth repossesses part of what she gave,
And the freed spirit mounts on wings of fire;
Each element partakes our scatter'd spoils;
As Nature, wide, our ruins spread; Man's death
Inhabits all things, but the thought of Man.　105

Nor Man alone; his breathing bust expires,
His tomb is mortal; empires die: Where now,
The Roman? Greek? They stalk an empty name!
Yet few regard them in this useful light;
Though half our learning is their epitaph.   110
When down thy vale unlock'd by midnight thought,
That loves to wander in thy sunless realms,
O Death! I stretch my view; what visions rise!
What triumphs, toils imperial, arts divine,
In wither'd laurels glide before my sight!   115
What lengths of far-fam'd ages, billow'd high
With human agitation, roll along
In unsubstantial images of air!
The melancholy ghosts of dead renown,
Whisp'ring faint echoes of the world's applause: 120
With penitential aspect, as they pass,
All point at earth, and hiss at human pride,
The wisdom of the wise, and prancings of the great.
    But, O LORENZO! far the rest above,
Of ghastly nature, and enormous size,   125
One form assaults my sight, and chills my blood,
And shakes my frame.   Of one departed world
I see the mighty shadow: Oozy wreath
And dismal sea-weed crown her; o'er her urn
Reclin'd, she weeps her desolated realms,   130
And bloated sons; and, weeping, prophesies
Another's dissolution, soon, in flames.
But, like CASSANDRA, prophesies in vain;
In vain, to many: not, I trust, to thee.
    For, know'st thou not, or art thou loth to know, 135
The great decree, the counsel of the skies?
Deluge and Conflagration, dreadful pow'rs!

Prime ministers of vengeance! chain'd in caves
Distinct, apart the giant furies roar;
Apart; or, such their horrid rage for ruin,   140
In mutual conflict would they rise, and wage
Eternal war, till one was quite devour'd.
But not for this, ordain'd their boundless rage:
When Heav'n's inferior instruments of wrath,
War, Famine, Pestilence, are found too weak   145
To scourge a world for her enormous crimes,
These are let loose, alternate: Down they rush,
Swift and tempestuous, from th' eternal throne,
With irresistible commission arm'd,
The world, in vain corrected, to destroy,   150
And ease creation of the shocking scene.
    Seest thou, LORENZO! what depends on Man?
The fate of Nature; as for Man, her birth.
Earth's actors change Earth's transitory scenes,
And make creation groan with human guilt.   155
How must it groan, in a new deluge whelm'd,
But not of waters! At the destin'd hour,
By the loud trumpet summon'd to the charge,
See, all the formidable sons of fire,
Eruptions, earthquakes, comets, lightnings, play 160
Their various engines; all at once disgorge
Their blazing magazines; and take, by storm,
This poor terrestrial citadel of Man.
    Amazing period! when each mountain-height
Out-burns VESUVIUS; rocks eternal pour   165
Their melted mass, as rivers once they pour'd;
Stars rush; and final Ruin fiercely drives
Her ploughshare o'er creation!—While aloft,
More than astonishment! if more can be!

Far other firmament than e'er was seen,   170
Than e'er was thought by Man! far other stars!
Stars animate, that govern these of fire;
Far other sun!—a sun, O how unlike
The Babe at BETHLE'M! how unlike the Man
That groan'd on CALVARY! Yet HE it is;   175
That Man of Sorrows! O how chang'd! What pomp!
In grandeur terrible, all heav'n descends!
And gods, ambitious, triumph in his train.
A swift archangel, with his golden wing,
As blots and clouds, that darken and disgrace   180
The scene divine, sweeps stars and suns aside.
And now, all dross remov'd, heav'n's own pure day,
Full on the confines of our æther, flames;
While, (dreadful contrast!) far, how far beneath!
Hell bursting, belches forth her blazing seas,   185
And storms sulphureous; her voracious jaws
Expanding wide, and roaring for her prey.
   LORENZO! welcome to this scene; the last
In Nature's course: the first in Wisdom's thought.
This strikes, if aught can strike thee; this awakes 190
The most supine; this snatches Man from death.
Rouse, rouse, LORENZO, then, and follow me,
Where truth, the most momentous Man can hear,
Loud calls my soul, and ardour wings her flight.
I find my inspiration in my theme;   195
The grandeur of my subject is my muse.
   At midnight (when mankind is wrapt in peace,
And worldly fancy feeds on golden dreams,)
To give more dread to Man's most dreadful hour,
At midnight, 'tis presum'd, this pomp will burst 200

From tenfold darkness; sudden as the spark
From smitten steel; from nitrous grain, the blaze.
Man, starting from his couch shall sleep no more!
The day is broke, which never more shall close!
Above, around, beneath, amazement all!   205
Terror and glory join'd in their extremes!
Our God in grandeur, and our world on fire!
All Nature struggling in the pangs of death!
Dost thou not hear her? Dost thou not deplore
Her strong convulsions, and her final groan?   210
Where are we now? Ah me! the ground is gone
On which we stood, LORENZO! While thou may'st,
Provide more firm support, or sink for ever!
Where—how—from whence? Vain hope! It is too late!
Where, where, for shelter, shall the guilty fly,   215
When consternation turns the good man pale?

    Great day! for which all other days were made;
For which earth rose from chaos, Man from earth;
And an eternity, the date of gods,
Descended on poor earth-created Man!   220
Great day of dread, decision, and despair!
At thought of thee each sublunary wish
Lets go its eager grasp, and drops the world;
And catches at each reed of hope in heav'n.
At thought of thee!—And art thou absent then?   225
LORENZO! no; 'tis here;—it is begun;—
Already is begun the grand assize,
In thee, in all: Deputed conscience scales
The dread tribunal, and forestals our doom;
Forestals; and, by forestalling, proves it sure.   230
Why on himself should Man void judgment pass?

Is idle Nature laughing at her sons?
Who Conscience sent, her sentence will support,
And GOD above assert that god in Man.
    Thrice happy they! that enter now the court   235
Heav'n opens in their bosom: But, how rare!
Ah me! that magnanimity, how rare!
What hero, like the man who stands himself;
Who dares to meet his naked heart alone;
Who hears, intrepid, the full charge it brings,   240
Resolv'd to silence future murmurs there!
The coward flies; and, flying, is undone.
(Art thou a coward? No:) The coward flies;
Thinks, but thinks slightly; asks, but fears to know;
Asks, " What is truth?" with PILATE; and retires;
Dissolves the court, and mingles with the throng; 246
Asylum sad! from Reason, Hope, and Heav'n!
    Shall all, but Man, look out with ardent eye,
For that great day, which was ordain'd for Man?
O day of consummation! mark supreme   250
(If men are wise) of human thought! nor least,
Or in the sight of angels, or their KING!
Angels, whose radiant circles, height o'er height,
Order o'er order, rising, blaze o'er blaze,
As in a theatre, surround this scene,   255
Intent on Man, and anxious for his fate.
Angels look out for thee; for thee, their LORD,
To vindicate his glory; and for thee,
Creation universal calls aloud,
To dis-involve the moral world, and give   260
To Nature's renovation brighter charms.
    Shall Man alone, whose fate, whose final fate,
Hangs on that hour, exclude it from his thought?

I think of nothing else; I see! I feel it!
All Nature, like an earthquake, trembling round! 265
All deities, like summer's swarms, on wing!
All basking in the full meridian blaze!
I see the JUDGE enthron'd! the flaming guard!
The volume open'd! open'd every heart!
A sun-beam pointing out each secret thought!   270
No patron! intercessor none! now past
The sweet, the clement, mediatorial hour!
For guilt no plea! to pain, no pause! no bound!
Inexorable, all! and all, extreme!

  Nor Man alone; the foe of GOD and Man,   275
From his dark den, blaspheming, drags his chain,
And rears his brazen front with thunder scarr'd;
Receives his sentence, and begins his hell.
All vengeance past, now, seems abundant grace;
Like meteors in a stormy sky, how roll   280
His baleful eyes! He curses whom he dreads;
And deems it the first moment of his fall.

  'Tis present to my thought!—And yet where is it?
Angels can't tell me; angels cannot guess
The period; from created beings lock'd   285
In darkness. But the process, and the place,
Are less obscure; for these may Man inquire.
Say, thou great Close of human hopes and fears!
Great Key of Hearts! great Finisher of Fates!
Great End! and great Beginning! say, where art thou?
Art thou in time, or in eternity?   291
Nor in eternity, nor time, I find thee.
These, as two monarchs, on their borders meet,
(Monarchs of all elaps'd, or unarriv'd!)
As in debate, how best their pow'rs ally'd   295

May swell the grandeur, or discharge the wrath,
Of HIM, whom both their monarchies obey.
   Time, this vast fabric for him built (and doom'd
With him to fall) now bursting o'er his head;
His lamp, the sun, extinguish'd; from beneath   300
The frown of hideous darkness, calls his sons
From their long slumber; from earth's heaving womb,
To second birth; contemporary throng!
Rous'd at one call, upstarting from one bed,
Prest in one crowd, appall'd with one amaze,   305
He turns them o'er, Eternity! to thee.
Then (as a king depos'd disdains to live)
He falls on his own scythe; nor falls alone;
His greatest foe falls with him; Time, and he
Who murder'd all Time's offspring, Death, expire. 310
   Time was! Eternity now reigns alone!
Awful Eternity! offended queen!
And her resentment to Mankind, how just!
With kind intent, soliciting access,
How often has she knock'd at human hearts!   315
Rich to repay their hospitality,
How often call'd! and with the voice of GOD!
Yet bore repulse, excluded as a cheat!
A dream! while foulest foes found welcome there!
A dream, a cheat, now, all things, but her smile. 320
   For, lo! her twice ten thousand gates thrown wide,
As thrice from INDUS to the frozen pole,
With banners, streaming as the comet's blaze,
And clarions, louder than the deep in storms,
Sonorous as immortal breath can blow,   325
Pour forth their myriads, potentates, and pow'rs,
Of light, of darkness; in a middle field,

Wide as creation! populous as wide!
A neutral region! there to mark th' event
Of that great drama, whose preceding scenes   330
Detain'd them close spectators, through a length
Of ages, rip'ning to this grand result;
Ages, as yet unnumber'd, but by GOD;
Who now, pronouncing sentence, vindicates
The rights of Virtue, and his own renown.   335
    Eternity, the various sentence past,
Assigns the sever'd throng distinct abodes,
Sulphureous or ambrosial: What ensues?
The deed predominant! the deed of deeds!
Which makes a hell of hell, a heav'n of heav'n. 340
The goddess, with determin'd aspect, turns
Her adamantine key's enormous size
Through destiny's inextricable wards,
Deep-driving ev'ry bolt, on both their fates.
Then, from the crystal battlements of heav'n,   345
Down, down, she hurls it through the dark profound,
Ten thousand thousand fathom; there to rust,
And ne'er unlock her resolution more.
The deep resounds, and hell, through all her glooms,
Returns, in groans, the melancholy roar.   350
    O how unlike the chorus of the skies!
O how unlike those shouts of joy, that shake
The whole ethereal! How the concave rings!
Nor strange! when deities their voice exalt;
And louder far, than when creation rose,   355
To see creation's godlike aim, and end,
So well accomplish'd! so divinely clos'd!
To see the mighty Dramatist's last act
(As meet) in glory rising o'er the rest.

No fancy'd god, a GOD indeed, descends,   360
To solve all knots; to strike the moral home;
To throw full day on darkest scenes of time;
To clear, commend, exalt, and crown the whole.
Hence, in one peal of loud, eternal praise,
The charm'd spectators thunder their applause;   365
And the vast void beyond, applause resounds.
    What then am I?——
                    Amidst applauding worlds,
And worlds celestial, is there found on earth,
A peevish, dissonant, rebellious string,
Which jars in the grand chorus, and complains?   370
Censure, on thee, LORENZO! I suspend,
And turn it on myself; how greatly due!
All, all is right, by GOD ordain'd or done;
And who, but GOD, resum'd the friends he gave?
And have I been complaining, then, so long?   375
Complaining of his favours: pain and death?
Who, without Pain's advice, would e'er be good?
Who, without Death, but would be good in vain?
Pain is to save from pain; all punishment,
To make for peace; and Death, to save from death; 380
And second death, to guard immortal life;
To rouse the careless, the presumptuous awe,
And turn the tide of souls another way;
By the same tenderness divine ordain'd,
That planted EDEN, and high-bloom'd for Man, 385
A fairer EDEN, endless in the skies.
    Heav'n gives us friends to bless the present scene;
Resumes them, to prepare us for the next.
All evils natural are moral goods;
All discipline, indulgence, on the whole.   390

M M

None are unhappy; all have cause to smile,
But such as to themselves that cause deny.
Our faults are at the bottom of our pains;
Error in act, or judgment, is the source
Of endless sighs: We sin, or we mistake,   395
And Nature tax, when false Opinion stings.
Let impious grief be banish'd, joy indulg'd,
But chiefly then, when grief puts in her claim.
Joy from the joyous, frequently betrays,
Oft lives in vanity, and dies in woe.   400
Joy, amidst ills, corroborates, exalts;
'Tis joy, and conquest; joy, and virtue too.
A noble fortitude in ills delights
Heav'n, earth, ourselves; 'tis duty, glory, peace.
Affliction is the good man's shining scene;   405
Prosperity conceals his brightest ray;
As night to stars, woe lustre gives to Man.
Heroes in battle, pilots in the storm,
And virtue in calamities, admire.
The crown of manhood is a winter-joy;   410
An evergreen, that stands the northern blast,
And blossoms in the rigour of our fate.

'Tis a prime part of happiness, to know
How much unhappiness must prove our lot;
A part which few possess! I'll pay life's tax,   415
Without one rebel murmur, from this hour,
Nor think it misery to be a Man;
Who thinks it is, shall never be a god.
Some ills we wish for, when we wish to live.

What spoke proud Passion?—"Wish my being lost!"
Presumptuous! blasphemous! absurd! and false! 421
The triumph of my soul is—That I am;

And therefore that I may be—What? LORENZO!
Look inward, and look deep; and deeper still;
Unfathomably deep our treasure runs   425
In golden veins, through all eternity!
Ages, and ages, and succeeding still
New ages, where this phantom of an hour,
Which courts, each night, dull slumber, for repair,
Shall wake, and wonder, and exult, and praise,   430
And fly through infinite, and all unlock;
And (if deserv'd) by Heav'n's redundant love,
Made half-adorable itself, adore;
And find, in adoration, endless joy!
Where thou, not master of a moment here,   435
Frail as the flow'r, and fleeting as the gale,
May'st boast a whole eternity, enrich'd
With all a kind Omnipotence can pour.
Since ADAM fell, no mortal, uninspir'd,
Has ever yet conceiv'd, or ever shall,   440
How kind is GOD, how great (if good) is Man.
No Man too largely from Heav'n's love can hope,
If what is hop'd he labours to secure.
    Ills?—There are none: All-Gracious! none from thee;
From Man full many! Num'rous is the race   445
Of blackest ills, and those immortal too,
Begot by Madness on fair Liberty;
Heav'n's daughter, hell-debauch'd! her hand alone
Unlocks destruction to the sons of men,
Fast barr'd by thine; high-wall'd with adamant, 450
Guarded with terrors reaching to this world,
And cover'd with the thunders of thy law;
Whose threats are mercies, whose injunctions, guides,
Assisting, not restraining, Reason's choice;

Whose sanctions, unavoidable results　　　　455
From Nature's course, indulgently reveal'd;
If unreveal'd, more dang'rous, nor less sure.
Thus, an indulgent father warns his sons,
" Do this; fly that"—nor always tells the cause;
Pleas'd to reward, as duty to his will,　　　　460
A conduct needful to their own repose.

　　Great GOD of wonders! (if, thy love survey'd,
Aught else the name of wonderful retains,)
What rocks are these, on which to build our trust!
Thy ways admit no blemish; none I find;　　　465
Or this alone—" That none is to be found."
Not one, to soften Censure's hardy crime;
Not one, to palliate peevish Grief's COMPLAINT,
Who, like a demon, murm'ring, from the dust,
Dares into judgment call her Judge.—SUPREME! 470
For all I bless thee; most, for the severe;
Her death—my own at hand—the fiery gulph,
That flaming bound of wrath omnipotent!
It thunders;—but it thunders to preserve;
It strengthens what it strikes; its wholsome dread 475
Averts the dreaded pain; its hideous groans
Join Heav'n's sweet hallelujahs in thy praise,
Great Source of good alone! How kind in all!
In vengeance kind! Pain, Death, GEHENNA, save.

　　Thus, in thy world material, mighty Mind!　　480
Not that alone which solaces, and shines,
The rough and gloomy, challenges our praise.
The winter is as needful as the spring;
The thunder as the sun; a stagnate mass
Of vapours breeds a pestilential air:　　　　485
Nor more propitious the Favonian breeze

To Nature's health, than purifying storms.
The dread volcano ministers to good;
Its smother'd flames might undermine the world.
Loud ÆTNAS fulminate in love to Man;   490
Comets good omens are, when duly scann'd;
And, in their use, eclipses learn to shine.
     Man is responsible for ills receiv'd;
Those we call wretched are a chosen band,
Compell'd to refuge in the right, for peace.   495
Amid my list of blessings infinite,
Stand this the foremost, " That my heart has bled."
'Tis Heav'n's last effort of good-will to Man;
When Pain can't bless, Heav'n quits us in despair.
Who fails to grieve, when just occasion calls,   500
Or grieves too much, deserves not be blest;
Inhuman, or effeminate, his heart:
Reason absolves the grief, which Reason ends.
May Heav'n ne'er trust my friend with happiness,
Till it has taught him how to bear it well,   505
By previous pain; and made it safe to smile!
Such smiles are mine, and such may they remain;
Nor hazard their extinction, from excess.
My change of heart a change of style demands;
The CONSOLATION cancels the COMPLAINT,   510
And makes a convert of my guilty song.
     As when o'er-labour'd, and inclin'd to breathe,
A panting traveller, some rising ground,
Some small ascent, has gain'd, he turns him round,
And measures with his eye the various vale,   515
The fields, woods, meads, and rivers, he has past;
And, satiate of his journey, thinks of home,

Endear'd by distance, nor affects more toil:
Thus I, though small, indeed, is that ascent
The muse has gain'd, review the paths she trod; 520
Various, extensive, beaten but by few:
And, conscious of her prudence in repose,
Pause; and with pleasure meditate an end,
Though still remote; so fruitful is my theme.
Through many a field of moral, and divine,   525
The muse has stray'd; and much of sorrow seen
In human ways; and much of false and vain;
Which none, who travel this bad road, can miss.
O'er friends deceas'd full heartily she wept;
Of love divine the wonders she display'd;   530
Prov'd Man immortal; shew'd the source of joy;
The grand tribunal rais'd; assign'd the bounds
Of human grief: In few, to close the whole,
The moral muse has shadow'd out a sketch,
Though not in form, nor with a RAPHAEL-stroke, 535
Of most our weakness needs believe, or do,
In this our land of travel, and of hope,
For peace on earth, or prospect of the skies.
      What then remains?—Much! much! a mighty debt
To be discharg'd: These thoughts, O Night! are thine;
From thee they came, like lovers' secret sighs,   541
While others slept.   So, CYNTHIA (poets feign,)
In shadows veil'd, soft sliding from her sphere,
Her shepherd cheer'd; of her enamour'd less,
Than I of thee.—And art thou still unsung,   545
Beneath whose brow, and by whose aid, I sing?
Immortal Silence!—Where shall I begin?
Where end? Or how steal music from the spheres,

To sooth their goddess?
                    O majestic Night!
Nature's great ancestor! Day's elder-born!   550
And fated to survive the transient sun!
By mortals, and immortals, seen with awe!
A starry crown thy raven brow adorns,
An azure zone, thy waist; clouds in Heav'n's loom
Wrought through varieties of shape and shade,   555
In ample folds of drapery divine,
Thy flowing mantle form; and, Heav'n throughout,
Voluminously pour thy pompous train.
Thy gloomy grandeurs (Nature's most august,
Inspiring aspect!) claim a grateful verse;   560
And, like a sable curtain starr'd with gold,
Drawn o'er my labours past, shall close the scene.
   And what, O Man! so worthy to be sung?
What more prepares us for the songs of Heav'n?
Creation of archangels is the theme!   565
What, to be sung, so needful? What so well
Celestial joys prepares us to sustain?
The soul of Man, His face design'd to see,
Who gave these wonders to be seen by Man,
Has here a previous scene of objects great,   570
On which to dwell; to stretch to that expanse
Of thought, to rise to that exalted height
Of admiration, to contract that awe,
And give her whole capacities that strength,
Which best may qualify for final joy.   575
The more our spirits are enlarg'd on earth,
The deeper draught shall they receive of Heav'n.
   Heav'n's KING! whose face unveil'd consummates
      bliss;

Redundant bliss! which fills that mighty void,
The whole creation leaves in human hearts!   580
THOU, who didst touch the lip of JESSE's son,
Rapt in sweet contemplation of these fires,
And set his harp in concert with the spheres!
While of thy works material the supreme
I dare attempt, assist my daring song.   585
Loose me from earth's inclosure, from the sun's
Contracted circle set my heart at large;
Eliminate my spirit, give it range
Through provinces of thought yet unexplor'd;
Teach me, by this stupendous scaffolding,   590
Creation's golden steps, to climb to THEE.
Teach me with Art great Nature to controul,
And spread a lustre o'er the shades of Night.
Feel I thy kind assent? And shall the sun
Be seen at midnight, rising in my song?   595
     LORENZO! come, and warm thee: Thou whose
            heart,
Whose little heart, is moor'd within a nook
Of this obscure terrestrial, anchor weigh.
Another ocean calls, a nobler port;
I am thy pilot, I thy prosp'rous gale.   600
Gainful thy voyage through yon azure main;
Main, without tempest, pirate, rock, or shore;
And whence thou may'st import eternal wealth;
And leave to beggar'd minds the pearl and gold.
Thy travels dost thou boast o'er foreign realms; 605
Thou stranger to the world! thy tour begin;
Thy tour through Nature's universal orb.
Nature delineates her whole chart at large,
On soaring souls, that sail among the spheres;

And Man how purblind, if unknown the whole! 610
Who circles spacious Earth, then travels here,
Shall own he never was from home before!
Come, my PROMETHEUS, from thy pointed rock
Of false ambition, if unchain'd, we'll mount;
We'll innocently steal celestial fire,   615
And kindle our devotion at the stars;
A theft, that shall not chain, but set thee free.
    Above our atmosphere's intestine wars,
Rain's fountain-head, the magazine of hail;
Above the northern nests of feather'd snows,   620
The brew of thunders, and the flaming forge
That forms the crooked lightning; 'bove the caves
Where infant tempests wait their growing wings,
And tune their tender voices to that roar,
Which soon, perhaps, shall shake a guilty world; 625
Above misconstru'd omens of the sky,
Far-travell'd comets' calculated blaze,
Elance thy thought, and think of more than Man.
Thy soul, till now, contracted, wither'd, shrunk,
Blighted by blasts of Earth's unwholesome air,   630
Will blossom here; spread all her faculties
To these bright ardours; ev'ry pow'r unfold,
And rise into sublimities of thought.
Stars teach, as well as shine.   At Nature's birth,
Thus, their commission ran—" Be kind to Man." 635
Where art thou, poor benighted traveller!
The stars will light thee; though the moon should fail.
Where art thou, more benighted, more astray,
In ways immoral? The stars call thee back;
And, if obey'd their counsel, set thee right.   640

N N

This prospect vast, what is it?—Weigh'd aright,
'Tis Nature's system of divinity,
And ev'ry student of the night inspires.
'Tis elder scripture, writ by GOD's own hand;
Scripture authentic, uncorrupt by Man.   645
LORENZO! with my radius (the rich gift
Of thought nocturnal!) I'll point out to thee
Its various lessons; some that may surprise
An un-adept in mysteries of Night;
Little, perhaps, expected in her school,   650
Nor thought to grow on planet, or on star.
Bulls, lions, scorpions, monsters here we feign;
Ourselves more monstrous, not to see what here
Exists indeed;—a lecture to mankind.
      What read we here?—Th' existence of a GOD? 655
—Yes; and of other beings, Man above;
Natives of æther! sons of higher climes!
And, what may move LORENZO's wonder more,
Eternity is written in the skies.
And whose eternity?—LORENZO! thine;   660
Mankind's eternity.   Nor Faith alone,
Virtue grows here; here springs the sov'reign cure
Of almost ev'ry vice; but chiefly thine;
Wrath, pride, ambition, and impure desire.
      LORENZO! thou canst wake at midnight too,   665
Though not on morals bent: Ambition, Pleasure!
Those tyrants I for thee so lately fought,
Afford their harass'd slaves but slender rest.
Thou, to whom midnight is immoral noon,
And the sun's noon-tide blaze, prime dawn of day;
Not by thy climate, but capricious crime,   671

Commencing one of our antipodes!
In thy nocturnal rove, one moment halt,
'Twixt stage and stage, of riot, and cabal;
And lift thine eye (if bold an eye to lift,   675
If bold to meet the face of injur'd Heav'n)
To yonder stars: For other ends they shine,
Than to light revellers from shame to shame,
And, thus, be made accomplices in guilt.
   Why from yon arch, that infinite of space,   680
With infinite of lucid orbs replete,
Which set the living firmament on fire,
At the first glance, in such an overwhelm
Of wonderful, on Man's astonish'd sight,
Rushes Omnipotence?—To curb our pride;   685
Our reason rouse, and lead it to that Pow'r,
Whose love lets downs these silver chains of light;
To draw up Man's ambition to Himself,
And bind our chaste affections to his throne.
Thus the three virtues, least alive on earth,   690
And welcom'd on Heav'n's coast with most applause,
An humble, pure, and heav'nly-minded heart,
Are here inspir'd:—And canst thou gaze too long?
   Nor stands thy wrath depriv'd of its reproof,
Or un-upbraided by this radiant choir.   695
The planets of each system represent
Kind neighbours; mutual amity prevails;
Sweet interchange of rays, receiv'd, return'd;
Enlight'ning, and enlight'ned! all, at once,
Attracting, and attracted! Patriot-like,   700
None sins against the welfare of the whole;
But their reciprocal, unselfish aid,
Affords an emblem of millenial love.

Nothing in nature, much less conscious being,
Was e'er created solely for itself: 705
Thus Man his sov'reign duty learns in this
Material picture of benevolence.

    And know, of all our supercilious race,
Thou most inflammable; thou wasp of men!
Man's angry heart, inspected, would be found   710
As rightly set, as are the starry spheres;
'Tis Nature's structure, broke by stubborn will,
Breeds all that uncelestial discord there.
Wilt thou not feel the bias Nature gave!
Canst thou descend from converse with the skies, 715
And seize thy brother's throat?—For what?—a clod?
An inch of earth? The planets cry, " Forbear."
They chase our double darkness; Nature's gloom,
And (kinder still!) our intellectual night.

    And see, Day's amiable sister sends   720
Her invitation, in the softest rays
Of mitigated lustre; courts thy sight,
Which suffers from her tyrant-brother's blaze.
Night grants thee the full freedom of the skies,
Nor rudely reprimands thy lifted eye;   725
With gain, and joy, she bribes thee to be wise.
Night opes the noblest scenes, and sheds an awe,
Which gives those venerable scenes full weight,
And deep reception in th' intender'd heart;
While light peeps through the darkness like a spy: 730
And darkness shews its grandeur by the light.
Nor is the profit greater than the joy,
If human hearts at glorious objects glow,
And admiration can inspire delight.
What speak I more, than I, this moment, feel!   735

With pleasing stupor first the soul it struck:
(Stupor ordain'd to make her truly wise!)
Then into transport starting from her trance,
With love and admiration how she glows!
This gorgeous apparatus! this display!   740
This ostentation of creative pow'r!
This theatre!—what eye can take it in?
By what divine enchantment was it rais'd,
For minds of the first magnitude to launch
In endless speculation, and adore?   745
One sun by day, by night ten thousand shine;
And light us deep into the DEITY;
How boundless in magnificence and might!
O what a confluence of ethereal fires,
From urns unnumber'd down the steep of Heav'n,
Streams to a point, and centres in my sight!   751
Nor tarries there; I feel it at my heart.
My heart, at once, it humbles and exalts;
Lays it in dust, and calls it to the skies.
Who sees it unexalted? Or unaw'd?   755
Who sees it, and can stop at what is seen?
Material offspring of Omnipotence!
Inanimate, all-animating birth!
Work worthy HIM who made it! worthy praise!
All praise! praise more than human! nor deny'd 760
Thy praise divine! But though Man, drown'd in sleep,
Withholds his homage, not alone I wake;
Bright legions swarm unseen, and sing, unheard
By mortal ear, the glorious Architect,
In this his universal temple hung   765
With lustres, with innumerable lights,
That shed religion on the soul; at once,

The temple, and the preacher! O how loud
It calls devotion! genuine growth of Night!
   Devotion! daughter of Astronomy!   770
An undevout astronomer is mad.
True; all things speak a GOD; but in the small,
Men trace out HIM; in great, he seizes Man;
Seizes, and elevates, and raps, and fills
With new enquiries 'mid associates new.   775
Tell me, ye stars! ye planets! tell me, all
Ye starr'd, and planeted, inhabitants! what is it?
What are these sons of wonder! say, proud arch!
(Within whose azure palaces they dwell)
Built with divine ambition! in disdain   780
Of limit built! built in the taste of Heav'n!
Vast concave! ample dome! wast thou design'd
A meet apartment for the DEITY?—
Not so; that thought alone thy state impairs,
Thy lofty sinks, and shallows thy profound,   785
And streightens thy diffusive; dwarfs the whole,
And makes an universe an orrery.
   But when I drop mine eye, and look on Man,
Thy right regain'd, thy grandeur is restor'd,
O Nature! wide flies off th' expanding round.   790
As when whole magazines, at once, are fir'd,
The smitten air is hollow'd by the blow;
The vast displosion dissipates the clouds;
Shock'd æther's billows dash the distant skies;
Thus (but far more) th' expanding round flies off, 795
And leaves a mighty void, a spacious womb,
Might teem with new creation; re-inflam'd
Thy luminaries triumph, and assume
Divinity themselves. Nor was it strange,

Matter high-wrought to such surprising pomp, 800
Such godlike glory, stole the style of gods,
From ages dark, obtuse, and steep'd in sense;
For, sure, to sense, they truly are divine,
And half-absolv'd idolatry from guilt;
Nay, turn'd it into virtue.., Such it was 805
In those, who put forth all they had of Man
Unlost, to lift their thought, nor mounted higher;
But, weak of wing, on planets perch'd; and thought
What was their highest, must be their ador'd.
    But they how weak, who could no higher mount!
And are there, then, LORENZO! those to whom 811
Unseen, and unexistent, are the same?
And if incomprehensible is join'd,
Who dare pronounce it madness, to believe?
Why has the mighty Builder thrown aside 815
All measure in his work; stretch'd out his line
So far, and spread amazement o'er the whole?
Then (as he took delight in wide extremes,)
Deep in the bosom of his universe,
Dropt down that reas'ning mite, that insect, Man, 820
To crawl, and gaze, and wonder at the scene?
That Man might ne'er presume to plead amazement
For disbelief of wonders in himself.
Shall GOD be less miraculous, than what
His hand has form'd? Shall mysteries descend 825
From unmysterious? Things more elevate,
Be more familiar? Uncreated lie
More obvious than created, to the grasp
Of human thought? The more of wonderful
Is heard in HIM, the more we should assent. 830
Could we conceive him, GOD he could not be;

Or he not God, or we could not be men.
A God alone can comprehend a God;
Man's distance how immense! on such a theme,
Know this, Lorenzo! (seem it ne'er so strange,) 835
Nothing can satisfy but what confounds;
Nothing, but what astonishes, is true.
The scene thou seest, attests the truth I sing,
And every star sheds light upon thy creed.
These stars, this furniture, this cost of Heav'n,   840
If but reported, thou hadst ne'er believ'd;
But thine eye tells thee, the romance is true.
The grand of nature is th' Almighty's oath,
In Reason's court, to silence Unbelief.

How my mind, opening at this scene, imbibes 845
The moral emanations of the skies,
While nought, perhaps, Lorenzo less admires!
Has the great Sov'reign sent ten thousand worlds
To tell us, He resides above them all,
In glory's unapproachable recess?   850
And dare Earth's bold inhabitants deny
The sumptuous, the magnific embassy
A moment's audience? Turn we, nor will hear
From whom they come, or what they would impart
For Man's emolument; sole cause that stoops   855
Their grandeur to Man's eye? Lorenzo! rouze;
Let thought, awaken'd, take the lightning's wing,
And glance from east to west, from pole to pole.
Who sees, but is confounded, or convinc'd?
Renounces Reason, or a God adores?   860
Mankind was sent into the world to see:
Sight gives the science needful to their peace;
That obvious science asks small learning's aid.

Wouldst thou on metaphysic pinions soar?
Or wound thy patience amid logic thorns?   865
Or travel history's enormous round?
Nature no such hard task injoins: She gave
A make to Man directive of his thought;
A make set upright, pointing to the stars,
As who should say, " Read thy chief Lesson there."
Too late to read this manuscript of Heav'n,   871
When, like a parchment-scroll, shrunk up by flames,
It folds LORENZO's lesson from his sight.
    Lesson how various! Not the God alone,
I see his ministers; I see, diffus'd   875
In radiant orders, essences sublime,
Of various offices, of various plume,
In heav'nly liveries distinctly clad,
Azure, green, purple, pearl, or downy gold,
Or all commix'd; they stand, with wings outspread,
List'ning to catch the Master's least command,   881
And fly through Nature, ere the moment ends;
Numbers innumerable!—well conceiv'd
By Pagan, and by Christian! O'er each sphere
Presides an angel, to direct its course,   885
And feed, or fan, its flames; or to discharge
Other high trusts unknown. For who can see
Such pomp of matter, and imagine, mind,
For which alone inanimate was made,
More sparingly dispens'd? That nobler Son,   890
Far liker the great SIRE!—'Tis thus the skies
Inform us of superiors numberless,
As much, in excellence, above mankind,
As above earth, in magnitude, the spheres.
These, as a cloud of witnesses, hang o'er us;   895

In a throng'd theatre are all our deeds;
Perhaps, a thousand demi-gods descend
On ev'ry beam we see, to walk with men.
Awful reflection! strong restraint from ill!
   Yet, here, our virtue finds still stronger aid   900
From these ethereal glories sense surveys.
Something, like magic, strikes from this blue vault;
With just attention is it view'd? We feel
A sudden succour, unimplor'd, unthought;
Nature herself does half the work of Man.   905
Seas, rivers, mountains, forests, deserts, rocks,
The promontory's height, the depth profound
Of subterranean, excavated grots,
Black-brow'd, and vaulted high, and yawning wide
From Nature's structure, or the scoop of Time;   910
If ample of dimension, vast of size,
Ev'n these an aggrandizing impulse give;
Of solemn thought enthusiastic heights
Ev'n these infuse.—But what of vast in these?
Nothing;—or we must own the skies forgot.   915
—Much less in Art.—Vain Art! thou pigmy pow'r!
How dost thou swell, and strut, with human pride,
To shew thy littleness! What childish toys,
Thy watry columns squirted to the clouds!
Thy bason'd rivers, and imprison'd seas!   920
Thy mountains moulded into forms of men!
Thy hundred-gated capitals! or those
Where three days travel left us much to ride;
Gazing on miracles by mortals wrought,
Arches triumphal, theatres immense,   925
Or nodding gardens pendent in mid-air!
Or temples proud to meet their gods half-way!

Yet these affect us in no common kind.
What then the force of such superior scenes?
Enter a temple, it will strike an awe: 930
What awe from this the DEITY has built?
A good man seen, though silent, counsel gives:
The touch'd spectator wishes to be wise:
In a bright mirror his own hands have made,
Here we see something like the face of GOD.   935
Seems it not then enough, to say, LORENZO,
To Man abandon'd, " Hast thou seen the skies?"
    And yet, so thwarted Nature's kind design
By daring Man, he makes her sacred awe
(That guard from ill) his shelter, his temptation   940
To more than common guilt, and quite inverts
Celestial Art's intent.   The trembling stars
See crimes gigantic, stalking through the gloom
With front erect, that hide their head by day,
And making night still darker by their deeds.   945
Slumb'ring in covert, till the shades descend,
Rapine and Murder, link'd, now prowl for prey.
The miser earths his treasure; and the thief,
Watching the mole, half-beggars him ere morn.
Now plots, and foul conspiracies, awake;   950
And, muffling up their horrors from the moon,
Havoc and devastation they prepare,
And kingdoms tott'ring in the field of blood.
Now sons of riot in mid-revel rage—
What shall I do? Suppress it—or proclaim—   955
Why sleeps the thunder? Now, LORENZO! now,
His best friend's couch the rank adulterer
Ascends secure; and laughs at gods and men.
Prepost'rous madmen, void of fear or shame,

Lay their crimes bare to these chaste eyes of heav'n;
Yet shrink and shudder at a mortal's sight.   961
Were moon, and stars, for villains only made?
To guide, yet screen them, with tenebrious light?
No; they were made to fashion the sublime
Of human hearts, and wiser make the wise.   965
   Those ends were answer'd once; when mortals liv'd
Of stronger wing, of aquiline ascent
In theory sublime.   O how unlike
Those vermin of the night, this moment sung,
Who crawl on earth, and on her venom feed;   970
Those ancient sages, human stars! They met
Their brothers of the skies, at midnight hour;
Their counsel ask'd; and, what they ask'd, obey'd.
The STAGYRITE, and PLATO, he who drank
The poison'd bowl, and he of TUSCULUM,   975
With him of CORDUBA, (immortal names!)
In these unbounded, and Elysian walks,
An area fit for gods, and godlike men,
They took their nightly round, through radiant paths
By seraphs trod; instructed, chiefly, thus,   980
To tread in their bright footsteps here below;
To walk in worth still brighter than the skies.
There, they contracted their contempt of Earth;
Of hopes eternal kindled, there, the fire;
There, as in near approach, they glow'd, and grew
(Great visitants!) more intimate with GOD,   986
More worth to men, more joyous to themselves.
Through various virtues, they, with ardour, ran
The zodiac of their learn'd, illustrious lives.
   In Christian hearts, O for a Pagan zeal!   990
A needful, but opprobrious pray'r! As much

Our ardour less, as greater is our light.
How monstrous this in morals! Scarce more strange
Would this phenomenon in nature strike, ·
A sun that froze us, or a star that warm'd.   995
    What taught these heroes of the moral world?
To these thou giv'st thy praise, give credit too;
These doctors ne'er were pension'd to deceive thee;
And Pagan tutors are thy taste.—They taught,
That, narrow views betray to misery: 1000
That, wise it is to comprehend the whole:
That, Virtue rose from Nature, ponder'd well,
The single base of Virtue built to Heav'n:
That, GOD, and Nature, our attention claim:
That, Nature is the glass reflecting GOD,   1005
As, by the sea, reflected is the sun,
Too glorious to be gaz'd on in his sphere:
That, mind immortal loves immortal aims:
That, boundless mind affects a boundless space:
That, vast surveys, and the sublime of things,   1010
The soul assimilate, and make her great:
That, therefore, Heav'n her glories, as a fund
Of inspiration, thus spreads out to Man.
Such are their doctrines; such the night inspir'd.
    And what more true? What truth of greater weight?
The soul of Man was made to walk the skies;   1016
Delightful outlet of her prison here!
There, disencumber'd from her chains, the ties
Of toys terrestrial, she can rove at large;
There, freely can respire, dilate, extend,   1020
In full proportion let loose all her pow'rs;
And, undeluded, grasp at something great.
Nor, as a stranger, does she wander there;

But, wonderful herself, through wonder strays;
Contemplating their grandeur, finds her own;   1025
Dives deep in their economy divine,
Sits high in judgment on their various laws,
And, like a master, judges not amiss.
Hence greatly pleas'd, and justly proud, the soul
Grows conscious of her birth celestial; breathes 1030
More life, more vigour, in her native air;
And feels herself at home among the stars;
And, feeling, emulates her country's praise.

    What call we, then, the firmament, LORENZO?—
As earth the body, since, the skies sustain   1035
The soul with food, that gives immortal life,
Call it, the noble pasture of the mind;
Which there expatiates, strengthens, and exults,
And riots through the luxuries of thought.
Call it, the garden of the DEITY,   1040
Blossom'd with stars, redundant in the growth
Of fruit ambrosial; moral fruit to man.
Call it, the breast-plate of the true High-Priest,
Ardent with gems oracular, that give,
In points of highest moment, right response;   1045
And ill neglected, if we prize our peace.

    Thus have we found a true astrology;
Thus have we found a new and noble sense,
In which alone stars govern human fates.
O that the stars (as some have feign'd) let fall 1050
Bloodshed, and havoc, on embattled realms,
And rescu'd monarchs from so black a guilt!
BOURBON! this wish how gen'rous in a foe!
Wouldst thou be great, wouldst thou become a god,
And stick thy deathless name among the stars,   1055

For mighty conquests on a needle's point?
Instead of forging chains for foreigners,
BASTILE thy tutor: Grandeur all thy aim?
As yet thou know'st not what it is: How great,
How glorious, then, appears the mind of man, 1060
When in it all the stars, and planets, roll!
And what it seems, it is: Great objects make
Great minds, enlarging as their views enlarge;
Those still more godlike, as these more divine. 1064
   And more divine than these, thou canst not see.
Dazzled, o'erpower'd, with the delicious draught
Of miscellaneous splendours, how I reel
From thought to thought, inebriate, without end!
An EDEN this! a Paradise unlost!
I meet the DEITY in ev'ry view, 1070
And tremble at my nakedness before him!
O that I could but reach the tree of life!
For here it grows, unguarded from our taste:
No flaming sword denies our entrance here;
Would man but gather, he might live for ever. 1075
   LORENZO! much of moral hast thou seen.
Of curious arts art thou more fond? Then mark
The mathematic glories of the skies,
In number, weight, and measure, all ordain'd.
LORENZO's boasted builders, Chance, and Fate, 1080
Are left to finish his aërial tow'rs;
Wisdom, and Choice, their well-known characters
Here deep impress; and claim it for their own.
Though splendid all, no splendour void of use;
Use rivals Beauty: Art contends with Pow'r; 1085
No wanton waste, amid effuse expense;
The great ECONOMIST adjusting all

To prudent pomp, magnificently wise.
How rich the prospect! and for ever new!
And newest to the man that views it most;   1090
For newer still in infinite succeeds.
Then, these aërial racers, O how swift!
How the shaft loiters from the strongest string!
Spirit alone can distance the career.
Orb above orb, ascending without end!   1095
Circle in circle, without end, inclos'd!
Wheel within wheel; EZEKIEL! like to thine!
Like thine, it seems a vision or a dream;
Though seen, we labour to believe it true!
What involution! what extent! what swarms   1100
Of worlds, that laugh at Earth! immensely great!
Immensely distant from each others' spheres!
What then the wondrous space thro' which they roll?
At once it quite ingulphs all human thought;
'Tis Comprehension's absolute defeat.   1105
    Nor think thou seest a wild disorder here;
Through this illustrious chaos to the sight,
Arrangement neat, and chastest order, reign.
The path prescrib'd, inviolably kept,
Upbraids the lawless sallies of mankind.   1110
Worlds, ever thwarting, never interfere;
What knots are ty'd! how soon are they dissolv'd,
And set the seeming married planets free!
They rove for ever, without error rove;
Confusion unconfus'd: Nor less admire   1115
This tumult untumultuous; all on wing!
In motion, all! yet what profound repose!
What fervid action, yet no noise! as aw'd
To silence, by the presence of their LORD;

Or hush'd, by his command, in love to Man,   1120
And bid let fall soft beams on human rest,
Restless themselves.   On yon cærulean plain,
In exultation to their GOD, and thine,
They dance, they sing eternal jubilee,
Eternal celebration of HIS praise.   1125
But, since their song arrives not at our ear,
Their dance perplex'd exhibits to the sight
Fair hieroglyphic of HIS peerless pow'r.
Mark, how the labyrinthian turns they take,
The circles intricate, and mystic maze,   1130
Weave the grand cypher of Omnipotence;
To gods, how great! how legible to Man!
     Leaves so much wonder greater wonder still?
Where are the pillars that support the skies?
What more than Atlantean shoulder props   1135
Th' incumbent load? What magic, what strange art,
In fluid air these pond'rous orbs sustains?
Who would not think them hung in golden chains?—
And so they are; in the high will of Heav'n,
Which fixes all; makes adamant of air,   1140
Or air of adamant; makes all of nought,
Or nought of all; if such the dread decree.
     Imagine from their deep foundations torn
The most gigantic sons of earth, the broad
And tow'ring ALPS, all tost into the sea;   1145
And, light as down, or volatile as air,
Their bulks enormous dancing on the waves,
In time, and measure, exquisite; while all
The winds, in emulation of the spheres,
Tune their sonorous instruments aloft;   1150
The concert swell, and animate the ball.

Would this appear amazing? What, then, worlds,
In a far thinner element sustain'd,
And acting the same part, with greater skill,
More rapid movement, and for noblest ends?　　1155
　　More obvious ends to pass, are not these stars
The seats majestic, proud imperial thrones,
On which angelic delegates of Heav'n,
At certain periods, as the Sov'reign nods,
Discharge high trusts of vengeance, or of love;　1160
To clothe, in outward grandeur, grand design,
And acts most solemn still more solemnize?
　　Ye citizens of air! what ardent thanks,
What full effusion of the grateful heart,
Is due from Man indulg'd in such a sight!　　1165
A sight so noble! and a sight so kind!
It drops new truths at ev'ry new survey!
Feels not LORENZO something stir within,
That sweeps away all period? As these spheres
Measure duration, they no less inspire　　　1170
The godlike hope of ages without end.
The boundless space, through which these rovers take
Their restless roam, suggest the sister-thought
Of boundless time.　Thus, by kind Nature's skill,
To Man unlabour'd, that important guest,　　1175
Eternity, finds entrance at the sight:
And an eternity for Man ordain'd,
Or these his destin'd midnight counsellors,
The stars, had never whisper'd it to Man.
Nature informs, but ne'er insults, her sons.　　1180
Could she then kindle the most ardent wish
To disappoint it?—That is blasphemy.
Thus, of thy creed a second article,

Momentous, as th' existence of a GOD,
Is found (as I conceive) where rarely sought;   1185
And thou may'st read thy soul immortal, here.
   Here, then, LORENZO! on these glories dwell;
Nor want the gilt, illuminated roof,
That calls the wretched gay to dark delights.
Assemblées?—This is one divinely bright;   1190
Here, unendanger'd in health, wealth, or fame,
Range through the fairest, and the sultan scorn.
He, wise as thou, no crescent holds so fair,
As that, which on his turban awes a world;
And thinks the moon is proud to copy him.   1195
Look on her, and gain more than worlds can give,
A mind superior to the charms of pow'r.
Thou muffled in delusions of this life!
Can yonder moon turn Ocean in his bed,
From side to side, in constant ebb and flow,   1200
And purify from stench his watry realms?
And fails her moral influence? Wants she pow'r
To turn LORENZO's stubborn tide of thought
From stagnating on Earth's infected shore,
And purge from nuisance his corrupted heart?   1205
Fails her attraction when it draws to Heav'n?
Nay, and to what thou valu'st more, Earth's joy?
Minds elevate, and panting for unseen,
And defecate from sense, alone obtain
Full relish of existence undeflower'd,   1210
The life of life, the zest of worldly bliss.
All else on earth amounts—to what? To this:
" Bad to be suffer'd; blessings to be left:"
Earth's richest inventory boasts no more.

Of higher scenes be, then, the call obey'd.   1215
O let me gaze!—Of gazing there's no end.
O let me think!—Thought too is wilder'd here;
In mid-way flight imagination tires;
Yet soon re-prunes her wings to soar anew,
Her point unable to forbear, or gain;   1220
So great the pleasure, so profound the plan!
A banquet this, where men, and angels, meet,
Eat the same manna, mingle earth, and heav'n.
How distant some of these nocturnal suns!
So distant (says the sage,) 'twere not absurd   1225
To doubt, if beams, set out at Nature's birth,
Are yet arriv'd at this so foreign world;
Though nothing half so rapid as their flight.
An eye of awe and wonder let me roll,
And roll for ever: Who can satiate sight   1230
In such a scene? In such an ocean wide
Of deep astonishment? Where depth, height, breadth,
Are lost in their extremes; and where to count
The thick-sown glories in this field of fire,
Perhaps a seraph's computation fails.   1235
Now, go, Ambition! boast thy boundless might
In conquest, o'er the tenth part of a grain.
      And yet LORENZO calls for miracles,
To give his tott'ring faith a solid base.
Why call for less than is already thine?   1240
Thou art no novice in theology;
What is a miracle?—'Tis a reproach,
'Tis an implicit satire, on mankind;
And while it satisfies, it censures too.
To common-sense, great Nature's course proclaims

A Deity: When mankind falls asleep,   1246
A miracle is sent, as an alarm,
To wake the world, and prove Him o'er again,
By recent argument, but not more strong.
Say, which imports more plenitude of pow'r   1250
Or Nature's laws to fix, or to repeal?
To make a sun, or stop his mid-career?
To countermand his orders, and send back
The flaming courier to the frighted East,
Warm'd, and astonish'd, at his ev'ning ray?   1255
Or bid the moon, as with her journey tir'd,
In Ajalon's soft, flow'ry vale repose?
Great things are these; still greater, to create.
From Adam's bow'r look down thro' the whole train
Of miracles;—resistless is their pow'r?   1260
They do not, cannot, more amaze the mind,
Than this, call'd un-miraculous survey,
If duly weigh'd, if rationally seen,
If seen with human eyes. The brute, indeed, 1264
Sees nought but spangles here; the fool, no more.
Say'st thou, " The course of Nature governs all?"
The course of Nature is the art of God.
The miracles thou call'st for, this attest;
For say, could Nature Nature's course controul?
   But miracles apart. who sees Him not,   1270
Nature's Controller, Author, Guide, and End?
Who turns his eye on Nature's midnight face,
But must inquire—" What hand behind the scene,
" What arm almighty, put these wheeling globes
" In motion, and wound up the vast machine? 1275
" Who rounded in his palm these spacious orbs?

" Who bowl'd them flaming through the dark pro-
          " found,
" Num'rous as the glitt'ring gems of morning dew,
" Or sparks from populous cities in a blaze,
" And set the bosom of old Night on fire?   1280
" Peopled her desert, and made horror smile?"
Or, if the military style delight thee
(For stars have fought their battles, leagu'd with Man,)
" Who marshals this bright host? Enrols their names?
" Appoints their posts, their marches, and returns,
" Punctual, at stated periods? Who disbands   1286
" These vet'ran troops, their final duty done,
" If e'er disbanded?"—HE, whose potent word,
Like the loud trumpet, levy'd first their pow'rs
In Night's inglorious empire, where they slept   1290
In beds of darkness; arm'd them with fierce flames,
Arrang'd, and disciplin'd, and cloth'd in gold;
And call'd them out of Chaos to the field,
Where now they war with Vice and Unbelief.
O let us join this army! Joining these,   1295
Will give us hearts intrepid, at that hour,
When brighter flames shall cut a darker night;
When these strong demonstrations of a GOD
Shall hide their heads, or tumble from their spheres,
And one eternal curtain cover all!   1300
    Struck at that thought, as new-awak'd, I lift
A more enlighten'd eye, and read the stars,
To Man still more propitious; and their aid
(Though guiltless of idolatry) implore;
Nor longer rob them of their noblest name.   1305
O ye dividers of my time! ye bright

Accomptants of my days, and months, and years,
In your fair kalendar distinctly mark'd!
Since that authentic, radiant register,   1309
Tho' Man inspect it not, stands good against him;
Since you, and years, roll on, tho' Man stand still;
Teach me my days to number, and apply
My trembling heart to wisdom; now beyond
All shadow of excuse for fooling on.
Age smooths our path to prudence; sweeps aside 1315
The snares, keen appetite, and passion, spread
To catch stray souls; and woe to that grey head,
Whose folly would undo what age has done!
Aid, then, aid, all ye stars!—Much rather, THOU,
Great Artist! THOU, whose finger set aright   1320
This exquisite machine, with all its wheels,
Though intervolv'd, exact; and pointing out
Life's rapid and irrevocable flight,
With such an index fair, as none can miss,
Who lifts an eye, nor sleeps till it is clos'd: 1325
Open mine eye, dread DEITY! to read
The tacit doctrine of thy works; to see
Things as they are, unalter'd through the glass
Of worldly wishes.   Time—Eternity—
('Tis these, mis-measur'd, ruin all mankind,)   1330
Set them before me; let me lay them both
In equal scale, and learn their various weight.
Let Time appear a moment, as it is:
And let Eternity's full orb, at once,
Turn on my soul, and strike it into heav'n.   1335
When shall I see far more than charms me now?
Gaze on creation's model in thy breast
Unveil'd, nor wonder at the transcript more?

When, this vile, foreign, dust, which smothers all
That travel Earth's deep vale, shall I shake off? 1340
When shall my soul her incarnation quit,
And, re-adopted to thy blest embrace,
Obtain her apotheosis in THEE?

    Dost think, LORENZO! this is wand'ring wide?
No, 'tis directly striking at the mark;   1345
To wake thy dead devotion was my point;
And how I bless Night's consecrating shades,
Which to a temple turn an universe;
Fill us with great ideas full of Heav'n,
And antidote the pestilential earth!   1350
In ev'ry storm, that either frowns, or falls,
What an asylum has the soul in pray'r!
And what a fane is this, in which to pray!
And what a GOD must dwell in such a fane!
O what a Genius must inform the skies!   1355
And is LORENZO's salamander-heart
Cold, and untouch'd amid these sacred fires?
O ye nocturnal sparks! ye glowing embers,
On Heav'n's broad hearth! who burn, or burn no more,
Who blaze, or die, as great JEHOVAH's breath   1360
Or blows you, or forbears; assist my song;
Pour your whole influence; exorcise his heart,
So long possest; and bring him back to Man.

    And is LORENZO a demurrer still?
Pride in thy parts provokes thee to contest   1365
Truths, which, contested, put thy parts to shame.
Nor shame they more LORENZO's head than heart;
A faithless heart, how despicably small!
Too strait, aught great, or gen'rous, to receive!
Fill'd with an atom! fill'd, and foul'd, with self! 1370

And self-mistaken! self, that lasts an hour!
Instincts and passions, of the nobler kind,
Lie suffocated there; or they alone,
Reason apart, would wake high hope; and open,
To ravish'd thought, that intellectual sphere,　1375
Where Order, Wisdom, Goodness, Providence,
Their endless miracles of love display,
And promise all, the truly great, desire.
The mind that would be happy, must be great;
Great in its wishes; great in its surveys.　1380
Extended views a narrow mind extend;
Push out its corrugate, expansive make,
Which, ere-long, more than planets shall embrace.
A man of compass makes a man of worth;
Divine contemplate, and become divine.　1385
　　As Man was made for glory, and for bliss,
All littleness is an approach to woe;
Open thy bosom, set thy wishes wide,
And let in manhood; let in happiness;
Admit the boundless theatre of thought .　1390
From nothing, up to GOD; which makes a Man.
Take GOD from Nature, nothing great is left;
Man's mind is in a pit, and nothing sees;
Man's heart is in a jakes, and loves the mire.
Emerge from thy profound; erect thine eye;　1395
See thy distress! How close art thou besieg'd!
Besieg'd by Nature, the proud sceptic's foe!
Inclos'd by these innumerable worlds,
Sparkling conviction on the darkest mind,
As in a golden net of Providence,　1400
How art thou caught, sure captive of belief!
From this thy blest captivity, what art,

What blasphemy to reason, sets thee free!
The scene is Heav'n's indulgent violence:
Canst thou bear up against this tide of glory?   1405
What is earth bosom'd in these ambient orbs,
But, faith in GOD impos'd, and press'd on Man?
Dar'st thou still litigate thy desp'rate cause,
Spite of these num'rous, awful witnesses,
And doubt the deposition of the skies?   1410
O how laborious is thy way to ruin!
        Laborious? 'Tis impracticable quite;
To sink beyond a doubt in this debate,
With all his weight of wisdom, and of will,
And crime flagitious, I defy a fool.   1415
Some wish they did; but no man disbelieves.
GOD is a spirit; spirit cannot strike
These gross, material organs: GOD by Man
As much is seen, as Man a GOD can see,
In these astonishing exploits of pow'r.   1420
What order, beauty, motion, distance, size!
Concertion of design, how exquisite!
How complicate, in their divine police!
Apt means! great ends! consent to gen'ral good!—
Each attribute of these material gods,   1425
So long (and that with specious pleas) ador'd,
A sep'rate conquest gains o'er rebel thought;
And leads in triumph the whole mind of Man.
        LORENZO! this may seem harangue to thee;
Such all is apt to seem, that thwarts our will.   1430
And dost thou, then, demand a simple proof
Of this great master-moral of the skies,
Unskill'd, or disinclin'd, to read it there?
Since 'tis the basis, and all drops without it,

Take it, in one compact, unbroken chain.   1435
Such proof insists on an attentive ear;
'Twill not make one amid a mob of thoughts,
And, for thy notice, struggle with the world.
Retire;—the world shut out;—thy thoughts call home;
Imagination's airy wing repress;—   1440
Lock up thy senses;—let no passion stir;—
Wake all to Reason; let her reign alone;—
Then, in thy soul's deep silence, and the depth
Of Nature's silence, midnight, thus inquire,
As I have done; and shall inquire no more.   1445
In Nature's channel, thus the questions run:

" What am I? And from whence?—I nothing know,
" But that I am; and, since I am, conclude
" Something eternal: Had there e'er been nought,
" Nought still had been: Eternal there must be.—
" But what eternal?—Why not human race?   1450
" And ADAM's ancestors without an end?—
" That's hard to be conceiv'd, since ev'ry link
" Of that long-chain'd succession is so frail;
" Can ev'ry part depend, and not the whole?   1455
" Yet grant it true; new difficulties rise;
" I'm still quite out at sea; nor see the shore.
" Whence earth, and these bright orbs?—Eternal too?
" Grant matter was eternal; still these orbs
" Would want some other Father:—Much design
" Is seen in all their motions, all their makes; 1460
" Design implies intelligence, and art:
" That cant be from themselves—or Man; that art
" Man scarce can comprehend, could Man bestow?
" And nothing greater, yet allow'd, than Man.   1465
" Who, motion, foreign to the smallest grain,

" Shot through vast masses of enormous weight?
" Who bid brute matter's restive lump assume
" Such various forms, and gave it wings to fly?
" Has matter innate motion? Then each atom, 1470
" Asserting its indisputable right
" To dance, would form an universe of dust:
" Has matter none? Then whence these glorious forms,
" And boundless flights, from shapeless, and repos'd?
" Has matter more than motion? Has it thought,
" Judgment, and genius? Is it deeply learn'd 1476
" In mathematics? Has it fram'd such laws,
" Which, but to guess, a NEWTON made immortal?—
" If so, how each sage atom laughs at me,
" Who think a clod inferior to a man! 1480
" If art, to form; and counsel, to conduct;
" And that with greater far than human skill;
" Resides not in each block; a Godhead reigns.—
" Grant, then, invisible, eternal, Mind;
" That granted, all is solv'd.—But, granting that,
" Draw I not o'er me a still darker cloud; 1486
" Grant I not that which I can ne'er conceive?
" A Being without origin, or end!
" Hail, human liberty! There is no GOD—
" Yet, why? On either scheme that knot subsists;
" Subsist it must, in GOD, or human race: 1491
" If in the last, how many knots beside,
" Indissoluble all?—Why choose it there,
" Where, chosen, still subsist ten thousand more?
" Reject it, where, that chosen, all the rest 1495
" Dispers'd, leave Reason's whole horizon clear?
" This is not Reason's dictate; Reason says,
" Close with the side where one grain turns the scale;

" What vast preponderance is here! Can Reason
" With louder voice exclaim—Believe a GOD? 1500
" And Reason heard, is the sole mark of Man.
" What things impossible must Man think true
" On any other system! And how strange
" To disbelieve, through mere credulity!"
 If in this chain LORENZO finds no flaw, 1505
Let it for ever bind him to belief.
And where's the link, in which a flaw he finds?
And, if a GOD there is, that GOD how great!
How great that Pow'r, whose providential care
Through these bright orbs' dark centres darts a ray!
Of Nature universal threads the whole! 1511
And hangs creation, like a precious gem,.
Though little, on the footstool of his throne!
That little gem, how large! A weight let fall
From a fixt star, in ages can it reach 1515
This distant earth? Say then, LORENZO! where,
Where ends this mighty building? Where begin
The suburbs of creation? Where the wall
Whose battlements look o'er into the vale
Of non-existence, Nothing's strange abode? 1520
Say, at what point of space JEHOVAH dropp'd
His slacken'd line, and laid his balance by;
Weigh'd worlds, and measur'd infinite no more?
Where, rears his terminating pillar high
Its extra-mundane head? And says to gods, 1525
In characters illustrious as the sun,
" I stand the plan's proud period; I pronounce
" The work accomplish'd; the creation clos'd:
" Shout, all ye gods! nor shout, ye gods, alone;
" Of all that lives, or, if devoid of life, 1530

" That rests, or rolls, ye heights, and depths, resound!
" Resound! resound! ye depths, and heights, resound!"
    Hard are those questions?   Answer harder still.
Is this the sole exploit, the single birth,
The solitary son of Pow'r divine?   1535
Or has th' ALMIGHTY FATHER, with a breath,
Impregnated the womb of distant space?
Has he not bid, in various provinces,
Brother-creations the dark bowels burst
Of Night primæval; barren, now, no more?   1540
And HE the central sun, transpiercing all
Those giant-generations, which disport,
And dance, as motes, in his meridian ray;
That ray withdrawn, benighted, or absorb'd,
In that abyss of horror, whence they sprung;   1545
While Chaos triumphs, repossest of all
Rival creation ravish'd from his throne?
Chaos! of Nature both the womb and grave!
    Think'st thou, my scheme, LORENZO, spreads too
      wide?
Is this extravagant?—No; this is just;   1550
Just, in conjecture, though 'twere false in fact.
If 'tis an error, 'tis an error sprung
From noble root, high thought of the MOST-HIGH.
But wherefore error? Who can prove it such?—
He that can set Omnipotence a bound.   1555
Can Man conceive beyond what GOD can do?
Nothing, but quite impossible, is hard.
He summons into being, with like ease,
A whole creation, and a single grain.   1559
Speaks HE the word? A thousand worlds are born!
A thousand worlds? There's space for millions more!

And in what space can his great fiat fail?
Condemn me not, cold critic! but indulge
The warm imagination: Why condemn?   1564
Why not indulge such thoughts, as swell our hearts
With fuller admiration of that Pow'r,
Who gives our hearts with such high thoughts to swell?
Why not indulge in his augmented praise?
Darts not his glory a still brighter ray,
The less is left to Chaos, and the realms   1570
Of hideous Night, where Fancy strays aghast;
And, though most talkative, makes no report?

　　Still seems my thought enormous? Think again
Experience' self shall aid thy lame belief.
Glasses (that revelation to the sight!)   1575
Have they not let us deep in the disclose
Of fine-spun Nature, exquisitely small,
And, though demonstrated, still ill-conceiv'd?
If then, on the reverse, the mind would mount
In magnitude, what mind can mount too far,   1580
To keep the balance, and creation poise?
Defect alone can err on such a theme;
What is too great if we the Cause survey?
Stupendous Architect! THOU, THOU art all!
My soul flies up and down in thoughts of THEE, 1585
And finds herself but at the centre still!
I AM, thy name! Existence, all thine own!
Creation's nothing; flatter'd much, if styl'd
" The thin, the fleeting atmosphere of GOD."
　　O for the voice—Of what? Of whom?—What voice
Can answer to my wants, in such ascent,   1591
As dares to deem one universe too small?
Tell me, LORENZO! (for now fancy glows,

Fir'd in the vortex of Almighty Pow'r)
Is not this home-creation, in the map   1595
Of universal Nature, as a speck,
Like fair BRITANNIA in our little ball;
Exceeding fair, and glorious, for its size,
But, elsewhere, far outmeasur'd, far outshone?
In fancy (for the fact beyond us lies)   1600
Canst thou not figure it, an isle, almost
Too small for notice, in the vast of being;
Sever'd by mighty seas of unbuilt space,
From other realms; from ample continents
Of higher life, where nobler natives dwell;   1605
Less northern, less remote from DEITY,
Glowing beneath the line of the SUPREME;
Where souls in excellence make haste, put forth
Luxuriant growths; nor the late autumn wait
Of human worth, but ripen soon to gods?   1610
     Yet why drown fancy in such depths as these?
Return, presumptuous rover! and confess
The bounds of Man; nor blame them, as too small.
Enjoy we not full scope in what is seen?
Full ample the dominions of the sun?   1615
Full glorious to behold! How far, how wide,
The matchless monarch, from his flaming throne,
Lavish of lustre, throws his beams about him,
Farther, and faster, than a thought can fly,
And feeds his planets with eternal fires!   1620
This HELIOPOLIS, by greater far,
Than the proud tyrant of the NILE, was built;
And HE alone, who built it, can destroy.
Beyond this city, why strays human thought?
One wonderful, enough for Man to know!   1625

One infinite, enough for Man to range!
One firmament, enough for Man to read!
O what voluminous instruction here!
What page of wisdom is deny'd him? None;
If learning his chief lesson makes him wise.   1630
Nor is instruction, here, our only gain;
There dwells a noble pathos in the skies,
Which warms our passions, proselytes our hearts.
How eloquently shines the glowing pole!
With what authority it gives its charge!   1635
Remonstrating great truths in style sublime,
Though silent, loud; heard earth around; above
The planets heard; and not unheard in hell:
Hell has her wonder, though too proud to praise.
Is earth, then, more infernal? Has she those,   1640
Who neither praise (LORENZO!) nor admire?
      LORENZO's admiration, pre-engag'd,
Ne'er ask'd the moon one question; never held
Least correspondence with a single star;
Ne'er rear'd an altar to the queen of heav'n   1645
Walking in brightness; or her train ador'd.
Their sublunary rivals have long since
Engross'd his whole devotion; stars malign,
Which made their fond astronomer run mad,
Darken his intellect, corrupt his heart;   1650
Cause him to sacrifice his fame and peace
To momentary madness, call'd delight.
Idolater, more gross than ever kiss'd
The lifted hand to LUNA, or pour'd out
The blood to JOVE!—O THOU, to whom belongs
All sacrifice! O THOU, great JOVE unfeign'd!   1656
Divine Instructor! Thy first volume this,

R R

For Man's perusal; all in capitals!
In moon and stars (Heav'n's golden alphabet!) 1659
Emblaz'd to seize the sight; who runs, may read;
Who reads, can understand. 'Tis unconfin'd
To Christian land, or Jewry; fairly writ,
In language universal, to mankind:
A language, lofty to the learn'd; yet plain   1664
To those that feed the flock, or guide the plough,
Or, from its husk, strike out the bounding grain.
A language, worthy the great MIND, that speaks!
Preface, and comment, to the sacred page!
Which oft refers its reader to the skies,
As pre-supposing his first lesson there,   1670
And scripture-self a fragment, that unread.
Stupendous book of wisdom, to the wise!
— Stupendous book! and open'd, Night! by thee.
      By thee much open'd, I confess, O Night!
Yet more I wish; but how shall I prevail?   1675
Say, gentle Night! whose modest, maiden beams
Give us a new creation, and present
The world's great picture soften'd to the sight;
Nay, kinder far, far more indulgent still,
Say, thou, whose mild dominion's silver key   1680
Unlocks our hemisphere, and sets to view
Worlds beyond number; worlds conceal'd by day
Behind the proud and envious star of noon!
Canst thou not draw a deeper scene?—And shew
The mighty Potentate, to whom belong   1685
These rich regalia pompously display'd
To kindle that high hope? Like him of Uz,
I gaze around; I search on every side—
O for a glimpse of HIM my soul adores!

_____ thou whose mild dominion's silver key

Unlocks our hemisphere, and sets to view

Worlds beyond number;

Page 106

London Published Sept 9th 1797 by T Heptinstall N 304 High Holborn

T Stothard del.   J Neagle sculp.

As the chas'd hart, amid the desert waste,   1690
Pants for the living stream; for HIM who made her,
So pants the thirsty soul, amid the blank
Of sublunary joys.   Say, goddess! where,
Where blazes his bright court? Where burns his throne?
Thou know'st; for thou art near him; by thee, round
His grand pavilion, sacred Fame reports   1696
The sable curtain's drawn.   If not, can none
Of thy fair daughter-train, so swift of wing,
Who travel far, discover where HE dwells?
A star his dwelling pointed out below.   1700
Ye PLEIADES! ARCTURUS! MAZAROTH!
And thou, ORION! of still keener eye!
Say ye, who guide the wilder'd in the waves,
And bring them out of tempest into port!
On which hand must I bend my course to find HIM?
These courtiers keep the secret of their King;   1706
I wake whole nights, in vain, to steal it from them.

    I wake; and waking, climb Night's radiant scale,
From sphere to sphere; the steps by Nature set
For Man's ascent; at once to tempt and aid;   1710
To tempt his eye, and aid his tow'ring thought;
Till it arrives at the great goal of all.
    In ardent Contemplation's rapid car,
From earth, as from my barrier, I set out.
How swift I mount! diminish'd earth recedes;   1715
I pass the moon; and, from her farther side,
Pierce Heav'n's blue curtain; strike into remote;
Where, with his lifted tube, the subtile sage
His artificial, airy journey takes,
And to celestial lengthens human sight.   1720
I pause at ev'ry planet on my road,

And ask for HIM who gives their orbs to roll,
Their foreheads fair to shine.   From SATURN's ring,
In which, of earths an army might be lost,
With the bold comet, take my bolder flight,   1725
Amid those sov'reign glories of the skies,
Of independent, native lustre, proud;
The souls of systems! and the lords of life,
Through their wide empires!—What behold I now?
A wilderness of wonders burning round;   1730
Where larger suns inhabit higher spheres;
Perhaps the villas of descending gods!
Nor halt I here; my toil is but begun;
'Tis but the threshold of the DEITY;
Or, far beneath it, I am groveling still.   1735
Nor is it strange; I built on a mistake;
The grandeur of his works, whence folly sought
For aid, to reason sets his glory higher;
Who built thus high for worms (mere worms to HIM;)
O where, LORENZO! must the Builder dwell?   1740
      Pause, then; and, for a moment, here respire—
If human thought can keep its station here.
Where am I?—Where is earth?—Nay, where art thou,
O Sun?—Is the sun turn'd recluse?—And are
His boasted expeditions short to mine?   1745
To mine, how short! On Nature's ALPS I stand,
And see a thousand firmaments beneath!
A thousand systems! as a thousand grains!
So much a stranger, and so late arriv'd,
How can Man's curious spirit not inquire,   1750
What are the natives of this world sublime,
Of this so foreign, un-terrestrial sphere,
Where mortal, untranslated, never, stray'd?

" O ye, as distant from my little home,

" As swiftest sun-beams in an age can fly!   1755

" Far from my native element I roam,

" In quest of new, and wonderful, to Man.

" What province this, of his immense domain,

" Whom all obey? Or mortals here, or gods?

" Ye bord'rers on the coasts of bliss! what are you?

" A colony from Heav'n? or only rais'd,   1760

" By frequent visit from Heav'n's neighb'ring realms,

" To secondary gods, and half-divine?—

" Whate'er your nature, this is past dispute,

" Far other life you live, far other tongue   1765

" You talk, far other thought, perhaps, you think,

" Than Man.   How various are the works of God!

" But say, What thought? Is reason here enthron'd,

" And absolute? Or sense in arms against her?

" Have you two lights? Or need you no reveal'd?

" Enjoy your happy realms their golden age?   1771

" And had your EDEN an abstemious EVE?

" Our EVE's fair daughters prove their pedigree,

" And ask their ADAMS—' Who would not be wise?'

" Or, if your mother fell, are you redeem'd?   1775

" And if redeem'd—is your REDEEMER scorn'd?

" Is this your final residence? If not,

" Change you your scene, translated? Or by death?

" And if by death; what death?—Know you disease?

" Or horrid war?—With war, this fatal hour,   1780

" EUROPA groans (so call we a small field,

" Where kings run mad.) In our world, Death deputes

" Intemperance to do the work of Age!

" And, hanging up the quiver Nature gave him,

" As slow of execution, for dispatch   1785

" Sends forth imperial butchers; bids them slay
" Their sheep (the silly sheep they fleec'd before,)
" And toss him twice ten thousand at a meal.
" Sit all your executioners on thrones?
" With you, can rage for plunder make a god? 1790
" And bloodshed wash out ev'ry other stain?
" But you, perhaps, can't bleed: From matter gross
" Your spirits clean, are delicately clad
" In fine-spun ether, privileg'd to soar,
" Unloaded, uninfected: How unlike   1795
" The lot of Man! How few of human race
" By their own mud unmurder'd! How we wage
" Self-war eternal!—Is your painful day
" Of hardy conflict o'er? Or, are you still
" Raw candidates at school? And have you those 1800
" Who disaffect reversions, as with us?—
" But what are we? You never heard of Man,
" Or Earth; the bedlam of the universe!
" Where Reason (undiseas'd with you) runs mad,
" And nurses Folly's children as her own;   1805
" Fond of the foulest.   In the sacred mount
" Of holiness, where reason is pronounc'd
" Infallible; and thunders, like a god;
" Ev'n there, by saints the demons are outdone;
" What these think wrong, our saints refine to right!
" And kindly teach dull Hell her own black arts;
" SATAN, instructed, o'er their morals smiles.—
" But this, how strange to you, who know not Man!
" Has the least rumour of our race arriv'd?
" Call'd here ELIJAH, in his flaming car?   1815
" Past by you the good ENOCH, on his road
" To those fair fields, whence LUCIFER was hurl'd;

" Who brush'd, perhaps, your sphere, in his descent,
" Stain'd your pure crystal ether, or let fall
" A short eclipse from his portentous shade?   1820
" O! that the fiend had lodg'd on some broad orb
" Athwart his way; nor reach'd his present home,
" Than blacken'd Earth with footsteps foul'd in Hell,
" Nor wash'd in ocean, as from ROME he past
" To BRITAIN's isle; too, too, conspicuous there!"
    But this is all digression: Where is HE,   1826
That o'er Heav'n's battlements the felon hurl'd
To groans, and chains, and darkness? Where is HE,
Who sees creation's summit in a vale?
HE, whom, while Man is Man, he can't but seek;
And if he finds, commences more than Man?   1831
O for a telescope his throne to reach!
Tell me, ye learn'd on earth! or blest above!
Ye searching, ye Newtonian angels tell! tell,
Where's your great Master's orb? His planets, where?
Those conscious satellites, those morning-stars,   1836
First-born of DEITY! from central love,
By veneration most profound, thrown off;
By sweet attraction, no less strongly drawn;
Aw'd, and yet raptur'd; raptur'd, yet serene;   1840
Past thought, illustrious, but with borrow'd beams;
In still approaching circles still remote,
Revolving round the sun's eternal Sire?
Or sent, in lines direct on embassies
To nations—in what latitude?—Beyond   1845
Terrestrial thought's horizon!—And on what
High errands sent?—Here human effort ends;
And leaves me still a stranger to his throne.

Full well it might! I quite mistook my road.
Born in an age more curious than devout;   1850
More fond to fix the place of heav'n, or hell,
Than studious this to shun, or that secure.
'Tis not the curious, but the pious path,
That leads me to my point: LORENZO! know,
Without or star, or angel, for their guide,   1855
Who worship GOD, shall find him.   Humble Love,
And not proud Reason, keeps the door of Heav'n;
Love finds admission where proud Science fails.
Man's science is the culture of his heart;
And not to lose his plummet in the depths   1860
Of Nature, or the more profound of GOD.
Either to know, is an attempt that sets
The wisest on a level with the fool.
To fathom Nature (ill-attempted here!)
Past doubt, is deep philosophy above;   1865
Higher degrees in bliss archangels take,
As deeper learn'd; the deepest, learning still.
For, what a thunder of Omnipotence
(So might I dare to speak!) is seen in all!
In Man! in earth! in more amazing skies!   1870
Teaching this lesson, Pride is loth to learn
   " Not deeply to discern, not much to know;
   " Mankind was born to wonder, and adore."
    And is there cause for higher wonder still,
Than that which struck us from our past surveys?
Yes; and for deeper adoration too.   1876
From my late airy travel unconfin'd,
Have I learn'd nothing? Yes, LORENZO! this;
Each of these stars is a religious house;

I saw their altars smoke, their incense rise,   1880
And heard Hosannas ring through ev'ry sphere,
A seminary fraught with future gods.
Nature all o'er is consecrated ground,
Teeming with growths immortal, and divine.
The great Proprietor's all-bounteous hand   1885
Leaves nothing waste; but sows these fiery fields
With seeds of reason, which to virtues rise
Beneath his genial ray; and, if escap'd
The pestilential blasts of stubborn will,
When grown mature, are gather'd for the skies. 1890
And is devotion thought too much on earth,
When beings, so superior, homage boast,
And triumph in prostrations to the Throne?
    But wherefore more of planets, or of stars?
Ethereal journies, and, discover'd there,   1895
Ten thousand worlds, ten thousand ways devout,
All Nature sending incense to the Throne,
Except the bold LORENZO's of our sphere?
Op'ning the solemn sources of my soul,
Since I have pour'd, like feign'd ERIDANUS,   1900
My flowing numbers o'er the flaming skies,
Nor see, of fancy, or of fact, what more
Invites the muse—Here turn we, and review
Our past nocturnal landscape wide:—Then say,
Say, then, LORENZO! with what burst of heart, 1905
The whole, at once, revolving in his thought,
Must Man exclaim, adoring, and aghast?
" O what a root! O what a branch is here!
" O what a father! what a family!
" Worlds! systems! and creations!—And creations,
" In one agglomerated cluster, hung,   1911
                    S S

" Great Vine, on THEE, on THEE the cluster hangs;
" The filial cluster! infinitely spread
" In glowing globes, with various being fraught;
" And drinks (nectareous draught!) immortal life.
" Or, shall I say (for who can say enough?)   1916
" A constellation of ten thousand gems,
" (And, O! of what dimension! of what weight!)
" Set in one signet, flames on the right-hand
" Of Majesty Divine! The blazing zeal,   1920
" That deeply stamps, on all created mind,
" Indelible, his sov'reign attributes,
" Omnipotence, and love! That, passing bound:
" And this, surpassing that. Nor stop we here, 1924
" For want of pow'r in GOD, but thought in Man.
" Ev'n this acknowledg'd, leaves us still in debt;
" If greater aught, that greater all is thine,
" Dread SIRE!—Accept this miniature of THEE;
" And pardon an attempt from mortal thought,
" In which archangels might have fail'd, unblam'd."
        How such ideas of th' ALMIGHTY's pow'r,   1931
And such ideas of th' ALMIGHTY's plan,
(Ideas not absurd) distend the thought
Of feeble mortals! Nor of them alone!
The fulness of the DEITY breaks forth   1935
In inconceivables to men, and gods.
Think, then, O think; nor ever drop the thought;
How low must Man descend, when Gods adore!
Have I not, then, accomplish'd my proud boast?
Did I not tell thee, " We would mount, LORENZO!
" And kindle our devotion at the stars?"   1941
        And have I fail'd? And did I flatter thee?
And art all adamant? And dost confute

All urg'd with one irrefragable smile?
LORENZO! Mirth how miserable here!　　　1945
Swear by the stars, by HIM who made them, swear,
Thy heart, henceforth, shall be as pure as they:
Then thou, like them, shalt shine; like them, shalt rise
From low to lofty; from obscure to bright;
By due gradation, Nature's sacred law.　　　1950
The stars, from whence?—Ask Chaos—He can tell.
These bright temptations to idolatry,
From darkness, and confusion, took their birth;
Sons of Deformity! From fluid dregs
Tartarean, first they rose to masses rude:　　　1955
And then, to spheres opaque; then dimly shone;
Then brighten'd; then blaz'd out in perfect day.
Nature delights in progress; in advance
From worse to better: But, when minds ascend,
Progress, in part, depends upon themselves.　　　1960
Heav'n aids exertion; greater makes the great;
The voluntary little lessens more.
O be a man! and thou shalt be a god!
And half self-made!—Ambition how divine!

　O thou, ambitious of disgrace alone!　　　1965
Still undevout? Unkindled?—Though high-taught,
School'd by the skies; and pupil of the stars;
Rank coward to the fashionable world!
Art thou asham'd to bend thy knee to heav'n?
Curst fume of pride, exhal'd from deepest hell! 1970
Pride in religion is Man's highest praise.
Bent on destruction! and in love with death!
Not all these luminaries, quench'd at once,
Were half so sad, as one benighted mind,
Which gropes for happiness, and meets despair. 1975

How, like a widow in her weeds, the Night,
Amid her glimm'ring tapers, silent sits!
How sorrowful, how desolate, she weeps
Perpetual dews, and saddens Nature's scene!
A scene more sad sin makes the darken'd soul,   1980
All comfort kills, nor leaves one spark alive.

　　Though blind of heart, still open is thine eye:
Why such magnificence in all thou seest?
Of matter's grandeur, know, one end is this,
To tell the rational, who gazes on it—   1985
" Though that immensely great, still greater He,
" Whose breast, capacious, can embrace, and lodge,
" Unburden'd, Nature's universal scheme;
" Can grasp creation with a single thought;
" Creation grasp; and not exclude its SIRE."— 1990
To tell him farther—" It behoves him much
" To guard th' important, yet depending, fate
" Of being, brighter than a thousand suns:
" One single ray of thought outshines them all."—
And if Man hears obedient, soon he'll soar   1995
Superior heights, and on his purple wing,
His purple wing bedropp'd with eyes of gold,
Rising, where thought is now deny'd to rise,
Look down triumphant on these dazzling spheres.

　　Why then persist?—No mortal ever liv'd   2000
But, dying, he pronounc'd (when words are true!)
The whole that charms thee, absolutely vain;
Vain, and far worse!—Think thou, with dying men;
O condescend to think as angels think!
O tolerate a chance for happiness!   2005
Our nature such, ill choice ensures ill fate;
And hell had been, though there had been no God.

Dost thou not know, my new astronomer!
Earth, turning from the sun, brings night to Man?
Man, turning from his God, brings endless night;
Where thou canst read no morals, find no friend,
Amend no manners, and expect no peace.
How deep the darkness! and the groan, how loud!
And far, how far, from lambent are the flames!
Such is LORENZO's purchase! such his praise! 2015
The proud, the politic, LORENZO's praise!
Though in his ear, and levell'd at his heart,
I've half read o'er the volume of the skies.

For think not thou hast heard all this from me;
My song but echoes what great Nature speaks. 2020
What has she spoken? Thus the Goddess spoke,
Thus speaks for ever—" Place, at Nature's head,
" A sov'reign which o'er all things rolls his eye,
" Extends his wing, promulgates his commands,
" But, above all, diffuses endless good;   2025
" To whom, for sure redress, the wrong'd may fly;
" The vile, for mercy; and the pain'd, for peace:
" By whom, the various tenants of these spheres,
" Diversify'd in fortunes, place, and pow'rs,
" Rais'd in enjoyment, as in worth they rise,   2030
" Arrive at length (if worthy such approach)
" At that blest Fountain-head, from which they stream;
" Where conflict past redoubles present joy;
" And present joy looks forward on increase;
" And that, on more; no period! ev'ry step   2035
" A double boon! a promise and a bliss."
How easy sits this scheme on human hearts!
It suits their make; it soothes their vast desires;
Passion is pleas'd, and Reason asks no more;

'Tis rational, 'tis great!—But what is thine?　　2040
It darkens! shocks! excruciates! and confounds!
Leaves us quite naked, both of help and hope,
Sinking from bad to worse; few years, the sport
Of fortune; then the morsel of despair.　　2044
　　Say, then, LORENZO! (for thou know'st it well)
What's Vice?—Mere want of compass in our thought.
Religion, what?—The proof of common sense;
How art thou whooted, where the least prevails!
Is it my fault, if these truths call thee fool?
And thou shalt never be miscall'd by me.　　2050
Can neither shame nor terror stand thy friend?
And art thou still an insect in the mire?
How, like thy guardian angel, have I flown;
Snatch'd thee from earth; escorted thee through all
Th' ethereal armies; walk'd thee, like a God,　2055
Through splendours of first magnitude, arrang'd
On either hand; clouds thrown beneath thy feet;
Close-cruis'd on the bright paradise of GOD;
And almost introduc'd thee to the Throne!
And art thou still carousing for delight,　　2060
Rank poison; first, fermenting to mere froth,
And then subsiding into final gall?
To beings of sublime, immortal make,
How shocking is all joy, whose end is sure!
Such joy more shocking still, the more it charms!
And dost thou chuse what ends are well begun, 2066
And infamous, as short? And dost thou chuse
(Thou, to whose palate glory is so sweet)
To wade into perdition, through contempt,
Not of poor bigots only, but thy own?　　2070
For I have peep'd into thy cover'd heart,

And seen it blush beneath a boastful brow;
For, by strong guilt's most violent assault,
Conscience is but disabled, not destroy'd.
   O thou most awful being, and most vain!   2075
Thy will, how frail! how glorious is thy pow'r!
Though dread Eternity has sown her seeds
Of bliss, and woe, in thy despotic breast;
Though Heav'n, and Hell, depend upon thy choice!
A butterfly comes cross, and both are fled.   2080
Is this the picture of a rational?
This horrid image, shall it be most just?
LORENZO! No: It cannot—shall not, be,
If there is force in reason; or, in sounds,
Chanted beneath the glimpses of the moon,   2085
A magic, at this planetary hour,
When slumber locks the gen'ral lip, and dreams,
Through senseless mazes, hunt souls uninspir'd.
Attend—The sacred mysteries begin—
My solemn night-born adjuration hear: 2090
Hear, and I'll raise thy spirit from the dust;
While the stars gaze on this enchantment new;
Enchantment, not infernal, but divine!
   " By Silence, Death's peculiar attribute;
" By Darkness, Guilt's inevitable doom;   2095
" By Darkness, and by Silence, sisters dread!
" That draw the curtain round Night's ebon throne,
" And raise ideas, solemn as the scene!
" By Night, and all of awful, Night presents   2099
" To thought, or sense; (of awful much, to both,
" The goddess brings!) By these her trembling fires,
" Like VESTA's, ever burning; and, like her's,
" Sacred to thoughts immaculate, and pure!

" By these bright orators, that prove, and praise,

" And press thee to revere the DEITY;   2105

" Perhaps, too, aid thee, when rever'd awhile,

" To reach his throne; as stages of the soul,

" Through which, at diff'rent periods, she shall pass,

" Refining gradual, for her final height,

" And purging off some dross at ev'ry sphere!   2100

" By this dark pall thrown o'er the silent world!

" By the world's kings, and kingdoms, most renown'd,

" From short ambition's zenith set for ever;

" Sad presage to vain boasters, now in bloom!

" By the long list of swift mortality,   2115

" From ADAM downward to this ev'ning knell,

" Which midnight waves in Fancy's startled eye;

" And shocks her with an hundred centuries,

" Round Death's black banner throng'd, in human
      " thought?

" By thousands, now, resigning their last breath,

" And calling thee—wert thou so wise to hear! 2121

" By tombs o'er tombs arising; human earth

" Ejected, to make room for—human earth;

" The monarch's terror! and the sexton's trade!

" By pompous obsequies, that shun the day,   2125

" The torch funereal, and the nodding plume,

" Which makes poor Man's humiliation proud;

" Boast of our ruin! triumph of our dust!

" By the damp vault that weeps o'er royal bones;

" And the pale lamp that shews the ghastly dead,

" More ghastly, through the thick incumbent gloom!

" By visits (if there are) from darker scenes,

" The gliding spectre! and the groaning grave!

" By groans, and graves, and miseries that groan

" For the grave's shelter! By desponding men, 2135
" Senseless to pains of death, from pangs of guilt!
" By guilt's last audit! by yon moon in blood,
" The rocking firmament, the falling stars,
" And thunder's last discharge, great Nature's knell!
" By second Chaos; and eternal night"—   2140
Be wise—Nor let PHILANDER blame my charm;
But own not ill-discharg'd my double debt,
Love to the living; duty to the dead.

   For know, I'm but executor; he left
This moral legacy! I make it o'er   2145
By his command; PHILANDER hear in me;
And heav'n in both.—If deaf to these, Oh! hear
FLORELLO's tender voice; his weal depends
On thy resolve; it trembles at thy choice;
For his sake—love thyself: Example strikes   2150
All human hearts; a bad example more;
More still a father's; that ensures his ruin.
As parent of his being, wouldst thou prove
Th' unnatural parent of his miseries,
And make him curse the being which thou gav'st?
Is this the blessing of so fond a father?   2156
If careless of LORENZO, spare, oh! spare,
FLORELLO's father, and PHILANDER's friend;
FLORELLO's father ruin'd, ruins him:
And from PHILANDER's friend the world expects
A conduct, no dishonour to the dead.   2161
Let passion do, what nobler motive should;
Let love, and emulation, rise in aid
To reason; and persuade thee to be—blest.

   This seems not a request to be deny'd;   2165
Yet (such th' infatuation of mankind!

T T

'Tis the most hopeless, Man can make to Man.
Shall I, then, rise in argument, and warmth;
And urge PHILANDER's posthumous advice,
From topics yet unbroach'd?—   2170
But oh! I faint! My spirits fail!—Nor strange!
So long on wing, and in no middle clime; ˙
To which my great Creator's glory call'd:
And calls—but, now, in vain. Sleep's dewy wand
Has strok'd my drooping lids, and promises   2175
My long arrear of rest; the downy god
(Wont to return with our returning peace)
Will pay, ere long, and bless me with repose.
Haste, haste, sweet stranger! from the peasant's cot,
The ship-boy's hammock, or the soldier's straw, 2180
Whence sorrow never chas'd thee; with thee bring,
Not hideous visions, as of late, but draughts
Delicious of well-tasted, cordial rest;
Man's rich restorative; his balmy bath,
That supples, lubricates, and keeps in play,   2185
The various movements of this nice machine,
Which asks such frequent periods of repair.
When tir'd with vain rotations of the day,
Sleep winds us up for the succeeding dawn;
Fresh we spin on, till sickness clogs our wheels, 2190
Or death quite breaks the spring, and motion ends.
When will it end with me?

———" THOU only know'st!

" THOU! whose broad eye, the future and the past,
" Joins to the present! making one of three   2195
" To mortal thought! THOU know'st, and THOU alone,

" All-knowing!—all unknown!—and yet well known!
" Near, though remote! and, though unfathom'd, felt!
" And, though invisible, for ever seen!
" And seen in all! the great, and the minute; 2200
" Each globe above, with its gigantic race,
" Each flower, each leaf, with its small people swarm'd,
" (Those puny vouchers of Omnipotence!)
" To the first thought, that asks, ' From whence?'
  " declare
" Their common Source. Thou Fountain running o'er
" In rivers of communicated joy!   2206
" Who gav'st us speech for far, far humbler themes!
" Say, by what name shall I presume to call
" Him I see burning in these countless suns,
" As Moses in the bush? Illustrious Mind!   2210
" The whole creation, less, far less, to THEE,
" Than that to the creation's ample round.
" How shall I name THEE?—How my labouring soul
" Heaves underneath the thought, too big for birth!
 " Great System of perfections! Mighty Cause 2215
" Of causes mighty! Cause uncaus'd! sole Root
" Of Nature, that luxuriant growth of GOD!
" First Father of effects! that progeny
" Of endless series; where the golden chain's
" Last link admits a period, who can tell?   2220
" Father of all that is or heard, or hears!
" Father of all that is or seen, or sees:
" Father of all that is, or shall arise!
" Father of this immeasurable mass
" Of matter multiform; or dense, or rare: 2225
" Opaque, or lucid; rapid, or at rest;
" Minute, or passing bound! In each extreme

" Of like amaze, and mystery, to Man.
" Father of these bright millions of the night!
" Of which the least full godhead had proclaim'd,
" And thrown the gazer on his knee—Or, say, 2231
" Is appellation higher still, thy choice?
" Father of matter's temporary lords!
" Father of spirits! nobler offspring! sparks
" Of high paternal glory; rich-endow'd   2235
" With various measures, and with various modes
" Of instinct, reason, intuition; beams
" More pale, or bright from day divine, to break
" The dark of matter organiz'd (the ware
" Of all created spirit;) beams, that rise   2240
" Each over other in superior light,
" Till the last ripens into lustre strong,
" Of next approach to Godhead.   Father fond
" (Far fonder than e'er bore that name on earth)
" Of intellectual beings! beings blest   2245
" With pow'rs to please THEE; not of passive ply
" To laws they know not; beings lodg'd in seats
" Of well-adapted joys, in diff'rent domes
" Of this imperial palace for thy sons;
" Of this proud, populous, well policy'd,   2250
" Though boundless habitation, plann'd by THEE;
" Whose several clans their several climates suit;
" And transposition, doubtless, would destroy.
" Or, oh; indulge, immortal King! indulge
" A title, less august indeed, but more   2255
" Endearing; ah! how sweet in human ears!
" Sweet in our ears, and triumph in our hearts!
" Father of immortality to Man!
" A theme that lately set my soul on fire.—   2259

" And THOU the next! yet equal! THOU, by whom
" That blessing was convey'd; far more! was bought;
" Ineffable the price! by whom all worlds
" Were made; and one, redeem'd! Illustrious light
" From light illustrious! THOU, whose regal power,
" Finite in time, but infinite in space,   2265
" On more than adamantine basis fix'd,
" O'er more, far more, than diadems, and thrones,
" Inviolably reigns; the dread of gods!
" And oh! the Friend of Man! beneath whose foot,
" And by the mandate of whose awful nod,   2270
" All regions, revolutions, fortunes, fates,
" Of high, of low, of mind, and matter, roll
" Through the short channels of expiring time,
" Or shoreless ocean of eternity,
" Calm, or tempestuous (as Thy Spirit breathes,)
" In absolute subjection!—And, O THOU   2276
" The glorious Third! distinct, not separate!
" Beaming from both! with both incorporate!
" And (strange to tell!) incorporate with dust!
" By condescension, as thy glory, great,   2280
" Enshrin'd in Man! of human hearts, if pure,
" Divine inhabitant! the tie divine
" Of heav'n with distant earth! by whom, I trust,
" (If not inspir'd) uncensur'd this address   2284
" To THEE, to Them—To whom? Mysterious Power!
" Reveal'd—yet unreveal'd! Darkness in light!
" Number in unity! Our joy! Our dread!
" The triple bolt that lays all wrong in ruin!
" That animates all right, the triple sun!
" Sun of the soul! her never-setting sun!   2290
" Triune, unutterable, unconceiv'd,

" Absconding, yet demonstrable, Great GOD!

" Greater than greatest; better than the best!

" Kinder than kindest! with soft Pity's eye

" Or (stronger still to speak it) with thine own,   2295

" From thy bright home, from that high firmament,

" Where THOU, from all eternity, hast dwelt;

" Beyond archangels' unassisted ken;

" From far above what mortals highest call;

" From elevation's pinnacle; look down   2300

" Through—What? Confounding interval! Through
     " all,

" And more than lab'ring fancy can conceive;

" Through radiant ranks of essences unknown;

" Through hierarchies from hierarchies detach'd

" Round various banners of Omnipotence,   2305

" With endless change of rapt'rous duties fir'd;

" Through wondrous beings interposing swarms,

" All clust'ring at the call, to dwell in THEE;

" Through this wide waste of worlds; this vista vast,

" All sanded o'er with suns; suns turn'd to night

" Before thy feeblest beam—Look down—down—
     " down,   2311

" On a poor breathing particle in dust,

" Or, lower,—an immortal in his crimes.

" His crimes forgive! forgive his virtues, too!

" Those smaller faults, half-converts to the right. 2315

" Nor let me close these eyes, which never more

" May see the sun (though night's descending scale

" Now weighs up morn), unpity'd, and unblest!

" In thy displeasure dwells eternal pain;

" Pain, our aversion; pain, which strikes me now;

" And, since all pain is terrible to Man,   2321

" Though transient, terrible; at thy good hour,
" Gently, ah gently, lay me in my bed,
" My clay-cold bed! by nature, now, so near;
" By nature, near; still nearer by disease!　　2325
" Till then, be this, an emblem of my grave:
" Let it out-preach the preacher; ev'ry night
" Let it out-cry the boy at PHILIP's ear;
" That tongue of death! that herald of the tomb!
" And when (the shelter of thy wing implor'd) 2330
" My senses, sooth'd, shall sink in soft repose;
" O sink this truth still deeper in my soul,
" Suggested by my pillow, sign'd by fate,
" First, in Fate's volume, at the page of Man— 2334
" Man's sickly soul, though turn'd and toss'd for ever,
" From side to side, can rest on nought but THEE;
" Here, in full trust; hereafter in full joy;—
" On THEE, the promis'd, sure, eternal down
" Of spirits, toil'd in travel through this vale.
" Nor of that pillow shall my soul despond;　　2340
" For—Love Almighty! Love Almighty! (sing,
" Exult, Creation!) Love Almighty, reigns!
" That death of death! that cordial of despair!
" And loud Eternity's triumphant song!　　2344
　　" Of whom no more: For, O Thou Patron-God!
" Thou GOD and Mortal! thence more GOD to Man!
" Man's theme eternal! Man's eternal theme!
" Thou canst not 'scape uninjur'd from our praise.
" Uninjur'd from our praise can he escape,
" Who, disembosom'd from the FATHER, bows 2350
" The heaven of heav'n's, to kiss, the distant earth!
" Breathes out in agonies a sinless soul!
" Against the cross, Death's iron sceptre breaks!

" From famish'd Ruin plucks her human prey!
" Throws wide the gates celestial to his foes!   2355
" Their gratitude, for such a boundless debt,
" Deputes their suff'ring brothers to receive!
" And, if deep human guilt in payment fails;
" As deeper guilt prohibits our despair!
" Injoins it, as our duty, to rejoice!   2360
" And (to close all) omnipotently kind,
" Takes his delight among the sons of men?"
    What words are these!—And did they come from
        Heav'n?
And were they spoke to Man? to guilty Man?
What are all mysteries to love like this!   2365
The song of angels, all the melodies
Of choral gods, are wafted in the sound;
Heal and exhilarate the broken heart,
Though plung'd, before, in horrors dark as night:
Rich prelibation of consummate joy!   2370
Nor wait we dissolution to be blest.
    This final effort of the moral muse,
How justly titled! Not for me alone;
For all that read; what spirit of support,
What heights of CONSOLATION crown my song!   2375
    Then farewell NIGHT! Of darkness, now, no more:
Joy breaks; shines; triumphs; 'tis eternal day.
Shall that which rises out of nought complain
Of a few evils, paid with endless joys?
My soul! henceforth, in sweetest union join   2380
The two supports of human happiness,
Which some, erroneous, think can never meet;
True taste of life, and constant thought of death;
The thought of death, sole victor of its dread!

Hope be thy joy; and probity thy skill;
Thy patron HE, whose diadem has dropp'd
Yon gems of heaven; Eternity, thy prize:　　2385
And leave the racers of the world their own,
Their feather, and their froth, for endless toils:
They part with all for that which is not bread;
They mortify, they starve, on wealth, fame, power;
And laugh to scorn the fools that aim at more.　2390
How must a spirit, late escap'd from earth,
Suppose PHILANDER's, LUCIA's, or NARCISSA's,
The truth of things new blazing in its eye,
Look back, astonish'd, on the ways of men,
Whose lives' whole drift is to forget their graves!
And when our present privilege is past,　　2396
To scourge us with due sense of its abuse,
The same astonishment will seize us all.
What then must pain us, would preserve us now.
LORENZO! 'tis not yet too late: LORENZO!　2400
Seize wisdom, ere 'tis torment to be wise;
That is, seize wisdom, ere she seizes thee.
For, what, my small philosopher! is hell?
'Tis nothing, but full knowledge of the truth,
When Truth, resisted long, is sworn our foe;　2405
And calls Eternity to do her right.
　Thus, darkness aiding intellectual light,
And sacred silence whisp'ring truths divine,
And truths divine converting pain to peace,
My song the midnight raven has outwing'd,　2410
And shot, ambitious of unbounded scenes,
Beyond the flaming limits of the world,
Her gloomy flight.　But what avails the flight
Of fancy, when our hearts remain below?

Virtue abounds in flatterers, and foes;   2415
'Tis pride, to praise her; penance, to perform.
To more than words, to more than worth of tongue,
LORENZO! rise, at this auspicious hour;
An hour, when Heav'n's most intimate with Man;
When, like a falling star, the ray divine   2420
Glides swift into the bosom of the just;
And just are all, determin'd to reclaim;
Which sets that title high, within thy reach.
Awake then, thy PHILANDER calls: Awake!   2424
Thou, who shalt wake, when the creation sleeps;
When, like a taper, all these suns expire;
When Time, like him of GAZA in his wrath,
Plucking the pillars that support the world,
In Nature's ample ruins lies intomb'd;
And Midnight, universal Midnight! reigns.   2430

NOTES,

CRITICAL AND EXPLANATORY,

ON

THE NIGHT THOUGHTS.

———————

CRITICISM has two leading objects; the one to point out the latent beauties of an author, which are apt to escape the observation of common readers; the other to detect his blemishes and defects. Though this last is far less agreeable to a liberal mind than the other, and has often the appearance of invidiousness, it is certainly the most useful, when done with candour and good humour; and it is to this species of criticism that many owe their excellence in composition, and some of the best writers have not blushed to acknowledge it.

Both these objects will be kept in view in the following Notes; and to these a third added, that of explaining such allusions as may appear obscure, and of supplying such facts and observations as may be necessary to elucidate the text.

———————

NIGHT I.

THE First Night was published in 1742, and is addressed to Arthur Onslow, Esq. then, and many years afterward, Speaker of the House of Commons; a situation which he supported with great reputation and respectability.

The opening of this Poem, though it has been objected to, I cannot help reckoning among its beauties; and the description of 'Night' upon her throne of ebony, is certainly poetical and sublime.

Though Young has less of imitation than any of our poets, these words, 'if dreams infest the grave,' (line 6) bring to our immediate recollection that fine passage of SHAKESPEARE in his HAMLET:

'———————To die;—to sleep;—
' To sleep! perchance to dream! aye, there's the rub;
' For in that sleep of death what dreams may come,
' When we have shuffled off this mortal coil,
' Must give us pause.'———————

It is difficult to be sublime, without bordering upon the extravagant : Young found it so. Line 15 introduces a sentiment far too hyperbolical. Another poet would have thought it sufficient to have said, his fate was ' dark as midnight,' but Young complains,

> '———————————And night,
> ' Ev'n in the zenith of her dark domain,
> ' Is *sunshine* to the colour of my fate:'

And all this on account only of an affliction common to human nature, the bereavement of his family.

Lines 29 and 30. We have a striking incongruity and confusion in the metaphors. Silence and darkness are said to

> '———————————*Nurse* the tender thought
> ' To reason, and on reason *build* resolve,'

Which resolve again is reckoned a

> ' Column of true majesty in man.'

The term *nurse* should have been exchanged for some other more applicable to building, as to *raise* or rear : Thus Pope,

> To *rear* the tender thought.

Line 39. There is something mean, though aspiring to grandeur, in comparing the creation of the sun to the striking a light with a tinder-box :

> ' O THOU! whose word from solid darkness *struck*
> ' That *spark*, the sun.'————

Nor is the application of the same figure to the *striking a light* in the *soul* (line 40) more happy. How much more dignified is the simple language of the inspired writer.

> He said—' Let light be, and light was.'

Another term censurable for its meanness occurs in line 105, where we are told

> ' For human weal Heav'n *husbands* all events.'

Which suggests a comparison between the conduct of Divine Providence, and the frugal management of a private family ; a comparison not very honourable to Deity, nor very consistent with some other parts of the poem, in which nature is supposed rather to be prodigal than parsimonious in her proofs and evidence.

Notwithstanding these blemishes, the First Night contains several passages of peculiar merit. The passage at line 55, beginning,

> ' The bell strikes one'————————

Is peculiarly forcible and solemn.

The paradox in human nature, line 68 and sequel, is a good specimen of our author's skill in the antithesis, which is his favourite figure. It may be too much dilated ; but in many parts it is striking and beautiful, and there is a world of import in this line,

> ' O what a miracle is man to man!'

One of Young's most conspicuous faults, is the crowding his images too fast on the imagination, as in line 123 and sequel, where the present life is considered as the bud—the dawn—the vestibule—the embryo of our future being; all which ideas, however, have their beauty, particularly the last, in which man, in his present state, is compared to an insect sleeping in its shell—till death bursts his confinement, and opens the way to immortality; like the moth and butterfly, when they first expand their wings, drop the worm in which they had been entombed, and sail at liberty in the open atmosphere.

The comparison (line 164 and sequel) between human life and a dream, though not new, is well wrought.

The answer to this question, ' Where is to-morrow?' (line 375) is pointed and poetic. And the reflections on procrastination, (line 390 and sequel) just, and for the most part, excellent.

Whoever was intended by PHILANDER, we learn that he died suddenly.

Line 384.—' ———A warning was denied.'

Line 430.—' Dark, tho' not blind like thee *Mæonides!*
            ' Or *Milton*, thee.'———————

MÆONIDES is a poetic name for Homer, who, as well as Milton, was blind in the latter part of his life.

It was POPE ' who made Mæonides our own,' (line 452) though the expression would now much better apply to Mr. COWPER.

From a letter preserved in JOHNSON, there appears to have subsisted an acquaintance, if not a friendship, between Pope and Young, [See Johnson, p. 366.] and that the latter requested from the former a prologue to one of his plays, which however does not appear to have been granted.

NIGHT II.

THIS is inscribed to the Earl of WILMINGTON. Our author has been accused, and not without reason, of flattery to the great: but when the charge has been carried to profaneness, as far as the Night Thoughts are in question, it appears unfounded. The famous line,

' And laughs at *Heaven*, O *Wilmington*, and thee.'

Appears simply to mean that this nobleman was on the side of heaven and virtue, and therefore exposed to the scorn of fools.

Line 1. " When the cock crew, he wept:" *i. e.* Peter. See Luke xxii. 60, 61.—SHAKESPEARE has some beautiful reflections upon ' the cock—the trumpet to the morn,' in Hamlet.

Line 40.—' That time is mine, O *Mead!* to thee I owe.'

The author appears to have been just recovered from a fit of illness, by the assistance of the celebrated Dr. *Mead*, then in full practice and high esteem.

Line 99.—" I've lost a day"—the prince who nobly cry'd :'

i. e. Vespasian, who thus exclaimed, whenever he let a day pass without some meritorious action.

Line 129.—' —————————As *Atlas* groan'd
' The world beneath.'——

Atlas, a son of Jupiter and King of Mauritania, for his skill in astrology, was poetically said to bear the globe upon his shoulders. He was supposed, in the heathen mythology, to be afterwards changed into a mountain. The fact is, *Atlas* is a ridge of high mountains whose tops are covered with the clouds, whence they were said poetically to support the heavens.

Line 139.—' Time in advance,' &c.

This picture of time is beautiful, and clear of our Author's too frequent fault—minuteness: which is always inimical to the sublime. Nor is the comparison (line 213) of ' hours, days, months, and years,' to the ' unequal plumes' that compose his ' ample pinions,' without its beauties, though there is some confusion of metaphor in the preceding lines.

Line 172.—' Lavish of *lustrums*,'

i. e. of sacrifices. The meaning is, though fond of life, we waste it in foolish sacrifices to vanity and trifles.

Line 256.—' O treacherous conscience !'

This is another beautiful portrait, which shews the hand of a master; and the succeeding idea of Death's reading the memorandums of Conscience to the dying, is original and striking.

The comparison between Night and Death, (line 286 and sequel) though not new is well conducted, and the subsequent lines exhibit an uncommon strength of language, as well as sublimity of ideas.

Line 406.—' Portentous as the written wall.'

The reader who unhappily knows but little of his Bible, may see the affecting narrative here alluded to, in the 5th chapter of Daniel.

There are several other fine passages in this poem, but I shall only point out the pathetic scene of a good man's death: which is finely drawn at line 633, and properly improved in the last paragraph but one. It is indeed a most important and instructive sight:

' Christians adore, and infidels believe.'

But, alas! how industrious are mankind to avoid, or to forget, rather than to improve it.

NIGHT III.

THIS Night was originally inscribed to the Dutchess of P———
which by line 46 must be PORTLAND, this lady it seems, at a recent
masquerade given by the Duke of Norfolk, hád worn the character of
CYNTHIA, or the Moon, (see line 29) and was therefore, the Author
hints, more properly selected as a patroness of Night Thoughts.

The character of NARCISSA, supposed to be Mrs. TEMPLE *, is
drawn with exquisite delicacy and tenderness, and while her loss was
yet fresh upon his memory, and his feelings still ' tremblingly alive.'—
I have already expressed a suspicion of Mr. Croft's dates †, and upon
reviewing the subject, I am strongly disposed to believe that PHI-
LANDER (Mr. Temple) died before his amiable NARCISSA; not only
because the poet has given this order to the events, but also because
we hear nothing of his accompanying her abroad, which it seems
natural to expect he would have done rather than her father, or at least
in company with him.

> Line 81.—' Sweet harmonist,' &c.

This is one of the finest examples of the figure of repetition I ever
remember to have read. And there is also a peculiar softness and
melody in the language.

> Line 116, &c.—' —————With haste, parental haste
> ' I flew, I snatch'd her from the rigid north,
> ' And bore her nearer to the sun.

That is, he accompanied her to the south of France; but from line 121,
it should seem the season was unfriendly to his wishes, ' The sun
denied his wonted succour,' and she died.

> Line 162.—' That mourn'd the dead, and this denied a grave.'

The circumstance of refusing christian burial to Protestants in Popish
Countries, and the manner in which the author stole a grave for his
daughter, is wrought up with much pathos: Perhaps however too much
dilated, and mingled with some exceptionable lines—and the author's
resentment is more like the poet than the christian. The story of
Michael and Satan is artfully introduced at line 201, compare Jude,
ver. 9, but it wants perspicuity.

> Line 172.—' With pious sacrilege a grave I stole.'

It appears by the extract of a letter just printed, that in order to
obtain this, the Doctor bribed the under Gardener, who dug the grave,
and let him in by a private door, bearing his beloved daughter, wrapt
up in a sheet, upon his shoulder. When he had laid her in this hole,
he sat down, and as the man expressed it, " rained tears."—It ap-
pears also, that sometime previous to this event, expecting the catas-

---

* See Life of the Author, page 12.   † Ibid. page 13.

trophe, he had been seen walking solitarily backward and forward in
this garden, as if to find the most solitary spot for his purpose.—*See
Evangelical Magazine for November*, 1797.

There is exquisite tenderness, and uncommon pathos in this passage,
which gives to each individual tear a distinct object of distress, and
magnifies each distress to a public and general calamity.

This alludes to a people of Italy, the *Cimmerii*, who are said to have
resided in a valley so deep that the sun never reached it. A very pro-
per emblem of the valley of the shadow of death.

Ajax, one of the most distinguished of the Grecian princes at the siege
of Troy, killed himself, but was afterward feigned to be changed into a
violet, the flower here alluded to.

Our Author often discovers much originality in the various lights in
which he places the same object, as here the death of friends; and in
this instance he has been careful to keep his images distinct, and not
spoiled them by confusedly running one into the other, as he some-
times did. Dying friends are a *cloud* to damp our improper ardour—
pioneers to prepare our way—*plumes* from the wing of human vanity—
and '*angels* sent on errands full of love.'

These concluding lines on Death have much point and animation,
intermixed with some feeble lines and quaint expressions; faults very
incidental to our Author; but which often serve as foils only to his
beauties.

NIGHT IV.

This Night is inscribed to the honourable Mr. YORKE, since Earl
of Hardwicke, to whom he acknowledges his muse to have been
' much indebted,' and who, it is said, intended to have laid our author
under farther obligations by the living of Shenfield in Essex, if it had
become vacant.

This Night has been decidedly preferred to the other eight; it cer-
tainly abounds with fine sentiments and beautiful imagery; but it is
not necessary to disparage the others in order to commend this.

This passage seems to have been prophetic, for if the Night Thoughts
were published in 1711, as Mr. Croft assures us, his age could not at

this time exceed sixty-three. It is observable, that fourteen years after this confession, the author solicited farther promotion, and received it exactly at fourscore. And yet, in this same Night, and but a few lines farther, (line 100) our Author tells us,

> ' If this song lives, posterity shall know
> ' One, tho' in Britain born, with courtiers bred,
> ' Who thought ev'n gold might come a day too late.'

Who can account for the inconsistencies even of wise and good men!

Line 166.—' With joy—with grief, that healing hand I see:'

In this passage there is much sublimity of thought, and strength of expression; yet weakened by hyperbole, and the love of paradox and antithesis. The Author's leading design is to form a strong contrast between the dignity and humiliation of our Redeemer; but in some parts it wants truth and propriety for its support. It was not the hand that bled upon the cross that ' formed the skies :' although the Creator and the Redeemer united in the same person : the different characters must be referred to diverse natures, the human and divine. In short, it was the same *person*, but *not* the same *nature*, that both *formed* and *bled*.

Line 197.—' Expended Deity on human weal.'

This verse has either no meaning or a false one : for Deity can suffer no change, no examination, nor exinanition : ' expended Deity' strikes me therefore as an impropriety that poetic licence will hardly justify.

Line 208.—' Thou, rather than thy justice should be *stain'd*,
' Didst *stain* the cross.'————

This is a *pun* very unworthy both of the Author and the subject and into which he appears to have been betrayed by the excessive love of antithesis.

Line 226.—' Not thus our infidels th' eternal draw.'

This, (if I may so speak) is a beautiful portrait of the Deity.

' Full orb'd, in his whole round of rays complete:'

Both the language and the sentiment are correct, and the allusion to the celestial orb ingenious and pertinent : but the succeeding lines to ' brainless wits,' discover again too much the Author's fondness for paradox and antithesis.

Line 246.—' The sun beheld it—No.'

This allusion to the supernatural darkness at our Saviour's crucifixion is admirable; and the idea of nature shuddering to behold it, is poetic and sublime. Who can read it without shuddering too?

Line 273.—' Hear, O ye nations! Hear it, O ye dead!'

There is uncommon animation in this passage; and it is one of a very few instances, I have observed, in which the *words* of scripture have been quoted by our poets without weakening them.

x x

Line 315.—' If, sick of folly, I *relent*, he writes

  ' My name in Heaven with that inverted spear
  ' (A spear deep-dipt in blood!) which pierc'd his side,
  ' And open'd there a fount for all mankind,
  ' Who *strive*, who combat crimes, to *drink* and live.'

The thought of writing the penitent's name with the spear that pierced our Lord's side, is new and striking; but I should have preferred the idea of *bathing* to drinking, as agreeing better with the idea of a font, and the more usual scripture phraseology—' to *bathe* and live.'

I object more strongly, however, against some parts of this passage as false divinity. It is not merely *striving* that forms the *Christian* penitent: since our Lord says, ' Many shall strive to enter in at the ' straight gate, and shall not be able.' The fact is, our exertions must be in God's strength, and not in our own, to be successful. A man is not crowned, says St. Paul, except he strive lawfully.

Line 321.—' Pardon for infinite offences,' &c.

This passage is one of the finest instances of poetic climax that I recollect; but the term *universe*, is too extensive for our Author's meaning: ' world' would have been better.

Line 345.—' So dear, so due to Heaven, shall praise descend

  ' With her soft plume————————
  ' ———————— to tickle mortal ears,
  ' Then diving in the pockets of the great.'

The conceit of tickling the ear with a feather, though puerile and hacknied, may, perhaps, be tolerated; but surely a feather is an odd instrument to pick pockets with! Here is then a confusion of metaphors; not to say that this, and several following ideas, are much below the subject, and the terms too mean for poetry.

Line 413.—' The great First-Last! pavilion'd high he sits,

  ' In darkness from excessive splendour.'——

Few readers need be told that these lines are borrowed from Milton; but the idea is amplified and improved in the following lines:

  ' His glory to created glory, bright
  ' As that to central horrors.'

Line 473.—' To man the bleeding cross has promised all.'

From this, to the end of this book, it is endless to point out the beauties of our Author. On other subjects he is great; but on redemption he is carried beyond himself; and though his sublime raptures are mixed with a few weak or exceptionable expressions, these serve but as a foil to his innumerable beauties.

Line 551.—' Religion's all.'

This portrait of Religion is drawn in Young's best manner, and not spoiled by overcolouring.

Line 582.—' He weeps!—the falling drop puts out the sun.

  ' He sighs!—the sigh earth's deep foundation shakes.'

These lines are very exceptionable. The conceit of blotting out the sun with a tear, and of producing an earthquake by a sigh, is puerile: and the expression *outré*.

> Line 756.—' Wrong not the Christian,' &c.

This defence of the reasonableness of Christianity is certainly just and excellent: but it must be guarded. Revelation promulgates nothing inconsistent with our reason, but many things beyond it. Besides, right reason must be distinguished from the false reasoning of infidels, which the author has exposed with exquisite irony at line 775 and sequel.

> Line 781.—' Talk they of morals,' &c.

No encomium can exceed the merit of this and the succeeding passages, whether they be weighed in the scales of poetic or theological criticism. The painting at verse 799, ' He calls his wish,' &c. is perfectly accurate, and from nature.

> Line 835.—' Like him they fable under Etna whelm'd :'

That is ; one of the giants whom the poets suppose to have been condemned to this station, and that from thence he belches up the flame and smoke that form the irruptions of that mountain.

NIGHT V.

LADY BETTY YOUNG was the daughter of the Earl of LITCH-FIELD, but it must be the young Earl to whom this Night is dedicated, because our author calls him (line 89) ' Illustrious youth !'

> Line 13.—' Wit, a true pagan, deifies the brute.'

Our Author's reflections on Wit and Pleasure, in the beginning of this Poem, are ingenious and poetical; and while they defend the application of poetry to sacred subjects, administer just reproof to those who pervert it to vicious and obscene purposes.

> ' There is in poesy a decent pride.'

> Line 97.—' O thou, blest Spirit! whether the supreme
> ' Great Antemundane Father!
> ' Or from his throne some delegated pow'r.'—

I am not aware that Dr. YOUNG's orthodoxy has been called in question: on the contrary, he speaks remarkably clear and strong upon the divinity of CHRIST in the preceding Night: yet certainly these lines look very favourable to Arianism, when he questions whether the Holy Spirit be the Supreme Being or a delegated power: a question that had no proper relation to his subject; and, perhaps, systematic theology is never more out of its place than in poetry.

Line 107.——————— ' A purer stream,
' And fuller of the god than that which burst
' From fam'd Castalia.'

That is, the Fountain of the Muses, at the foot of Mount PARNASSUS, supposed to inspire all who drank of it.

Line 243.—' Like him whom fable fledg'd with waxen wings.'

Namely; ICARUS, the son of DÆDALUS, who having made himself waxen wings to fly with, flew so near the sun that the wax melted, and he fell into the sea, and was drowned.

Line 272.—' Crassus but sleeps; Ardelio is undone.'

That is, men of a busy, active, lively temper, are exposed to more dangers than the phlegmatic and the dull: so our Author adds in the next line:

' Wisdom less shudders at a fool than wit.'

Line 310.—' The man how bless'd,' &c.

These lines have been universally admired, and often quoted; but not more than they deserve.

Line 317.—' Lorenzo, read with me Narcissa's stone,
' Narcissa was thy fav'rite.'———

I think we may gather from these words, that LORENZO and NARCISSA were real characters, and acquainted; but not intimately related, as has been commonly supposed; otherwise our poet might have probably called her his *sister* rather than his *favourite*.

Line 323.—' See from her tomb, as from an humble shrine,
' *Truth*, radiant goddess!'———

This painting is inimitably beautiful, and the idea as just as beautiful. The amplification also aggrandizes, instead of enervating the sentiment, as sometimes is the misfortune of our Author.

Line 360.—' As worldly schemes resemble Sibyls leaves,
' The good man's days to Sibyls books compare.'

The ancient story here alluded to runs thus: about five centuries before the Christian Æra, a strange old woman came to TARQUIN the Proud (the last Tyrant of ROME under the name of king) and offered to sell him nine books, which, she said, were the oracles of the SIBYLS. But he disputing the price, she went away and burned three of them, and returning with the other six, asked the same sum as before. TARQUIN only laughed at the humour, upon which she left him again, and burned another three, and then came the third time and demanded the same price for the remaining three as at first for all the nine. TARQUIN, beginning now to think there might be something extraordinary in the business, consulted the AUGURS, who reproved his impiety, and directed him to pay the sum demanded: This he did, and the story says, the woman immediately vanished; and the books were delivered to the care of two of the nobility appointed to be their keepers.

Some years afterward these oracles were all burned; but fresh ones were collected, some of which are still preserved, but intermixed with the grossest forgeries.

Some authors assert, that the original oracles were written upon the leaves of trees, subject to be wafted with every breath of air, whence our Author's comparison between these and worldly schemes.

Line 339.—' The brave, the gallant Altamont!'

In the third letter of our Author's ' Centaur not Fabulous,' (dated November 1754) is described the death-bed of the ' gay, young, noble, ' ingenious, accomplished, and most wretched ALTAMONT.' His last words were—' My principles have poisoned my friend, my extrava- ' gance has beggared my boy, my unkindness has murdered my wife.' By the NIGHT THOUGHTS, it appears that profligacy led to despair, and despair to suicide, the natural career of *Vice* and *Infidelity*. Pub- lic rumour considered this character as drawn from Lord EUSTON, but heightened, no doubt (like LORENZO) in the colouring.

Line 442.—' O Britain! infamous for suicide!'

Our country is unhappily proverbial for this crime all over the con- tinent; and ' to die like an Englishman,' is a common periphrasis for self-murder.—How horrid is it that one of our first writers for literary genius, should have been the advocate of this crime!—I mean the elegant, but sceptic HUME.

YOUNG argues against it with all his force of genius and of elo- quence; and no doubt brought it on the stage in order to render it more shocking; for it forms the catastrophe of all his tragedies. Ex- perience has, however, I conceive, sufficiently demonstrated that the natural effect of theatrical representations is the reverse. Crimes may be rendered less shocking, nay, even fashionable, by being exhibited on the stage; but I know of no man who ever took a hearty aversion to vice, and fled from it, in consequence of such exhibitions.

Line 545.———————— ' Egypt's wanton queen,
' Carousing gems, herself dissolv'd in love.'

CLEOPATRA, successively the mistress of JULIUS CÆSAR and MARC ANTHONY, was equally famous for her beauty, eloquence, and wit on the one hand, and for her pride, lewdness, and extravagance on the other. She is said to have drank pearls dissolved by chymical art, which is the circumstance here alluded to.

Line 568.—' Half-round the globe the tears *pump'd up* by death,
' Are spent in wat'ring vanities of life.'

There is something beautiful in the general idea of watering our vanities with the tears shed for the death of our friends: but the ex- pression of *pumping up* tears, is low, and borders on the burlesque.

Line 586.—' So wept Lorenzo fair Clarissa's fate,
' Who gave that angel-boy on whom he doats;
' And dy'd to give him, orphan'd in his birth.'

By this it seems LORENZO had been married—Had lost his lady in child-birth—but that her offspring was spared, and was the father's darling:—all which circumstances abundantly prove that this character could not intend the Author's son, who was yet a boy himself; and they confirm the common opinion, that LORENZO was a real character.

Line 619.—' Of age the glory is to wish to die:'

But this was very far from the Author's own case, who was seeking fame, riches, and promotion to his latest years. What illustrious characters would poets be if they could live up to all the great maxims they inculcate!

The remainder of this Night is a fine specimen of didactic poetry, and abounds with fine sentiments and beautiful apothegms.

Line 780.—' That, like the Jews' fam'd oracle of gems,
                ' Sparkles instruction:'————

A reference to the breast-plate of the Jewish high-priest, which was composed of twelve different gems, and gave oracular answers, as many learned men have supposed, by a particular lustre of certain letters engraved on them.

Line 815.—' Tiberian arts his purposes wrap up,
                ' In deep dissimulation's darkest night.'

The artifices of death are described here and in the context with inimitable wit and ingenuity: the above allusion is to the character of the Emperor TIBERIUS, a man famous, or rather infamous, for dissimulation.

Line 836.—' Such peace has Innocence in death:'

It would have better become Dr. YOUNG as a Christian divine, and have been more consistent with the doctrine of Night the Fourth, to have substituted Piety for Innocence. The Christian's peace in death, does not arise from a review of the innocence either of his heart or life: but from his sense of pardoning mercy through the atonement and mediation of JESUS CHRIST.

Line 846.—' 'Twas in a circle of the gay I stood'————

The following portrait of death, and the history of his adventures, is beyond encomium; and inferior to no passage of the kind I ever met with. The moral is good, the wit exquisite, and the painting betrays the hand of a master in every line.

Line 958.—' See high in air the sportive goddess,' &c.

This picture is intended as a contrast to the preceding, to which it forms a proper companion, and must be admitted to be well drawn, though it does not equally strike us with its novelty.

Line 1053.—' Lysander————
                Woo'd the fair Aspasia.'

This story is exquisitely tender. It was probably form'd by the imagination of the poet; but is so much like real life, that it interests us equally as if we knew the fact. The application of it to the Author's own distress is pathetic: it reminds him of his loss in the death of Lady Young: Lysander and Aspasia, Philander and Narcissa, are all, for the moment, now forgot and lost in the recollection of her death; this

———————— ' cures all other woe,'

by absorbing it.

———————— ' When such friends part,
' 'Tis the survivor dies.—My heart, no more!'

NIGHT VI.

The Preface to this Poem gives a just view of the Author's design and plan. It is inscribed to Henry Pelham, then prime minister; a very celebrated statesman, and a worthy character.

Our Author has drawn his portrait in two distinct lines, the first his abilities.

' So P—— [Pelham] thought: think better if you can.'——Night viii. l. 372.

And in this Poem (line 282)

' What is a Pelham's head to Pelham's heart!'

Line 1.—' She—for I know not yet her name in heav'n.'—

Our Author refers here to the conclusion of his former Poem, and continues to bewail his lady in very pathetic numbers.

' Too dark the sun to see it!'——

These few lines go beyond hyperbole; they are mere bombast. Our Author's strong imagination hurried him frequently into this fault.

Line 52.——————— ' Who can take
' Death's portrait true?'

There is inimitable beauty in these lines, with that kind of obscurity, which, according to our best critics, is essential to the sublime.

Line 128.—' Revere thyself—and yet thyself despise.'

This is an admirable precept, and founded upon a just estimate of human nature, the true dignity of which consists in its immortality and mental powers. As to moral rectitude, it is absurd and contradictory to ascribe this to a fallen creature, until restored by grace.

Line 261.—' Dedalian engin'ry!'

Our Author compares Genius and Art to the artificial wings that, according to remote antiquity, Dædalus formed to fly with: intimating that, without integrity and virtue, these can be of little use to their possessors.

The whole of this Poem abounds with solid argument, forcible expression, and beautiful imagery; but affords little scope for notes, having few obscurities to explain—no striking faults—nor any passages eminently excellent: it is all good; but neither sinks into the errors, nor rises into the sublimities of the former Poems.

Line 603.—' Enthusiastic this? Then all are weak
' But rank enthusiasts.'

Enthusiasm is one of those equivocal terms which may be taken either in a good or bad sense. When it expresses only ardour in the esteem of objects beautiful and excellent in the arts and sciences, it always is commended, and why not in religion? But when taken for that ' wildfire of the soul,' which, disregarding both reason and revelation, leads its subjects into extravagancies inconsistent with both, it cannot be too cautiously avoided, or too pointedly condemned.— Enthusiasm, in its original import, implies *inspiration*: when the spirit is from GOD, it is divine: when from the opposite quarter—diabolical.

Line 702.—' Matter immortal, and shall spirit die?'

If there is a weak place in our Author's argument, it is here. Many of the heathen reasoning from analogy in a similar manner, formed a very dangerous conclusion. They supposed that as our material part originated from the earth, and after a variety of revolutions returns thither; so our spirits, being a kind of ethereal flame, kindled from the great Spirit of the universe, after animating human bodies, and, perhaps, those of various other animals, return again and are absorbed in its original source—which they called the soul of the world and of the universe. But this is a species of Atheism, and abhorrent from Christianity.

Analogical reasoning is good so far only as the analogy is clear and just: but the analogy between matter and spirit, if any, is too remote to found an argument; and if it were not it should seem it would rather infer the mortality of the soul than its immortality, since all matter is subject to corruption, though not to annihilation. The argument from the revolutions of nature is, however, more favourable to the doctrine of a resurrection, and that implies our immortality.

NIGHT VII.

Line 6.—' *Pope*, who couldst make immortals, art thou dead?'

THE preface to this Night is dated, July 7, 1744, soon after Mr. POPE's death, between whom and our Author there was certainly an acquaintance if not a friendship. YOUNG on one occasion applied to

him for a favour, which is supposed to have been a prologue to one of
his tragedies: but it is not known that this was granted. YOUNG
addressed two Poetical Epistles to him, and speaks of him always with
high respect: yet the Author of the ‘ Essay on the Genius and Writ-
‘ ings of POPE,’ who is thought to have depreciated his merit, dedi-
cated that work to him, which, if done with his knowledge and con-
sent, is supposed to involve an inconsistency.

> Line 24.—‘ Unconscious bears, Bellerophon! like thee,
> ‘ His own indictment.’

BELLEROPHON, after he had killed his brother, put himself under
the protection of the King of ARGOS, who sent him with letters to his
father-in-law, desiring he might be punished.

> Line 126.—‘ Hence the world’s master, from ambition’s spire,
> ‘ In Caprea plung’d; and div’d beneath the brute.’

This alludes to the Emperor TIBERIUS, who at first bore an honour-
able character; but in the close of his life, he retired to CAPREA, a
small island in the MEDITERRANEAN, where he indulged himself in
every species of debauchery and vice.

> Line 161.—‘ Die for thy country? Thou romantic fool!’

The Author means to say, that to deny the immortality of the soul,
annihilates at once all public and private virtues. With infidels, who
deny a future state, patriotism is a jest, as well as other virtues.

> Line 170.—‘ His first command is this:—Man love thyself.’

That is, the love of existence and of happiness is implanted in our
nature: but this must be distinguished from that sordid principle
which not only begins but ends in self.

> ‘ Self-love but serves the virtuous mind to wake,
> ‘ As the small pebble stirs the peaceful lake;
> ‘ The centre mov’d, a circle straight succeeds,
> ‘ Another still, and still another spreads:
> ‘ Friend, parent, neighbour, first it will embrace,
> ‘ His country next; and next all human race.’
>   POPE.

> Line 290.————————————— ‘ Go, man!
> ‘ And bow to thy superiors of the stall.’

This is an admirable specimen of the Author’s talent at irony and
satire. It is not epigrammic, for it stings in *every* line.

> Line 396.—‘ Echo the proud Assyrian in their hearts.’

Read Daniel chap. iv. from verse 28 to the end.

> Line 574.—‘ A bed of roses, or the burning bull.’

This line alludes to two anecdotes of a very different nature. Phalaris,
a celebrated tyrant of antiquity, had a brazen bull so constructed as
to hold men in its inside, which, by heating it with a slow fire, were
roasted to death in it. The only act of justice recorded of this man is,

Y Y

that he obliged the inventor to make the first experiment. But his subjects performed another act no less just, when they roasted the tyrant himself in the same machine.

The first part of the above verse, refers to one of the English martyrs in the reign of the tyrant Henry VIII. (Counsellor Bainham) who while roasting in the flames at Smithfield, for the cause of God and truth, cried out—' O ye papists! ye look for miracles—behold one ' here! for in this fire I feel no more pain than if I were on a bed of ' down. To me it is a bed of roses.'

Line 652.—' In this black channel would my ravings run.'

There is something characteristically great and wild in the subsequent specimen of Infidel reasonings; and the concluding epitaph on the demolished universe is admirable.

Line 931.—' An all-prolific, all-preserving God!
    ' This were a God indeed—and such is man.'

The ascription of deity to man, may be poetic, but it is hardly Christian. The subsequent comparison of the dead wakened by the last trumpet, to bees collected by a warming-pan, (line 938 and sequel) reminds us of HOMER's use of the like simile; (ILIAD, Book II.) but it suits much better with the design of the bard than the divine: and gives an air of ridicule to the serious numbers of our Author.

Line 994.—' Know'st thou th' importance of a soul immortal?'

There is great beauty, strength, and justice, in this calculation of the worth of immortality, taking for granted that metaphysical axiom, that matter is incapable of sensation; for on this principle alone is the calculation just. All the insensible creation is not of equal value with one rational intelligence; nor all mortal concerns, comprehended in one great aggregate, of comparable importance with the concerns of one immortal soul; for this plain reason—there will arise a period in eternity, when the existence of each individual will be of longer duration than the temporal existence of all perishable beings summed together. Well, therefore, has Dr. DODDRIDGE estimated, ' that the ' eternal salvation of one soul is of more importance than the temporal ' salvation of all the nations of the earth until the end of time.'

    ' The devastations of one dreadful hour,
    ' shall the Creator's six day's work devour.
    ' A mighty, mighty ruin! yet one *soul*
    ' Has more to boast, and far outweighs the whole.

Line 1034.—' Hence, Heaven looks down on earth *with all her eyes.*'

The latter part of this verse is a low proverbial form of expression, and ought to have been avoided.

Line 1108.—' Witness, thou Sinai!'——

This refers to the giving of the law to MOSES. Exodus XIX. XX.

Line 1110.—' Witness, ye billows.'

Namely those of the RED SEA, in which PHARAOH and his host were drowned. Exodus XIV. 27.

Line 1113.—' Witness, ye flames, th' Assyrian tyrant blew
' To seven-fold rage.'

Viz. The fiery furnace of NEBUCHADNEZZAR. Daniel III. 19.

Line 1115.—' And thou, Earth, witness.'——

This alludes to the earthquake by which KORAH and his rebellious company were devoured, with all their property.

Line 1119.—' Renounce St. Evremont, and read St. Paul.'

Mons. ST. EVREMONT, was a celebrated free-thinker, and popular French writer of the last century.

Line 1139.—' The grave, like fabled Cerberus, has op'd
' A triple mouth.'

CERBERUS was a monstrous three-headed dog which the mythologists placed at the mouth of the infernal regions: the Poet compares the grave to this monster on account of its devouring ' LUCIA, NAR-
' CISSA, and PHILANDER,' as it were at once. LUCIA is evidently intended for Lady YOUNG, whose real name was ELIZABETH. (See Life, Page 11.) But why denominated LUCIA, I am at a loss to say. See above line 614, also Night VIII. line 1356.

Line 1268.—' There, there, Lorenzo! thy Clarissa sails.'

CLARISSA was LORENZO'S lady, and died in childbed, as observed above.

Line 1290.—' Not man alone, all rationals, heaven arms
' With an illustrious, but tremendous pow'r,
' To counteract its own most gracious ends;
' And this of strict necessity, not choice.'

Our Author here ventures upon the knotty subject of necessity and free-agency, which is not well adapted to his purpose. Without following him into this inextricable maze, we may venture to observe and censure the rashness of his assertion; that free-agency counteracts the designs of heaven. Both scripture and philosophy, on the contrary agree, that it is by the instrumentality of free agents that Providence effects its great designs, and in nothing is infinite wisdom more beau-tifully displayed, than in the controul of the guilty passions of mankind, and in the superintendance of the moral world. Though we admit the Author's general principle, that sinners are the cause of their own destruction, yet the proposition cannot be inverted, to say that they are also the cause of their own salvation. ' The wages of
' sin is death, but the gift of GOD eternal life, through JESUS CHRIST
' our Lord.'

Line 1354.—' A Christian dwells, like Uriel, in the sun.'

This sentiment is beautiful, and would bear amplification. MILTON (Paradise Lost, Book III.) makes URIEL, the angel of the sun, a resident in that celestial luminary; and Young compares a Christian to Uriel. His dwelling in the sun may be referred both to the meridian evidence of christianity, particularly to the doctrine of immortality, and to that glory which true piety casts around his character.

Line 1390.—' You know its *title* flatters you, not me.'

That is, the title of this Poem—' The Infidel Reclaimed.'

Line 1416, &c.—' Admit a God ——————
' —————— All other wonders cease ;
' Deny him—all is mystery besides.'

This is an accurate state of the controversy, as to the being of a God, and merits the most serious attention of every free-thinker. For in denying the existence of a Supreme Being, men certainly take the *harder*, as well as the *darker* side.

Line 1476.—' Though quite forgotten half your Bible's praise.'

That is, the poetic half, which includes the Psalms, Proverbs, the prophecies, and various other passages of scripture, which are evidently poetic in the original.

NIGHT VIII.

Dr. Young in his ' True Estimate of Human Life' (See Life, page 10.) attempted to weigh the world, ' and all that it contains,' in the balances of the sanctuary. His design never was completed ; but this Poem, in some measure, supplies the deficiency ; for here he estimates ' the love of this life ; the ambition and pleasure, with the wit and wisdom of the world ;' and having maturely weighed them, pronounces them altogether ' lighter than vanity.'

Line 14.—' Sprinkled with dews from the Castalian font.'

The Fountain of the Muses.—Urania (line 25) is the Muse that is supposed to inspire celestial themes.

Line 34.—————— ' Eternal is at hand
' To swallow Time's ambitious ; as the vast
' Leviathan the bubbles vain.'——————

By the *Leviathan* our Author understands the crocodile of Egypt in his paraphrase of Job ; but the comparison here better agrees with the whale. As this monster swallows the bubble that rides upon the wave, so Eternity devours all the trifling concerns of time.

Line 46.—' By him who foibles in archangels sees.'

This verse alludes to the expression of Elihu, in Job, chap. iv. 18. ' He putteth no trust in his servants, and his angels he charged with ' folly.'

Line 172.—' Who lately feasted high at Albion's cost.'

This alludes to the unhappy fate of Admiral BALCHEN, who was shipwrecked on the rocks of SCILLY, in the year 1744, in the VICTORY, a first-rate man of war; and more than a thousand persons perished with him.

Line 210.—' The boy has virtue by his mother's side.'

FLORELLO is the son of LORENZO by poor CLARISSA—' orphan'd ' in his birth;' and the manner in which he is introduced is a strong evidence that these are real characters.

Line 277.—' Men of the world, the terræ-filial breed:'

That is, ' the sons of earth;' This and the following verses are a very just description of the CHESTERFIELD School, where want of manners is the only vice, and politeness and simulation are the primary virtues. See farther, line 1266.

Line 329.—' Poor Machiavel! who labour'd hard his plan,
' Forgot that genius need not go to school.'

This consummate politician was the first, perhaps, that reduced the diabolical principles of tyranny and dissimulation to a system, and taught them as a science; not considering, that in vice and hypocrisy man is ' without a tutor wise.'

Line 419.—' Prometheus'

In the Greek mythology, the son of IÆPETUS and the Nymph ASIA, an exquisite artist, who having formed a man of clay, animated it with celestial fire, which, by the assistance of MINERVA, he had stolen from heaven; for which presumption he is fabled to have been chained by JUPITER to mount CAUCASUS, with a vulture constantly preying upon his liver, which grew by night as fast as it was devoured by day.—Our Author here compares ambition to this Mount CAUCASUS, the ' Mountain of Torments.'

Line 492.—' Fain would he make the world his pedestal;
' Mankind the gazers; the sole figure he.'

An admirable picture this of an ambitious man! and finely ridiculed; but debased by the following paltry lines:

Line 499, and sequel.—' Knows this all-knower, that from *itch* of praise,
' Or from an *itch* more sordid, when he shines
' Taking his country *by* five hundred *ears*.'

Line 522.—' Like Kouli Khan, in plunder of the proud.'

A famous tyrant of PERSIA, who like most conquerors, was celebrated by the extent of his massacres and plunder, and in the end, by his enormous cruelties brought down upon himself the vengeance of his subjects, being assassinated in 1747.

Line 549.—' Think you there's but one whoredom:'

Though this language is too coarse for the dignity of the subject, yet there is much merit in the succeeding imagery.

Line 602.—' Who think'st thyself a Murray———
    ' ——————— my Demosthenes '

MURRAY, the late Earl of MANSFIELD, celebrated both for his legal knowledge and graceful eloquence, and who was at this time at the head of his profession at the bar.

DEMOSTHENES the first orator of GREECE, and indeed of all antiquity, as well as the chief pleader of his time.

Line 609.—' Tell not Calista: she will laugh thee dead ;
    ' Or send thee to her hermitage with L.——.'

Mr. CROFT thinks this initial refers to the real name of LORENZO, and that this is a decisive proof that some real character was intended. Of this last fact I have no doubt, but suppose few persons who attentively peruse the context will think that this mysterious initial can refer to LORENZO, though I cannot pretend to say to whom it does refer.

Line 710.—' A soul in commerce with her God is heav'n.'

A finer sentiment than this never dropped from the pen of an uninspired writer. To have GOD *with us*, is heaven *here*: to be *with* GOD, is heaven *hereafter*.

Line 771.—' Retire and read thy Bible to be gay;
    ' There truths abound of sov'reign aid to peace.'

How salutary and how seasonable this advice! there is no book in the world calculated like the Bible to administer consolation, especially to the afflicted, oppressed, and broken-hearted.

Line 804.—' Can joy like thine meet accident unshock'd?'

This is the true test of peace and joy; the pleasures of the world may serve to flatter in the times of prosperity and ease ; but to ' meet ' accident unshocked, to open the door to poverty, or to talk with ' threatening death,' requires the consolation of the gospel. In all these cases we may say to the joys of sense and worldly pleasures, as JOB said to his friends, ' miserable comforters are ye all, and physi- ' cians of no value !'

Line 930.—' That like the fabled, self-enamour'd boy.'

Namely, NARCISSUS, who, according to the poets, fell in love with his own image in the water, and pined away into a *daffodil*.

Line 946.——————' Like angels seen of old
    ' In Israel's dream :'

See Genesis XXVIII.

Line 993.—' Imagination is the Paphian shop.'

The poets fable that VULCAN, the God of Subterraneous Fire, and husband of VENUS, kept a smith's shop at PAPHOS, made poisoned arrows, and forged thunderbolts for JUPITER.

Line 1011.—' That persecuting priest, the Turk of Rome.'

This alludes to some circumstances unknown at present: it seems that the Pope prohibited the exportation of some articles of luxury intended for the tables of the rich, which (poor creatures) disappointed them.

Line 1030.—————' Like Yorke
' Demurs on what it passes :——

Alluding to the Honourable Mr. YORKE, to whom the Fourth Night is dedicated.

Line 1051.————— ' The pillars, thefe :
' But those of Seth not more remote from thee.'

This alludes to a fabulous story in JOSEPHUS, who tells us (Antiq. lib. i. c. 2.) that SETH and his descendants applied to the study of the sciences, and being informed by ADAM, that the world should be destroyed twice, by water and by fire, they erected two pillars, one of stone and the other of brick, on which they inscribed their knowledge, supposing that one or other of them might remain for their posterity.

Line 1151.—' And when he falls writes *Vici* on his shield.'

That is; *I have conquered:* the Christian alone can sing of victory in death.

Line 1310.—————' As Athens' fool,
' Grinn'd from the port on ev'ry sail his own.'

A famous ideot, who pleased himself with the idea that every ship which came into port was his, and seemed to enjoy it as much as if it had been really so.

Line 1393.—' And headlong leap, like Curtius, down the gulph.'

M. CURTIUS, was a noble Roman youth, who, in the fourth Century before CHRIST, sacrificed his life for the salvation of his country, on the following occasion: a violent earthquake having opened a dreadful chasm in the Forum, the oracle declared it would not close till some noble youth was thrown into it; CURTIUS, therefore, being armed and mounted on a stately horse, leaped directly into it.

NIGHT IX.

THIS last Poem is dedicated to the Duke of NEWCASTLE, a celebrated statesman, and prime-minister under GEORGE II. who died in 1768.

Line 92.—' Where is the dust that has not been alive?'

This passage is inimitably beautiful and pathetic; and the following paragraph rises to the sublime.

Line 127.——————— ' Of one departed world
' I see the mighty shadow.————

This is a beautiful allusion to the deluge, which is elegantly personi-
fied in the succeeding verses. It was well imagined to make the
Deluge predict the final conflagration, and agrees with the scripture,
which represents ENOCH, the patriarch, as predicting the latter event
before the former took place. See Jude ver. 14, &c.

Line 133.—' But, like Cassandra, prophesies in vain.'

CASSANDRA was endued with the gift of prophesy by APOLLO,
but afterwards, for deceiving, had this curse entailed upon her, that
no one should believe her.

Line 159.—See all the formidable sons of fire.'

There is sublimity and force in this description superior to that in
our Author's ' LAST DAY,' because less minute. The Introduction of
CHRIST himself, as infinitely more resplendant than the sun, has a
grand effect.

Line 179.—' A swift arch-angel, with his golden wing,
' . . . .
' . . . . Sweeps stars and suns aside.'

This is a striking proof how easy it is, by an injudicious line, to
reduce the sublime to the ludicrous and extravagant. Our Author
was proceeding admirably, when the sudden thought of comparing the
wing of the archangel to a *besom* spoiled his imagery, and set him to
sweeping suns and stars, not, however, as dust and rubbish, but ' as
' blots and clouds,' as if these were the proper objects for the besom!
But HOMER sometimes nodded, and if our Author drops his wing
here, it is speedily to rise the higher; for the succeeding passage, at
ver. 197, is one of the most sublime in the whole work.

Line 229.——————— ' Deputed conscience scales
' The dread tribunal, and forestalls our doom.'

Here again our Author flags, his muse forsakes him, and the poet
degenerates into the tradesman, and talks of forestalling like a cheese-
monger or a butcher. Nothing can palliate such gross impro-
prieties.

Line 243.—' Asks, " What is truth " with Pilate, and retires.'

See John XVIII. 38.

Line 353.—' Eternity, the various sentence past
' Assigns the sever'd throng distinct abodes.'

Another passage which discovers great depth of thought, and strong
powers of imagination.

' Line 471.—' Her death.'————

That is; the death of LUCIA, which, as before observed, evidently
intends Lady YOUNG. This he considers as a dispensation, painful,
but instructive :

' For all I bless thee, most for the severe.'

Line 543.——————— ' So Cynthia, (poets feign;) &c.

The fable of ENDYMION's amour with DIANA, or the Moon, arises from ' his knowledge of astronomy; and as he passed the night ' on some high mountain, to observe the celestial bodies, it was re- ' ported that he was courted by the Moon.'

Line 549.——————— ' O majestic Night!'

This portrait is in the true spirit of poetry, sublime and beautiful.

Line 720.—' And see Day's amiable sister.'

That is, the MOON, whose beams are poetically represented as re- freshing the vegetable creation, fainting from the intenseness of the sun's rays.

Line 884.——————' O'er each sphere
' Presides an angel:'

It was by this hypothesis many of the ancients, ignorant of the ma- chinery of nature, accounted for the motions of the heavenly bodies.

Line 926.—' Or nodding gardens pendant in mid-air.'

This alludes to the *hanging gardens* (as they were called) in BABY- LON, which were raised to a great height on arches, and so thickly covered with mould, as to grow the largest trees, as well as shrubs and flowers.

Line 974.—' The Stagyrite, and Plato, he—who drank
' The poison'd bowl, and him of Tusculum,
' With him of Corduba.'————

Of this string of philosophers, the first intends ARISTOTLE, the chief of the peripatetic philosophers, born at STATYRA, in MACEDON —The 3d, SOCRATES, put to death by poison—The 4th, CICERO, whose country residence was TUSCULUM.—and the 5th, SENECA, the preceptor of NERO, and a sacrifice to his cruelty.

Line 1045.—' Call it the breast-plate of the true High-Priest.'

An allusion to the sacred ornaments of AARON—See Exodus XXVIII.

Line 1053.—' Bourbon ———————
' Wouldst thou be great?'————

This address is to LEWIS XV. of FRANCE, who copied the vices of his grandfather without his glory.

Line 1122 ——————— ' On yon cærulean plain:'

That is; the ethereal expanse of the skies, where the planets in ' mystic maze' perform their various revolutions.

Line 1257.—' In Ajalon's soft flow'ry vale repose:'

See Joshua x. 12, 13.

Line 1258.——————— ' Ye glowing embers,
' On heaven's broad hearth,' &c.

This comparison is mean in itself, and rendered more so by the manner in which it is dilated. Many figures will bear to be touched that will not bear to be amplified.

Line 1687.——————— ' Like him of Uz
' I gaze around!'

An allusion to Job's words, ' O that I knew where I might find
him !' as the following verses allude to the 42d Psalm.

Line 1715—' How swift I mount!'——— —

There is something very sublime and animated in this ethereal tour;
and the subsequent address is (in some parts at least) carried as high
as human language seems capable of rising.

Line 1780.——————' With war this fatal hour
' Europa groans.————————

The reader will recollect that this was just before the unhappy
rebellion of 1745, when FRANCE conspired with other powers to seat
a Pretender on the English throne; a period of remarkable commo-
tion in EUROPE. Would to GOD the language were not equally appli-
cable to our own times !

The following reflection on conquerors and tyrants are remarkably
severe; but who will say they are unjust or false ?

Line 1900.——————— ' Like feign'd Eridanus:

A constellation in the form of a river of the same name in ITALY.

Line 1910.——————— ' Creations
' In one agglomerated cluster hung
' Great Vine on thee.'

Dr. JOHNSON calls this ' an unlucky thought:'—' when it dropped
' into his mind (says the critic) that the orbs floating in space might
' be called the cluster of creation, he thinks on a cluster of grapes,
' and says they all hang on the great VINE,' that is, the Deity: but
this idea was no doubt borrowed from the scriptures, where our
LORD applies it to himself as the head of union with his people: but
our Author extends the idea to the union and dependance between
the Deity and the whole creation. See John xv.

Line 2070.—' For I have peep'd into thy cover'd heart:'

The word peep'd is highly improper and even ludicrous, spoiling a
sentiment otherwise just and beautiful.

Line 2200.—' Each flower, each leaf, with its small people swarm'd '

That is, the animalculæ, which the microscope discovers swarming
upon every leaf, and every flower.

Line 2508.—' All sanded o'er with suns:'———

A mean idea ! though evidently intended for sublime. The heavens
have been poetically called, ' the floor of his abode,' but our Poet is
the first, I presume, to inform us, that this *floor* is *sanded!*

Line 2326.—' Let it outcry the boy at Philip's ear.'

It is said, that Philip of Macedon, father of Alexander the Great, employed a boy to admonish him every morning of his mortality in these words—' Philip, thou art a man!'

Line 2425.—When time, like him of Gaza in his wrath,' &c.

Alluding to Sampson's taking away the gates of the Philistines. See Judges xvi. 29, 30. The allusion here is not improper in itself; but I cannot altogether admire it as a final conclusion of the Night Thoughts; which, instead of opening into eternal day, abruptly close the subject in ' universal midnight.'

The Reader, however, who has perused the work with a taste for serious reflection, and has condescended to take these remarks with him as a guide, will not close the work without confessing, that among all the Author's blemishes he has found a great variety of beauties, uncommon originality of thought, many passages of the true sublime, and, above all, the finest moral sentiments, and the most interesting religious truths; may they rest with all their just and infinite importance on our minds!

END OF THE NOTES.

INDEX.

9. 634. Prove the being of a God, 9. 1298. Supposed to be suns, 9.
746. From whence sprung, 9. 1753. How kept in their places, 9.
1136. Address to them, 9. 1306. What intended for, 9. 1156.
Starry heavens, benefits arising from a view of the, 9. 753.

Statesmen, the wiles of, 8. 344.

Station, high, described, 6. 288.

St. Evremont, implied censure on, 7. 1219.

Stoics, opinion of the, adduced by infidels as an argument against immortality, 7. 559.

Subjects insisted on in the Night Thoughts, 5. 73.

Suicide, peculiar propensity of the English to, 5. 442. A picture of, 8.
1326. The cause of defined, 5. 475. Despair, the chief reason of, 8.
1324. The instruments used in, 8. 1330.

Superstition, the cruelty and popish bigotry of, displayed, 3. 161.

T.

Tears, their different sources, 5. 522. Indulged, deserve shame, 3. 109.

Thought, a superfluity and misery, if the grave closes all our prospects,
7. 759. Serious, the importance of, 8. 1360. And reason, insufficiency of, in man, 1. 84. Of death, how beneficial, 3. 303.

Thoughts, the importance of guarding our, 2. 95.

Time, fine description of the end or fall of, 9. 308. Noted from its loss
alone, 1. 55. The avarice of, recommended, 2. 52. Its value, 2. 28.
51. Never duly estimated, 2. 98. The waste and use of, what, 2.
150. The nature of, explained, 2. 194. Its treachery to man, 8. 119.
And eternity, the meeting of, 9. 293. See Allegory.

To-day, its deceptive resemblance to yesterday, 5. 397.

Tombs, instruction derived from the, 5. 310.

Truth, description of, where it is deposited, and what it is in itself,
4. 825.

Truth, signed by fate, 9. 2330.

U.

Unbelief defined, 7. 1144.

Understanding, the benefits and use of, 6. 449.

Universe, the threshold of the Deity, 9. 1734.

V.

Vice, in what instance it is virtue, 7. 146. A definition of, 9. 2045.

Vicious men, their enjoyments destitute of stability, 9. 49.

Virtue, alone, can inspire us with confidence in death, 2. 651. The
want of, want of thought, 3. 351. Attended with what consequences,
3. 353. Gives variety to life, 3. 368. The frailty of, 5. 139. A crime
if the doctrine of a future state is rejected, 7. 710. Suffers here below,
8. 386. The fruit of piety, 8. 692. When to be admired, 9. 409.
Springs from self-love, 7. 143. Lightens the evils of life, 3. 382. 6.
477. The nature of, an argument of immortality, 7. 141. Its durability, 6. 312.

W.

Warnings, the use of, 2. 402.

Wealth, true, described, 6. 411.

Winter, as necessary and beneficial as the spring, 9. 483.

Wisdom, her admonitions, when most prevalent, 5. 275. And wit,
properly distinguished, 8. 1233. Worldly and divine compared, 5.
344. And folly, the difference between, 8. 1368. True, the operations and advantages of, 8. 1247.

Wishes, proofs of immortality, 7. 113.

Wishing, the folly of, 4. 70.

www.ingramcontent.com/pod-product-compliance
Lightning Source LLC
Chambersburg PA
CBHW020240110726
47898CB00004B/1330